DYNASTIES

Myer

Durack

De Bortoli

Macarthur

Murdoch

Downer

DYNASTIES

Julie Browning &
Laurie Critchley

ABC
Books

To our families for their love and
support beyond the call of duty

Published by ABC Books for the
AUSTRALIAN BROADCASTING CORPORATION
GPO Box 9994 Sydney NSW 2001

First published July 2002

National Library of Australia
Cataloguing-in-Publication entry
Browning, Julie.
    Dynasties.
    Bibliography.
    ISBN 0 7333 1068 0.
    1. Macarthur family. 2. Durack family. 3. Myers family.
    4. Murdoch family. 5. De Bortoli family. 6. Australia –
    History. 7. Australia – Genealogy. I. Critchley, Laurie.
    II. Australian Broadcasting Corporation. III. Title.
994.0099

Cover images from the Murdoch and Myer families and Patsy Millett
Back cover images: Courtesy Lady Mary Downer, State Library of New South Wales,
the De Bortoli family
Designed by Kerry Klinner
Edited by Julie Stanton
Set in 12/15pt Bembo by Midland Typesetters, Maryborough, Victoria
Colour reproduction by Colorwize, Adelaide
Printed and bound in Australia by Griffin Press, Adelaide

5 4 3 2 1

CONTENTS

INTRODUCTION

What matters is influence, power and money. Culture, pedigree and tradition are also important, of course, but without power and money they are meaningless.

Dino Frescobaldi, fourteenth-century Italian aristocrat

MOST of us create some chronicle of our lives and our families, even if simply in a shoebox of photographs. These images—of grandparents, family holidays and the like—serve as props for a random and partial personal history and often bring a host of bittersweet memories.

But for a few families such personal memorabilia carry added weight. When the child in the photograph is Rupert Murdoch or Alexander Downer, the photograph holds a more public significance. In these families, photographs are stored and family trees maintained not only for the family's own pleasure but also in appreciation of their wider importance on the national stage. The Duracks might never have been known outside the East Kimberleys if Mary Durack had not retrieved her ancestors' records and turned them into best-selling accounts of her family's pioneering endeavours.

It is in the nature of dynasties—those families who, for three generations or more, have exerted public influence—to preserve and maintain a shared family heritage and identity. This quest may seem anachronistic in the 'lucky country', where the vernacular rings with stories of mateship and digger heroism, and where aristocracy and hereditary privilege are regarded as belonging to the old world. But if notions of dynasty run contrary to popularly held perceptions of Australia as a new and classless society, there is no escaping the fact that since colonisation this country has provided fertile soil for dynastic ambitions. From European settlement, the interests of influential families and their progenitors have shaped our development as a nation. These families still influence our lives—from what we buy and where we shop, to what we read and watch, to the politicians we elect.

Australia may not have the chateaux of France, but most of the wine we drink carries a family name. True, in some cases, it is only the name that remains. The Penfold and Hardy vineyards, for example, are now retained by large public companies in which the families have limited, if any, involvement. But many wine labels, among them Brown Brothers, McWilliams and De Bortoli, represent a sturdy family tradition going back generations, and with their eyes fixed firmly on the future.

These families, whose names are better known than most, represent the tip of an iceberg of family connections. In an age of global finance, some 80 per cent of Australia's wealth is still generated by family businesses. And within this pool swim some enormous fish. While these families may not rule Australia per se, at the height of their power they have had a considerable influence in its administration. Wool baron John Macarthur, while still a budding dynast in the fledgling colony of New South Wales, engineered the removal of several governors. Two hundred years later, father-and-son media team Rupert and Lachlan Murdoch are among a handful of private individuals able to visit the prime minister, John Howard, while he recovers from the flu at home—to discuss the government's cross-media laws.

Few if any governments have proved immune to the influence of elite families. Even the Labor Party, for all its professed dislike of dynastic power and privilege, has embraced its share of powerful mates. Kerry Packer, a third-generation media magnate and one of the richest men in Australia, was assiduously courted by Labor politicians who considered him outside Australia's old establishment clique.

These days media dynasties loom large in the power and influence they wield—not only, as in the case of the Packers, on the national stage but, as with the Murdoch family, across the globe. They are in some ways the new kids on the block, although Australia can also lay claim to the oldest media dynasty in the world, the Fairfaxes. Notwithstanding the loss of their flagship newspaper the *Sydney Morning Herald*, the family is still going strong under the auspices of John and Tim Fairfax's billion-dollar enterprise, Rural Press. These players have joined, and in many ways eclipsed, earlier dynastic families whose fortunes were built on pastoral enterprise and above all, land.

Today, while land remains a significant indicator of wealth—the Packer family is the Northern Territory's largest private landholder—it is no longer the great generator of family fortunes it once was. And this is perhaps one of the interesting things about Australian dynasties, for the business activities of our pre-eminent families have altered significantly since the early years of the colony, as have the names. No longer does the Macarthur family, once at the summit of a nascent colonial gentry, hold the political, social and economic clout that the Packers or Murdochs now do. Instead, it and other old pastoral families have had to make way for more recent dynasts, born of the country's twentieth-century wave of immigrants who immediately set to work building family empires in the boom industries of property, construction, food, textiles and media. These more recent dynasties are part of an increasingly diverse national elite, no longer dominated exclusively by old Anglo-Australian family wealth.

In just over two hundred years Australia's boom-and-bust economy has created a more porous dynastic establishment than that of its European or even American counterparts. In part, this may reflect the vagaries of fortune in a land plagued by cycles of flood and drought. In part it also reflects the difficulty of transplanting European notions to a country so far removed from the financial and cultural powerhouses of these traditions. Either way, family fortunes here have been built on relatively shallow foundations, the result of easy opportunities grasped which have just as quickly crumbled and been blown away by the winds of change.

Indeed it is often difficult to predict from one generation to the next whether a dynasty will collapse or strengthen. When Sir Keith Murdoch died he was the most powerful media boss in Australia and many observers thought that his maverick son Rupert would never be able to 'better' his father. How wrong they were. Rupert Murdoch's steely nerve and gambling instinct have driven the expansion of the family enterprise beyond all expectations. His basic philosophy is, he says, since his father's death, to keep pushing when things are going well and to pull out and 'go home' when losing. Rupert's winning streak has secured extraordinary power and influence on the international stage for himself and for the next generation of Murdochs.

But for most, the old adage 'shirtsleeves to shirtsleeves in three generations' holds true. Fewer than 40 per cent of Australian family companies are passed on to the second generation and only 13 per cent to the third. And it's often downhill from there. Consider the collapse of one of the country's great pastoral dynasties when third-generation patriarch David Wright, in an attempt to build on his inheritance, gambled away a family enterprise worth more than $16 million. Seeking to expand, he borrowed millions in the confident expectation of fulfilling a national demand for fine beef. Drought, a depressed cattle market and the failure of his retail deal to materialise brought his dynastic dreams and hubris crashing down when, in 1996, the bank placed the family empire and all its assets into receivership.

This book, however, looks primarily at those families whose dedication to a family enterprise or tradition has been sustained over three or more generations, with expectations of a continuance in the future. And despite the many failures, the fortunes of some of Australia's older dynasties have held remarkably strong in the face of national and global downturns and a vastly changed economic landscape. A significant number of families, among them the Myers (as well as their cousins by marriage, the Baillieus), have held their place among the nation's richest families for more than three generations, and retain a dynastic identity, despite the loss of the family's flagship enterprise. They have been joined by more recent entries, such as the De Bortoli wine family, who have gradually made their presence felt over three generations.

Moreover, while older pastoral elites such as the Macarthurs may be regarded as dynasties in decline, they remain pillars of the establishment, with wealthy connections that arise from their unique position, private schooling, work and clubs. They may no longer have the public presence they once did, but after seven generations their social standing is hardly questioned. Nor is the working of Australia's democratic process as chary of dynastic notions as we may think. In the 2001 federal election, two third-generation politicians were comfortably returned to office. In South Australia Alexander Downer easily held the seat of Mayo, in the Adelaide Hills, where both his politician father and grandfather had lived before him. Meanwhile, in the New South Wales seat of Richmond, Larry Anthony came one term closer to living up to the legacy of his father and grandfather, who between them had held the seat for more than half a century. As one among many voters confided to the press when Larry junior took up the political reins: 'I've been voting for Anthonys all my life. It's nice to have one back.'

And yet what is perhaps of greater significance than a family's enduring success is that the rise and fall of dynastic fortunes in Australia provides a fascinating glimpse of a wider historical canvas, as seen through the window of the family home. From early colonial 'blue bloods' such as the Macarthurs and pastoral adventurers such as the Duracks, to the arrival of early urban entrepreneurs such as Sidney Myer and the domination of powerful media families such as the Murdochs, the manner by which these families have established their wealth and influence illuminates critical moments in our national development. Their personal stories and shifting fortunes reflect in part the wider struggles, values and trends that have shaped our society. Accordingly, the families chosen for this book come from all over the country and their ascendancy reflects different periods in our history. In focusing on six families and telling their stories more completely, we have endeavoured to bring out their distinctive qualities, as well as important points of commonality.

The book begins with one of Australia's oldest dynasties, the Macarthur family, who, in founding the nation's wool industry, became one of the great pastoral, political and social forces of their day. Their trail is traced from colonial beginnings to current travails. While the Macarthurs once represented the elite of a new colony whose eyes remained tightly focused on England and its accustomed hierarchies and prejudices, the Duracks, who arrived sixty years later, were cut from very different cloth. They were Irish Catholic immigrants, escaping famine and dispossession at the hands of the English. The Duracks sought new opportunities on the far side of the continent where they, in turn, would wrest control of an ancient land from its original inhabitants.

The book then looks to South Australia, created not as a convict colony but with a visionary belief in colonial reform that could create an idealised and improved-upon England. Here pastoral wealth found expression in *noblesse oblige* and colonial leadership, giving rise to one of our foremost political dynasties, the Downers.

If South Australia was home to the high-minded, Victoria was the heartland of the land boomers and a new wave of entrepreneurs who made their fortune in property speculation, banking and industry. By the end of the nineteenth century, Melbourne had overtaken Sydney as a magnet for migrants, among them a penniless Russian, Sidney Myer, who would ride the wave of industrialisation and urbanisation to found one of the world's great department stores. He would also make charitable work an integral part of the Myer company and dynasty, so that today one of the great unifying factors of this now large and diverse family is its philanthropy through the Myer Foundation.

In the tradition of many great patriarchs Sidney Myer broke through the ranks of society in a single generation. But even he has been overshadowed by Rupert Murdoch, the present-day patriarch of the mightiest media dynasty Australia has ever produced. In less than three generations this close-knit, ambitious family has moved from the respectable fringes of Melbourne society to become one of the world's most powerful clans. Although no longer a strictly Australian dynasty, the family maintains its antipodean roots, and we chart its rise from archetypal Anglo-Australian traditions.

Vittorio De Bortoli, who arrived in Melbourne from Italy in the 1920s, brought with him very different customs. He was an illiterate peasant farmer in search of land to till. He found this in Griffith, a small rural outpost equidistant from Melbourne and Sydney, where, over three generations, the family would emerge as one of Australia's most successful postwar migrant dynasties.

Common to all these families is the figure of the dynastic patriarch. Australia's oldest dynasties trace their origins to the arrival of the country's first entrepreneurs, eager to grasp whatever opportunities were to be wrung from a new colony. With few prospects and little status or money, they left their homelands determined to make their fortunes. The precursors of Australia's leading families were thus inherently different to their European counterparts: these were not men with aristocratic connections, but aspiring go-getters prepared to travel to the ends of the earth to succeed in their ambitions.

While political patronage and a dose of good luck may be among the ingredients for dynastic success, drive, determination, vision and a keen eye for the main chance are attributes equally well represented among Australia's founding dynasts. John Macarthur arrived in New South Wales £200 in debt and died its most influential private land holder. Patrick Durack, against all odds, acquired a pastoral empire the size of Belgium in the space of a single lifetime. Rupert Murdoch has gone from owning a part share in an Adelaide newspaper to becoming the head of one of the world's largest cross-media empires.

In view of these extraordinary achievements, it is hardly surprising that in most, if not all of our dynasties, the founding patriarch casts a long shadow. It is he who determines the basis of the dynasty's identity for generations to come. John Macarthur's success in establishing himself among the colony's first landed gentry ensured that his family, generations later, has remained part of a small propertied class for whom the need to inherit and manage land has been a central tenet of their lives. 'Newspapers,' observes Dame Elisabeth Murdoch, 'are in my children's blood,' and it is hard to imagine the Murdochs as anything but a media family. One of the most fascinating aspects of Sidney Myer's story concerns his ability to broaden his family's sense of identity from 'the Store' to philanthropy.

For the successful dynastic family, there is little distinction between business and home. The 'family business' is what the family 'does' whenever it is together. Alexander Downer says he learned the 'art of politics' at his parents' knee. Every weekday, the extended De Bortoli family eats lunch and talks business over meals cooked by the current matriarch, Emeri. For Lachlan Murdoch, having dinner with Dad means dining with the chairman of the board. He recalls as a schoolboy listening to his father and famous dinner guests thrash out business strategies. 'We're a private family,' reflects Lachlan. 'We don't talk about our personal affairs. But we can talk about business forever.'

Opting out of the business can mean opting out of the family. Those who don't object to the status quo tend to follow in their father's footsteps. The sons of most dynastic patriarchs grow up with an abiding admiration of their sires—however volatile their fathers may seem to a wider audience—resulting in a fervent desire to emulate them. 'Rupert is a modern version of his father. Absolutely,' claims Dame Elisabeth Murdoch of her son, the present-day patriarch of the family empire. In turn, her grandson James professes the hope that there are more similarities than differences between himself and his father Rupert.

In truth, however, the stronger the personality of the patriarch, the harder it can be for successive generations to step outside his shadow. Instead, they often become the servants of their father's vision. Successive generations are similarly caught in the blinding glare of the dynast's accomplishments. Novelist Martin Boyd, the third-generation descendant of an Anglo-Australian dynasty, writes tellingly in his novel *The Cardboard Crown* of the shock experienced when a great-grandson dares critique a portrait of the family patriarch. The young man observes that here was someone who 'looks very important, but not quite at ease with himself'. At these remarks, comments the novel's narrator, 'the balloon-like ghost of my grandfather suddenly shrank to its proper size in history. With the collapse of the bubble, I felt that I began to see him as he really was, and that in his shrunken image I began to perceive the nature of the treasures and calamities he had left us.'

There is little room for such reflection in most dynasties striving to maintain their elevated place in the order of things. Few are willing to find fault with their antecedents. Perhaps this kind of critical appraisal can come only at some distance— as shown by Mary Durack's endeavours in *Kings in Grass Castles*, written after the loss of the family's pastoral enterprise. More usually, a family's efforts are directed, over successive generations, to upholding the dynastic vision to which they owe their continuing prestige.

This in itself is a source of curious tension. Much as a dynasty may want to continue along the path established for it by its founding patriarch, a degree of reinvention is often required to keep a family from falling behind the times. Without the entrepreneurial contributions of successive generations, a dynasty can quickly find itself becoming obsolete, the reasons for its original success no longer relevant. When first seeking to hold his father's seat of Richmond, Larry Anthony took to the hills around Lismore, Nimbin and Ballina on a mountain bike in order to convince a new generation of voters that the medium, if not the message, had changed. Alexander Downer, as Minister for Foreign Affairs, declares himself a very different politician to his small 'l' liberal forebears.

The need to embrace change is particularly pertinent to business dynasties. The De Bortoli family owes its success precisely to the ability of each of its three generations to expand on the vision of its predecessor. While father Deen De Bortoli increased the family fortunes by leading the charge into bulk wine production, his eldest son Darren has taken the company to new heights by spearheading its entry into the quality wine market. Neither venture was without risk, yet both have paid off. In contrast, attempts by heirs apparent Lachlan Murdoch and James Packer to take their family companies into new technologies by investing in a telecommunications company, OneTel, proved disastrous, costing their family enterprises approximately $860 million. This failure, however, has not stopped either dynasty from continuing to appraise new media opportunities.

In fact, not grasping opportunities and taking risks is the death knell for a dynasty, as many have discovered when their assets have been whittled away over successive generations. The Macarthurs, who have done well indeed to keep their estate in the family for seven generations, have found themselves facing precisely this conundrum. 'As the older generations died, the shares split and became smaller and smaller,' observes one descendant of the empire begun by John and Elizabeth Macarthur.

In seeking to maintain their influence, perhaps all dynasties are battling against the odds. As early as 1377, the great Muslim historian and sociologist Muqaddin Ibn Khaldun declared that most dynasties would decline after three generations as a result of three interrelated and insurmountable evils: the indulgence in luxury, the loss of cohesiveness and group feeling, and financial trouble. But even as the power that once supported it fades, the determination to cleave to a family identity remains—and often grows inversely more significant. Successive generations of Macarthurs have changed their name by deed poll in order to preserve their cultural legacy.

It is this dedication to the past that makes many dynasties, in the final analysis, bastions of conservatism. While women are slowly starting to challenge traditional male rights of succession, the story of dynasties in Australia, as elsewhere, is more often than not the story of patriarchs and their sons. This is despite the fact that in almost every instance a family's initial success has been based on a successful partnership. Even in the most traditional marriages, women have performed the vital role of ensuring a family's cohesion while the patriarch expanded the empire. Rupert Murdoch's second wife Anna sat on the News Corporation board during their long marriage, insisting this was 'an assurance policy' in the event of Rupert dying before his children were fully blooded.

Other partnerships have been stronger working alliances still, forged on shared ambition and complementary skills. During his ongoing battles with colonial powerbrokers and his extended periods of exile, John Macarthur's wife Elizabeth administered the family holdings and at the same time established herself and her family as above reproach. Similarly, Giuseppina De Bortoli is credited by her daughters as being equally responsible for establishing the family enterprise, although it is her husband, Vittorio, whose portrait is given pride of place above the cellar door.

Neither of these women's daughters would inherit the dynastic mantle. Instead, this passed to the family's sons. Even today, it is Rupert Murdoch's eldest son Lachlan and not either of his older sisters who has been deemed the 'first among equals' as his father's successor in business. Women, it would seem, despite their tireless contributions to the dynastic endeavour, are favoured only in the absence of a male heir.

And it is this need by successive generations to come to terms with their place within a dynastic legacy that makes the families in this book so fascinating. Most of us have had to negotiate our identity within an understanding of familial expectations.

Imagine, however, the pressures of doing so within the context of a legacy handed down over generations. For it is only through an abiding sense of intergenerational identity that a dynasty maintains continuity.

The Murdoch family, despite the overwhelming presence of its current patriarch, has a strong collective identity as being, by nature, anti-establishment, hardworking and risk-taking. However accurate these self-descriptions may be, they are precisely the traits needed to manage the family business, News Corporation. The incentive to live up to such an identity must be powerful indeed—carrying with it the alluring possibility of great triumph but, equally, of great and public catastrophe.

The place of the family is complex and generally regarded as private and off limits to the public. But the trials and tribulations of our dynastic families are inevitably of wider interest—an interest that the families themselves accept as in keeping with their own understanding of their historic significance. Their personal stories provide insight into how individuals are shaped by the expectations of others, as well as by our own perceptions of self within the context of family, community and society. They offer a mirror to wider social forces that influence us all, for theirs is a history of family tradition, played out in the national arena and subjected to the pressures of changing times. From this crucible have arisen six remarkable histories.

THE MACARTHUR FAMILY

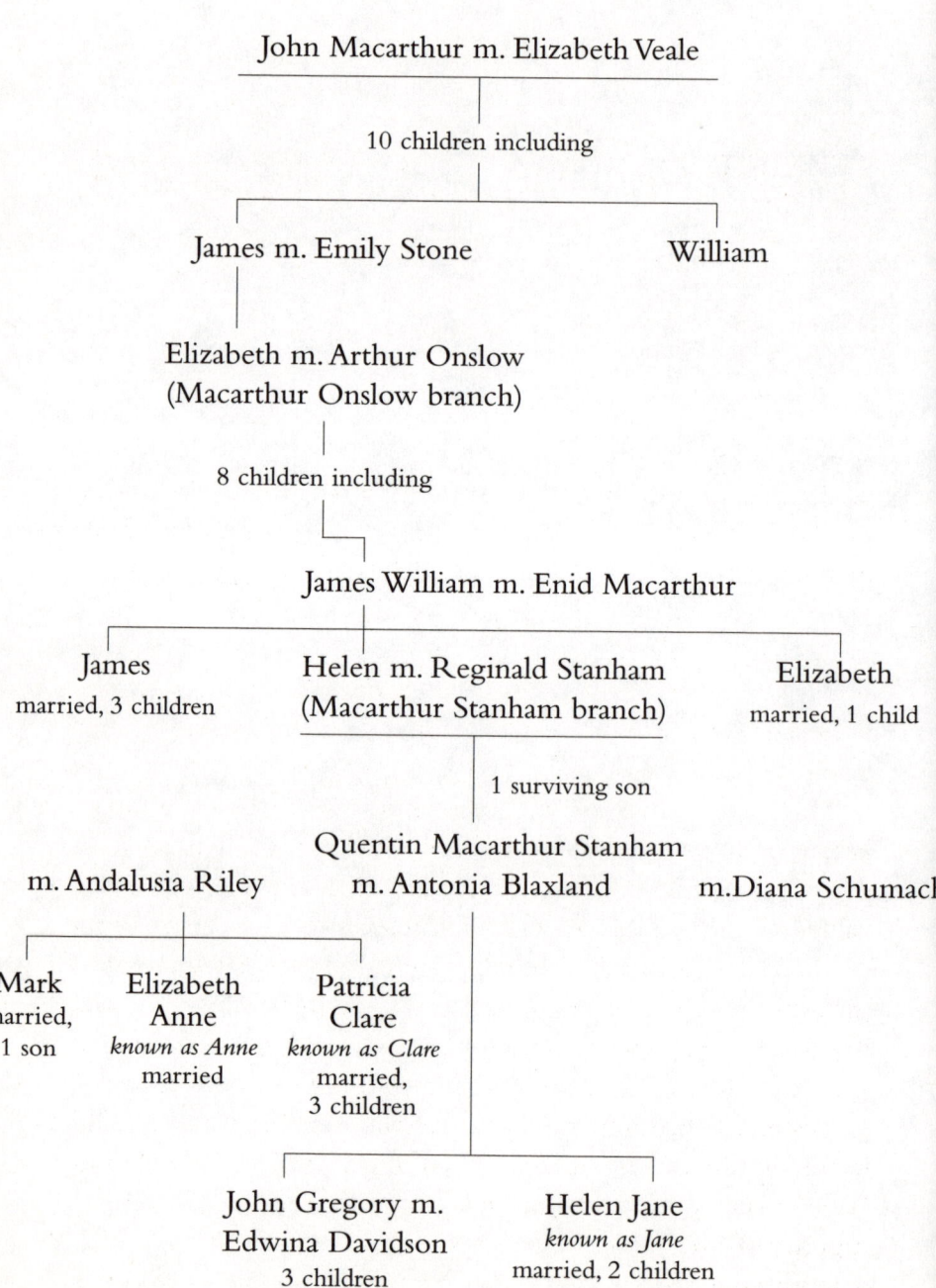

John Macarthur m. Elizabeth Veale

10 children including

James m. Emily Stone   William

Elizabeth m. Arthur Onslow
(Macarthur Onslow branch)

8 children including

James William m. Enid Macarthur

James
married, 3 children

Helen m. Reginald Stanham
(Macarthur Stanham branch)

Elizabeth
married, 1 child

1 surviving son

Quentin Macarthur Stanham

m. Andalusia Riley   m. Antonia Blaxland   m. Diana Schumach

Mark
married,
1 son

Elizabeth
Anne
known as Anne
married

Patricia
Clare
known as Clare
married,
3 children

John Gregory m.
Edwina Davidson
3 children

Helen Jane
known as Jane
married, 2 children

TO THE MANOR BORN

———— ■ ————

THE MACARTHURS

IT IS a warm spring morning, and the only sounds are the hum of cicadas and the crunch of feet on gravel as a well-mannered queue forms on the circular carriageway. The scent of wisteria, dust and hay lingers in the air. A face peers out of a ground-floor window, and the porticoed front door swings slowly open. For just one weekend each year Camden Park, the family home of the Macarthur dynasty for over seven generations, is open to the public.

This homespun affair, which takes place with almost no marketing or advertising, will bring hundreds of visitors eager for a peek at our colonial past. In a society obsessed with real estate values, Camden Park offers something more. The closest thing Australia has to an aristocratic heritage, it stands as testament to the aspirations of Australia's earliest mogul, John Macarthur, and his family, who saw themselves as the first of a new landed gentry. Driven by a burning ambition and keen entrepreneurial instincts, this aspiring dynast established his fortunes, and those of the emerging colony, by transforming New South Wales from a distant penal outpost into England's foremost supplier of fine wool.

Commissioned in 1831, Camden Park was built to celebrate

and confirm Macarthur's position as the colony's largest private landholder—an achievement that would keep his descendants at the forefront of society until late in the twentieth century. In a country of few historic buildings, it offers a vision of Australia that we barely recognise today; a glimpse of the good life as it once was for the tiny, elite cartel that helped shape the foundations of a nation. An hour's drive from Sydney's central business district, the house stands in a park-like landscape of paddocks and trees, its outlook punctuated only by the steeple of a distant church, 'built to the glory of God and to enhance the Macarthurs' view'.[1] There is an air of substance and permanence, a sense of serene graciousness and place, of belonging built up over generations.

Of course, this could simply be the enduring illusion of Georgian architecture, for later colonists would continue to build in this style as if, by invoking an earlier age and respectability, they could disguise the tenuous nature of their antipodean roots. But Camden Park's impact is undeniable—perhaps because, to contemporary eyes, it seems extraordinary to encounter such a splendid testament to English traditions in the Australian landscape.

The reigning head of the Macarthur dynasty, Quentin Macarthur-Stanham, is rarely present during Camden Park's open weekends. Spring usually finds him in Rhode Island, the home of his third wife, Diana, whom he met while on a croquet tour of the United States. When in Camden, he lives in the dowager's cottage, a short walk from the main house. With his starched English accent, beetling eyebrows and gentlemanly air, Quentin cuts as striking a figure as the house to which he has devoted his life.

His children are more recognisably part of a contemporary Australian landscape. On the back lawn, John Macarthur-Stanham—Quentin's son by his second marriage—is overseeing the sausage sizzle. His half-brother Mark, the child of an earlier marriage, directs traffic in the car park with a more parochial good humour. Heavier set and ten years John's senior, Mark is as dark as his brother is fair. Nonetheless, the two men bear a striking family resemblance, both to each other and to their antecedents. Both share their father's craggy features as well as his passion for Camden Park. Both grew up here. But their lives since then have taken very different turns.

As the eldest, Mark came to adulthood believing Camden Park was his birthright. But it is his younger sibling who occupies the house and John's children who will one day inherit. While there is always a bedroom for him, Mark will only ever be a guest at Camden Park. The house and the farmlands surrounding it are forever beyond his reach, for Quentin passed over his eldest child when Mark was in his early thirties, making John his sole heir.

Today, Mark lives in Cowra where, as Macarthur Farming Services, he works as a farm labourer and runs a small haulage company. His younger brother, meanwhile, shoulders the responsibility of safekeeping what remains of the family's heritage—an endowment that has shaped his life as much as its dispossession has shaped his brother's. For while the family's fortunes may have steadily diminished with the passing of generations, its custodianship of an iconic Australian heritage beckons as strongly as ever before.

From a European perspective, this dynastic legacy carries considerably less gravitas than those of the old world. As any member of the British peerage will tell you, Camden Park with its eighty-odd rooms is merely the home of a draper's son who made good on the sheep's back—a relatively recent upstart whose fortunes depended on the patronage of colonial power-brokers. Contrast this with the dynastic imperative of an estate such as Chatsworth, home of the Duke of Marlborough, with its imposing mansion of two hundred plus rooms—a heritage that has been held by the same family for over twelve generations.

And yet no other private house in Australia can boast such significance, age or lineage. In its heyday Camden Park was the nerve point of a pastoral empire that stretched over thousands of hectares and the headquarters of a family that, in shaping the colony's economic and political direction, were among its most influential citizens. Above all else, its history mirrors the success of early efforts to adapt English ideas to a new and contested landscape, as played out by one of the colony's most powerful families.

Today only 400 hectares remain, devoted mainly to dairy and poultry farming. The rest is illusion—old Macarthur land that was bought by the state government for an agricultural college, the grounds of which hold at bay the rapidly encroaching town of Camden, named after the family estate. Surrounded by this buffer, Camden Park is the Macarthurs' last link to a glorious dynastic past. And perhaps this is what makes the house such an enduring drawcard, because it is not a museum but an evolving repository of family history and secrets, as each visitor soon discovers.

That the present-day Macarthur dynasty has the makings of soap opera comes as less of a surprise when one considers that the family's early history is in itself worthy of a Regency melodrama. Dominating this drama is the character of John Macarthur who, in a portrait painted at the high point of his career, exudes an arrogance that is palpable centuries later. With an assessing stare, he gazes disdainfully down his aquiline nose at the rest of the world, the embodiment, it would seem, of an autocratic English gentleman.

And yet he was born the second son of a Plymouth draper on 13 August 1767. Unlike his older brother, who would follow his father into the family trade, John was encouraged to seek his future elsewhere. His father's mercantile success secured him the upward mobility of a private school education, followed, at the age of fifteen, by an ensign's commission in the army, traditionally the chosen vocation of second sons of the nobility. But John's fledgling career prospects stumbled to a halt a year later when America won its war of independence against Britain and his corps was disbanded.

Unable to sell his commission, which was of little value in peacetime, he spent the next five years living a desultory existence near the Devon–Cornwall border, riding and hunting, studying history, contemplating a legal career and working occasionally as an assistant teacher to supplement his meagre income. (In short, providing himself with a wide-ranging liberal education that would advantage his later career.)

It took a woman to get him out of this rut. Elizabeth Veale was twenty, the same age as John, when they met. She was the daughter of a Devonshire farmer who had died when she was six—to the detriment of her own social and economic standing. As one of her biographers observes, 'Like many of Jane Austen's poor heroines with inadequate family connections, her prospects of marriage were uncertain. Like them, she looked for strangers, newcomers to the village, army and navy men on half pay trying to make something of farming.'[2] But while the couple may have been well matched in terms of their place in the rigid social hierarchies of the day, their alliance was viewed with some pessimism by the bride's relatives. 'I was considered indolent and inactive; Mr Macarthur too proud and haughty for our humble fortune or expectations,' reflected Elizabeth of their marriage in October 1788. As an officer consigned to half pay, her husband lacked the means to support himself, let alone a wife—or the family that was rapidly upon them when Elizabeth gave birth to a son a mere five months later.

Had this been a Jane Austen novel, John and Elizabeth would no doubt have fallen into further obscurity, in keeping with the class politics of the day. Instead, whether as the result of desperation, the scandal of a child conceived out of wedlock, or a shared vision, their alliance seems to have empowered them both. Accordingly, in June 1789 Macarthur seized the opportunity to transfer his commission, becoming a lieutenant in the New South Wales Corps. It was a posting filled with risk and danger, for the penal colony had been founded only eighteen months earlier, and the fate of its first shipment of officers and convicts was uncertain. Indeed, one imagines that only the most unenviable of prospects could have motivated someone to embark on an enterprise that would put no less than six months of perilous voyage between themselves and all they had known, with little assurance of what lay in wait. (Let alone to do so with a baby.) But Elizabeth, despite her self-proclaimed 'timid and irresolute' appearance, was an ardent advocate of the scheme. As she enthused in a letter to her mother, it was a decision from which 'we have every reasonable expectation of reaping the most material advantage'.[3] She would be the first woman to embark on such a journey of her own free will.

The young family sailed with the Second Fleet on 17 January 1790. But even before they had left British waters, John Macarthur would fight the first duel of his Australian career with the captain of their ship, the *Neptune*, over the unsanitary conditions on board. It marked the start of a voyage notorious in the history of transportation to Australia for the suffering endured. Locked away in her small cabin, where the heat and stench soon became insupportable, Elizabeth wrote vividly of their plight, for 'no imagination could conceive the misery I experienced'. But she expressed no empathy for the welfare of others, lamenting that only a 'slight partition' separated her family from the women convicts, 'their dreadful imprecations' and 'attendant filth and vermin'.[4]

After protracted arguments with his commanding officer, John Macarthur was able to secure upgraded quarters on a sister ship, the *Scarborough*. Nevertheless, for the remainder of the voyage their son Edward was gravely ill. John also contracted a raging fever from which he nearly died—and on which his subsequent bouts of depression were blamed. A daughter born prematurely on the voyage lived less than an hour. When they disembarked half a year later, on 28 June 1790, the Macarthurs knew themselves fortunate to survive. Of the thousand prisoners transported on the Fleet's three vessels, one quarter had died, half were landed sick, and many died soon after—having been brutally beaten, starved and placed in irons. There was little joy on land either, for the thousand-strong penal colony was in the grip of famine and the supply ship accompanying the Second Fleet had hit ice and sunk.

Even at the best of times, the new settlement was a gossipy, avaricious and venal place. The small society was highly polarised between the 'haves' of the officer class and the convict 'have-nots'. At the same time, the colony's social structure, despite the inherent constraint of the convict taint, was remarkably fluid in contrast to English society. Those who migrated to New South Wales were 'precisely those who would not be accepted into the best society at home'[5] and even ex-convicts could attain wealth and prestige, if not respectability. The latter was reserved for free settlers, although as he rose through the ranks, Macarthur's sturdy bourgeois origins would be sneered at by his detractors. But Jack Bodice, as Macarthur was nicknamed in snide reference to his draper father, had gambled well. Unlike the colony's governors, who came and went, the New South Wales Corps was the enduring and dominant force in the small and isolated community. Its officers controlled all aspects of colonial life; they ran the courts, managed the convicts, and organised provisions. Nor was Macarthur alone in hoping to advance his fortunes. For the ambitious young men of the corps, even the assignment of convict labour became an instrument of profit, and they resisted any attempts to moderate their power. This often placed them at odds with the governors of the day—most of whom were more concerned with the colony's stable administration as a penal outpost than its economic future.

Few officers, however, made as early, decisive or lucrative an impact on the colony's affairs as John Macarthur. Although he quarrelled almost immediately with Governor Phillip, who promptly barred him from all social gatherings at Government House, he befriended his ageing commanding officer, who promoted him to regimental paymaster (at more than double his lieutenant's salary) and shortly thereafter Inspector of Public Works for Parramatta and Toongabbie. These assignments gave Macarthur extensive control over the colony's rudimentary resources, including the government stores. He capitalised on this with admirable filial allegiance by immediately directing orders for the regiment's slops—the clothing and other supplies sold to seamen from the ship's stores—to his elder brother in Plymouth.

Macarthur's position also enabled him to make the most of his own land grants and, using the convict labour under his command, he was soon able to double his original entitlement of 20 hectares as a reward for being the first to clear his land. But his vigorous pursuit of self-advancement was not without its benefits to the colony, insists historian Alan Atkinson, who points to Macarthur's progressive agricultural and employment practices.[6] By the same token, the practical administration of his farm-bred wife was equally decisive in transforming their property, Elizabeth Farm, into the best-run agricultural estate in the colony. (It did not perhaps take much to excel; Macarthur was the first man in the colony to import and use a plough.)

By 1796, the colony numbered just over three thousand Europeans, close to two thousand of whom were convicts. The officers of the New South Wales Corps, including Macarthur, made up a small and privileged caste, for they owned nearly a third of the colony's land, three-quarters of its livestock, and enjoyed a monopoly over the importing and sale of food, liquor, clothing and tobacco. For Elizabeth, the prosperity this brought easily made up for her isolation as the first free woman to have arrived in the settlement. As she happily admitted in a letter home to her best friend on 1 September 1798, 'This country possesses numerous advantages to persons holding appointments under Government.'[7] Her only qualm was the difficulty of educating her children—and the necessity of sending her boys to London to study. She would farewell her eldest, Edward, when he was twelve. Her second son, John, considered the brightest and most beautiful of her children, would leave when he was seven. She would never see him again.

John junior accompanied his father back to England in 1801. It was an ignominious departure, for Macarthur was returning home to face court martial after seriously wounding his new commanding officer in a duel. He was by now a veteran of a series of battles with the colony's governors. Phillip's successor,

John Hunter, had already been precipitately recalled after Macarthur—regarded by his adversary as 'restless, ambitious and litigious'—had mounted a campaign of complaint against him. Relations with the colony's third governor grew almost as sour when Governor King failed to support Macarthur in a dispute with another officer. In response, Macarthur organised a boycott of all social activities at Government House—only to extend the brawl to his commanding officer when the latter refused to comply.

Certainly his new superiors felt that, as one of the colony's wealthiest men, Macarthur had already exceeded his station. 'He came here in 1790 more than £500 in debt and he is now worth at least $20 000 pounds,' complained Governor King in an emotional yet prescient letter to the Colonial Office. 'His employment during the 11 years he has been here has been that of making a large fortune and helping his brother officers make small ones . . . If Captain McArthur returns here in any official character it should be that of Governor, as one half of the Colony already belongs to him and it will not be long before he gets the other half.'[8]

But King's hopes of seeing Captain John Macarthur receive his just desserts would be dashed. In the course of a slow year-long journey back to England, Macarthur met and befriended Robert Farquhar, the British Resident at Amboyna in the Indonesian archipelago, whose father, Sir Walter, was physician to the Prince of Wales. These new friends brought their considerable influence to bear in Macarthur's favour, ensuring that while he was officially censured, he avoided a trial. Ironically, Macarthur's forced return could not have been better timed to advance his interests. The Napoleonic wars had robbed Britain's lucrative textile industry of its continental source of wool and the country was desperate to secure an alternative supply. Seeing an opportunity, Macarthur seized it.

Resigning his commission, and investing himself with a monopoly of authority in the wool industry, Macarthur campaigned vigorously for a scheme of colonial wool production under his personal supervision. He made a convincing case, stressing the advantage to British industry as well as its necessity to a colony that remained dependent on British imports for its survival and which was constantly on the brink of starvation. 'This small population,' he argued, 'can have no prospect of success unless it can raise the export of some raw material in considerable demand, which can be produced with little labour, and be capable of bearing the expense of the longest sea voyage.'[9] With his new entree into royal circles, Macarthur took his case to the highest authorities and won the ear of Lord Camden, the colonial secretary.

Official history has it that Macarthur also brought with him samples of the fine wool he was already producing at Elizabeth Farm (proof of his credentials in the trade). But some historians who take issue with Macarthur's standing as the father of the Australian wool industry, question whether these samples ever existed. They argue that others—notably Governor King and the Reverend Samuel Marsden, who notwithstanding his religious calling was one of the colony's largest land- and stock-holders—did more to encourage an early wool industry in the colony.[10] And, in fact, it was Marsden who would send the first commercial shipment of wool to England from New South Wales in 1811. None of this, however, detracts from the fact that not only was Macarthur in the right place at the right time, but that he had the entrepreneurial instincts to exploit a small window of opportunity, predominantly for his own, but also others', benefit.

One can only imagine Governor King's immense chagrin when his *bête noire* returned to the colony in June 1805, aboard his own ship—a former whaler which, with poetic licence, Macarthur had renamed the *Argo*—more powerful than ever before. Macarthur brought with him merinos from the king's royal flock and Lord Camden's approval of a grant of 2000 hectares of the colony's best pastures—the largest entitlement by far allowed in the colony to date. Moreover, Camden had promised Macarthur a further 2000 hectares if his plans for a fine-wool industry in the colony came to fruition. King immediately wrote to the colonial secretary, begging him to reconsider, but to no avail. He went the way of all governors, back to England, while Macarthur stayed and prospered.

One would imagine that Macarthur was by now secure in his position as the colony's pre-eminent pastoral baron. But further conflict and controversy were soon to follow. Having survived the mutiny on the *Bounty*, William Bligh, King's successor, would make the grave mistake of challenging Macarthur's ascendancy. Bligh, who throughout his career had demonstrated a remarkable imperviousness to the opinions of others, envisaged New South Wales as a relatively static and stable society that would slowly develop as its convicts progressed gratefully up a truncated social ladder to the status of small-scale farmers or labourers. It was a cosy, paternalistic vision, at odds with the trading interests of the colony's business elites and with realities on the ground.

From the penal colony's inception, the officers of the New South Wales Corps had been the only people in the settlement to receive financial payment for their services in British sterling, as convicts were not considered to need money. They had quickly transformed this fiscal monopoly into a monopoly on the importation and distribution of all the colony's goods, enjoying mark-ups (at wholesale) of anywhere from 100 to 500 per cent.[11] At the centre of this trade was rum, which became the major currency in the colony and soon held much of the population in its thrall. The result, as historian Manning Clark vividly describes it, was that 'in the eyes of the moralisers, gaming, whoring and drunkenness stalked in broad daylight without least check; religion was laughed at, the Sabbath profaned. The more elemental passions went unrestrained.'[12] Governor King, himself an alcoholic, was the first to bemoan the ill effects of liquor on the colony. Bligh, as his successor, was determined that 'the pernicious customs of the place shall be checked by every means in my power'.[13]

The new governor established port regulations to tighten up the government's control of ships, their cargoes—including spirits—and their crews, which may have included possible escaping convicts. He then declared the bartering of spirits for grain, food or labour illegal, and ordered that all promissory notes should be drawn 'payable in sterling money'. Bligh also reissued an earlier ban on the use of private stills. These reforms placed him on a collision course with the colony's budding entrepreneurs, including the officers of the corps and Macarthur. The two men already held each other in deep suspicion, for Bligh had also made clear his scepticism of Macarthur's enthusiasm for the colony's fledgling wool industry and challenged his right to the land granted him by Lord Camden.[14] Only a few months later, in October 1807, Bligh further alienated Macarthur and his peers by declaring that all private houses and buildings on the leasehold crown land of Sydney Town were illegal and would be removed. Macarthur responded by building a fence round his leasehold property in a flagrant and popular act of civil disobedience.

Matters came to a head when Macarthur was brought to trial for permitting some of the crew of the *Parramatta*, a ship of which he was part owner, to land, contrary to regulations. In what had clearly become, among other things, a clash of personalities, Macarthur now found himself facing a long-time adversary, and one of the least reputable of Bligh's few allies. Richard Atkins, the fifth son of an English baronet, had fled to New South Wales to escape his creditors. As Macarthur publicly pronounced, 'this aristocratic relic, sent out hidden from other eyes, this befuddled buffoon full of demon drink, this human ruin, this vague bewildered wreck'[15] had been made the colony's highest judicial authority, its judge-advocate. Macarthur's scathing opinion of Atkins was widely shared, not least by Bligh himself, who nonetheless continued to support Atkins's findings against their common enemy. It would prove the governor's undoing.

In the lead-up to his hearing, Macarthur sponsored a petition urging the governor's removal. The request was well received, for Bligh had angered the corps' officers and enlisted men by challenging its status in the colony, arguing that it was becoming a dangerous militia and needed replacing. When the trial commenced on 25 January 1808, Macarthur (who had a better grasp of the law than his adversary) immediately challenged Atkins's right to adjudicate—a claim quickly supported by the officers on the Bench who had uncovered suggestions that Atkins had prepared fabricated evidence. The judge-advocate retaliated by insisting that the officers be charged with treason, a recommendation Bligh adopted, thereby precipitating his own downfall. The next day, on the twentieth anniversary of the colony's foundation, the commander of the New South Wales Corps freed Macarthur, and William Bligh, for the second time in his career, found himself at the mercy of his own men. After a swift and bloodless military coup which he had done much to engineer, Macarthur assumed the title of colonial secretary and became, for a time, the virtual administrator of the colony.

The Rum Rebellion, as it has since been known, remains one of the most controversial episodes in Australian colonial history. But irrespective of the rights or wrongs of the case, the coup confirms our protagonist's aptitude for political intrigue and self-preservation. Although like everyone else in the colony, including the clergy and the governor himself, Macarthur used rum as currency, he had gone on record condemning the traffic in liquor. Moreover, as colonial secretary he would anger his fellow revolutionaries by trying to suppress it. Indeed, Macarthur would soon prove almost as unpopular an administrator as the man he had toppled. Smaller settlers particularly fretted at his political dominance, arguing that his 'monopoly and extortion have been injurious to the inhabitants of every description'.[16]

Macarthur had also overestimated his support among the colonial authorities. When he returned to London in 1810 to rebut charges of treason, bringing with him his two youngest sons, William and James, who were due to commence their

English schooling, he found himself condemned to virtual exile. Although as a civilian Macarthur could not be courtmartialled, instructions were sent to the colony's new governor, Lachlan Macquarie, that as the 'leading Promoter and Instigator of the Mutinous measures' he was to be arrested if he returned to New South Wales and tried before a criminal court'.[17]

Macarthur would spend the next seven years campaigning for his return to the colony. To add insult to injury, this setback coincided with a low point in his fortunes for his most recent commercial speculations had failed, leaving him with debts the family's wool trade barely covered. Macarthur focused his attention on promoting his wool and ensuring that it established itself competitively in the British market, demonstrating a degree of circumspection and diplomacy that was remarkable for its absence in New South Wales.

Elizabeth, meanwhile, remained at home loyally tending the family's estates and flocks. Both flourished under her care. Despite complaining that 'the management of our concerns gets troublesome to me in the extreme', and bemoaning the lack of any assistance from the men in her family, Elizabeth was an able manager. In theory she followed her husband's advice; in practice a year or more could pass between letters, and Elizabeth relied on her own judgment and that of her convict workers.

It was Elizabeth who bought, tended and bred up the flock of fine wool merinos upon which the family fortunes increasingly depended. She also developed new methods of washing wool and was responsible for the building of the first large-capacity woolshed at Camden. Elizabeth's 'excellent and prudent management', acknowledged her grateful husband, was such that 'not many men would be capable of conducting so successfully as you have done, so much to your own credit, and to the advantage of your Family'.[18] Observes Quentin Macarthur-Stanham generations later, 'The vision of it was unquestionably John's, but the mechanics of making it work almost entirely Elizabeth's.'[19]

John's absence might even have been to his wife's advantage, for Elizabeth was as even-keeled as John was volatile. 'Where he was angry and abrasive, she was charming and diplomatic. He took things personally. She saw them as part of politics,' reflects one biographer.[20] As a result, Elizabeth Macarthur was as well regarded in the colonies as her husband was controversial. She was without doubt far more conventional than he, and her keen interest in social order and rank was reflected in her frequent requests for up-to-date copies of *Debrett's* and other such lists of the British peerage for her library. Intensely aware of her own social standing, Elizabeth assiduously cultivated her position as 'the First Lady of the colony' through her army of connections and friendships with the governors and their wives. Hers was one of the most gracious private homes in New South Wales, emulating 'as near as possible that of minor country gentry as they had known it in England. The rarity and beauty of this family life within the context of the colonial situation so impressed even John's most extreme political enemies that it purchased immunity for his family . . . Elizabeth Macarthur, her ordered home, her carefully nurtured children, always escaped any criticism levelled against John, as they escaped any possible reprisal for his part in the rebellion against Governor Bligh.'[21] It was a measure of her status that she was the only private citizen who did not have to bring her own bread to dinners at Government House.

Elizabeth was fifty-one when John returned from England in 1817, with their two youngest sons still in tow. Their youngest daughter, Emmeline had never met her father. With the return of her menfolk, Elizabeth would step back from active management, although she continued to exercise a strong influence over the family's public and private affairs. But after nearly a decade as her own woman, one wonders how easy Elizabeth found her retirement, for her correspondence suggests she was not only fully conversant with the wool business but enjoyed her involvement.

One also wonders what she made of her husband's growing antipathy towards the latest in a long line of governors. Elizabeth had enjoyed a long and warm association with Lachlan Macquarie and his wife, and their friendship secured her, among other things, an additional land grant of 240 hectares. Macarthur, however, soon took umbrage at Macquarie's reluctance to endow the family with yet more property as well as his liberal attitude to convicts, not least his eccentric if egalitarian practice of inviting prisoners to dinner.[22] Despite having undertaken to play no further part in the colony's public affairs as a condition of his sanctioned return, Macarthur would once more set out to undermine the crown's representative, successfully calling for an external investigation into Macquarie's emancipist practices.

In Macarthur's opinion, a lamentable and dangerous 'democratic feeling' had taken root in the colony as a consequence of 'the absurd and mischievous policy pursued by Governor Macquarie'. This, he insisted, could only be set right by supporting the interests 'of really respectable settlers—Men of real Capital—not needy adventurers' who, with government support and land grants 'of at least 10 000 Acres', could become as wealthy and powerful 'as an Aristocracy'.[23] While this might suggest a breathless and self-serving hypocrisy, Macarthur no doubt believed that, in keeping with the prejudices of the day, the mere absence of any convict taint bestowed unlimited credibility on his own personal endeavours.[24] In 1821, a 'dejected Macquarie'[25] left New South Wales to answer to a commission of inquiry in London, while Macarthur secured further imperial support for his pastoral ambitions.

Macarthur's determination to entrench the established hierarchies of the colony and see off any nascent competition was well in keeping with prevailing attitudes of the day. Indeed, it has been argued that Macarthur was more progressive than many free settlers in his association with ex-convicts, and for a time he counted 'the bastard son of a highway robber by a convict whore'[26] among his close friends. William Charles

Wentworth, who in character and contribution was at least as strong a colonial personality as Macarthur, would go on to found his own dynasty. But the two men fell out after Wentworth was refused the hand in marriage of Macarthur's eldest daughter, Elizabeth. That the refusal had come from the girl herself (though who can say how much influence her mother exerted in the background) and that Wentworth had sought this alliance on purely dynastic grounds made no difference to the rejected suitor's animosity. Henceforth, he would accuse his erstwhile friend of rank prejudice at every turn.

Wentworth would eventually marry the daughter of an emancipated convict and, as a consequence, would suffer far more entrenched snobbery. In order to secure his own daughters' marriages, Wentworth would have to assure their prospective husbands that they would have no further contact with their mother. Sarah Wentworth would work as her daughters' laundrywoman in order to maintain contact with her children—no matter that, at the time, she was wife to one of the richest men in the colony, as Wentworth had become. While the Wentworth dynasty would secure an enduring place for itself in Australia's conservative establishment, such was the convict taint that their ancestry remained an unspoken family secret for five generations.

Viewed against bigotry such as this, Macarthur could almost be regarded as generous in acclaiming the diligence and perseverance of former convicts, and upholding their contribution to the colony. Moreover, he happily entrusted responsibility to those in his employ and, as a local newspaper acknowledged, 'his prisoner servants never had cause to complain of deficient sustenance'.[27] But one does not establish a dynasty by promoting the interests of others in advance of one's own, and Macarthur's loyalties were firstly, firmly and exclusively allied to himself and his offspring. While he accepted that ex-convicts should be able to purchase small landholdings, he reserved for himself and his family a superior entitlement to honours and free land. Of the country's indigenous occupants there was no consideration.

Future governors would learn to work with this status quo, and even come to admire Macarthur, despite his hair-trigger temper. Increasingly sure of his power within the colony, Macarthur would boast to Governor Darling of his ability to rid himself of any man who had become obnoxious to him. (Darling evidently believed him, remarking with considerable restraint that here was a man of 'violent passions; his friendship strong, his hatred invincible'.[28]) Now in his sixties, Macarthur had come to regard the colony as home, and in 1831 he commissioned the distinguished colonial architect John Verge to design a mansion at Camden Park to be the family's principal place of residence. But, as his wife observed in a letter to their eldest son, Edward, 'Your poor Father cannot do anything in a quiet orderly way.'[29] Indeed, Macarthur's outbursts were becoming increasingly frenzied and frequent. Less than a year later, in June 1832, Elizabeth's 'long previous apprehensions'[30] about her husband's state of mind were realised when he was confined to his apartments at Elizabeth Farm convinced he was being robbed by his daughters, deserted by his sons, poisoned by his sons-in-law and cuckolded by his wife.

Elizabeth, that 'best beloved wife', the 'one woman in a thousand', who had so assiduously tended his fortune and flock, was banished from the house. The couple would never meet again. Two months later, in August 1832, John Macarthur was officially declared insane, despite his physical health and lucid intervals. He was moved to Camden in 1833 where, under the charge of his sons William and James, he continued to take an interest in the building of his new home. However, as Elizabeth somewhat acidly observed, 'I do not hear that he makes any enquiries or notices anything in relation to the sheep.'[31] Nor would John Macarthur live in the mansion of his dreams. As his condition deteriorated, he was confined to a small cottage on the estate's farm. He died there on 11 April 1834 and was buried on a small hill overlooking the site where the house was still being built, and where he has since been joined by many of his descendants.

There was little notice of his passing—although that year the colony's producers exported four and a half million pounds of fine wool to Britain, double that which came from Spain and other sources. Nor had Macarthur's exertions gone unrewarded, for he died one of the richest men in the colony, and his estate was declared at probate at more than £400 000. Very little of this would go to the women in his family. His three daughters received a modest annuity, and Elizabeth only a small income from his estates, his shares in the faltering Bank of Australia, and the use for as long as she wanted of the homestead at Elizabeth Farm. As her biographer would later bemoan on her behalf, 'Not a single sheep of the flocks she had nurtured, not an acre of the thousands she had acquired would belong to her.'[32]

Instead, in a spirit of chauvinistic egalitarianism, which some might argue remains a defining national characteristic, the family estates would be divided among John's surviving three sons. In this, Macarthur was clearly not concerned with emulating the British aristocratic tradition of preserving the hereditary privileges of its class by ruthlessly safeguarding the sole inheritance rights of the eldest male heir. Perhaps, in a colony that still abided by imperial arrangements, the fact that he was not a peer of the realm meant Macarthur never entertained such pretensions. Perhaps, in this land of opportunity, he never saw the need. Either way, neither here nor in other elite colonial families would the notion of primogeniture take root. Rather, Macarthur would leave his sons partners in an increasingly lucrative family business.

None of John Macarthur's heirs would match his volatile entrepreneurship, nor would they need to. Indeed, from this second generation on, the Macarthur dynasty would assume a far more restrained public face, aspiring on the one hand to social respectability while bound on the other by a common veneration of their mercurial ancestor. Although later individuals might occasionally lay claim to, or be accused of having, the famous Macarthur temper, there would be no successor to cut such a dramatic swathe through the society of their day. Highly strung (if not, as some historians quietly speculate, struggling with a degenerative mental illness) and 'suffering all the anxious doubts of those who depend on favours'[33] John Macarthur had revelled in his contentious reputation, believing that a certain arrogance and unpopularity were essential to one's public persona.[34]

His descendants, however, have since emphasised his more conventional qualities. 'He's portrayed as being a bit of a maverick and a leader of the Rum Rebellion and so on, but I don't think that is an accurate portrayal of John Macarthur as I understand him from being a descendant,' insists present-day patriarch Quentin Macarthur-Stanham. 'He undoubtedly didn't suffer fools gladly. But, at the same time, I think he was a man of very strict upbringing and extremely sound morality. I think in his dealings, he really did take an awful lot of trouble to make certain that all the people who were working for him were well treated. And he was certainly one of the first people to look after the local Aborigines. In fact, so much so, that when Bligh was trying to curtail his power and his landholdings, the local Aborigines came to him and said, "Look, we can easily go to Parramatta and we'll kill the governor for you. Wouldn't that make it easier for you?" And that was the relationship between John and the local indigenous people.'

This very different image of John Macarthur was one upheld by his relatives almost immediately upon his death. Indeed, while Macarthur seems to have inspired considerable loyalty among his employees and associates, none come close to the devotion expressed by his immediate family. Elizabeth may have endured much, particularly towards the end of her husband's life, but she was also his greatest supporter. However much theirs might have been a partnership of opposites bound by ambition, there is little doubting the genuine affection and admiration that existed between them. He was an even better parent—if the sentiments of his children are anything to go by. In a written record soon after Macarthur's death, his son James extolled the virtues of a loving father who had taught his children by reading them the classics, and who was 'loath to enter into a quarrel but bold and uncompromising when assailed—at all times ready to take arms against oppression and injustice'.[35]

While his daughters seem to have looked first to their mother, John Macarthur was the pre-eminent influence in his sons' lives, a constant and defining presence. He shaped their progress into adulthood, guiding their education and careers within the framework of the family enterprise and in keeping with his estimation of their skills and personalities. Indeed, if the words of his youngest, William, are to be believed, the boys even as grown men saw themselves as 'but humble instruments . . . endeavouring to carry into effect' their father's 'wise and beneficent plans'.[36] (In contrast, John and Elizabeth's three daughters, despite their mother's example, played no further part in the family business or the dynastic story.)

Macarthur would send his first son, Edward, into the army (a curious reversal of the English aristocratic tradition, which generally safeguards the eldest male as the heir apparent while sacrificing his younger brothers as cannon fodder). Edward would prove a more successful career soldier than his father. He would also become the family's London representative when his younger brother John died in 1831.

The death of his adored second son and namesake was perhaps the greatest tragedy of the elder Macarthur's life—and many believe it hastened his mental decline. Repatriated while still a young child, John junior was, in the opinion of a then amicable Wentworth, 'a complete chip off the old block'.[37] As his father fondly observed in a letter home to his wife, 'the too prominent parts of his character, which he derives from a person you well know, makes me shudder for his safety on the voyage of life'.[38]

In fact, young John's career would never be marked by the enmities that stamped his father's, but would hold out the promise of establishing the family among the upper echelons of British (as opposed to colonial) society. Having excelled at school, John would become a successful barrister who nonetheless spent much of his working life managing the family's business dealings in England. He was an effective ambassador for his father, and diligently promoted his interests among an increasingly influential network of friends and associates, including the commissioner charged with investigating Macquarie's emancipist leanings. But his ambition was to enter parliament where he believed he would be able to 'procure grants for James and William—to aid Edward in his profession and perhaps to influence the disposal of some of the colonial offices'.[39] His early and unexpected death, probably of a stroke, denied the family these services.

Nevertheless, in the new colony, a second generation of Macarthurs would prosper, thanks largely to the talents of younger brothers James and William. Born on 15 December, but two years apart, in 1798 and 1800 respectively, the two men would remain close friends and partners all their lives. To them fell the job of administering and overseeing the Macarthur estates—a task that their father would 'break them into' on their return from England in 1817. Judged a 'good tempered thoughtless fellow' by his father, William would prove an innovative agriculturist who took the family successfully into winemaking, and who taught himself the onerous task of wool sorting. James, 'grave and thoughtful', would provide the Macarthur enterprise with administrative skills, and would become the acknowledged head of the family on his father's death, and its public and political face.

With none of their father's good looks—miniatures of the two men suggest remarkably plain features—and none of his extremes of personality, William and James assiduously consolidated and advanced the dynasty's fortunes, helped by Edward in England. As the old adage would have it, the first generation might have made the wealth, but this second generation most certainly increased it. Indeed, within the family the contribution made by Macarthur's sons is seen as equally important to the family's long-term success as that of John and Elizabeth. 'People tend to try and single out somebody, and up until about five or ten years ago, people would say, "Oh, John Macarthur was the founder of the wool industry." Now the vogue is to say, "Eliz-abeth Macarthur did this and that, while John was in exile." I think the truth of the matter is that distances were so vast and communication so poor that you needed a group of competent people at the right place and time, and that's what the early Macarthurs are about . . . it was a combination of several gen-erations making a great deal of effort. I think you take away from the legacy of the early members of the family by singling out one person.'[40]

With James at the helm, the three brothers would work together for more than two decades, much as their father had no doubt intended. Together, they took the family to the zenith of its fortunes, negotiating a trajectory of growth and affluence through the wool boom of the 1830s. Not only would they make their produce the finest and most expensive in the colony, but James and William also dramatically extended their estate at Camden Park to some 11 000 hectares. This was freehold title in keeping with the family's original idea of itself as part of a new landowning class after the aristocratic European model. But the two brothers also showed themselves flexible to the exigencies of the day, negotiating substantial grazing leases further afield and forging an uneasy political alliance with the colony's emerging squattocracy. With the cessation of transportation in the 1840s, the brothers focused their attention on bringing skilled agricultural and artisan families from Britain and Germany to settle at Camden Park. It was an expensive under-taking but one that reflected their understanding of the family's place as a benevolent oligarchy, developing its vast private estates by leasing land to loyal tenants. As historian Robert Hughes notes rather acerbically in *The Fatal Shore*: 'The colonial elite after 1800 had arrived at an idea of gentility that was already becoming if not obsolete, then certainly old-fashioned in England. It was feudal and rural.'

It would become a feudal estate of two, however, when James and William dissolved their business partnership with Edward in 1858. Their older sibling had grown increasingly dissatisfied with the estate's falling revenues as the colonial economy had swung from boom to bust (unaware that James and William were also using its income to prop up the failing fortunes of their brother-in-law who, along with many of the colony's pastoral elite, had been bankrupted). In accordance with their father's will, Edward would keep Elizabeth Farm, while James and William would share Camden Park. (Edward's widow in England would later sell the Macarthur family's first home, and today only the homestead and a fraction of the original garden remain as a state-owned museum.)

Their eldest brother's defection confirmed William and James as the most influential members of their generation. But their pre-eminence was perhaps always assured by virtue of their joint residency of Camden Park, henceforth the family's dynastic focal point.[41] Both men would live out their lives in the house their father had begun but never completed, and their influence lingers even today. Their library remains the family's main living room, and while the furniture may have changed, the room still reflects the interests and outlook of two well-educated, steadfastly respectable, nineteenth-century gentlemen who, while residing on the fringes of empire, nonetheless saw themselves at the centre of current imperial issues and debates. Their paintings—oil colours of romantic Italian vistas collected while on a European tour—are still on the walls. Their books still fill the floor-to-ceiling cedar bookcases.

Living at Camden Park, acknowledges the present-day occupant John Macarthur-Stanham, James's great-great-great-grandson, is to live with constant reminders of their presence. 'Six months ago, my wife was looking through some things in the library and suddenly found a slim volume of maps of the exploration of Ludwig Leichhardt, who was a friend of William Macarthur, and had stayed here to write up his journals. So there were some of his maps, with a little poem to William. So you're finding fascinating things all the time—and it's great to be able to go and scrummage in those things.'

Most importantly James and William established Camden Park

as the repository of the family's archives. It is perhaps a defining feature of any would-be dynasty that the family recognises its own importance and duly records its progress, aspirations and achievements, and in this the Macarthurs have proved more self-aware than most. With the possible exception of the patriarch himself—who saved only one of his wife's letters—the early generations carefully preserved a first-hand record of their lives for posterity. Elizabeth Macarthur's journals and correspondence—unlike her husband, she kept her spouse's letters—would establish the foundations of this archive. Her sons would improve on this, most notably James and William who saved all their personal papers—thirty boxes and 296 large volumes of which are now in the State Library of New South Wales. William would also become one of the colony's first amateur photographers and as such would produce an extensive pictorial record of family life on the estate, his self-titled 'Camden Albums'.

As James's biographer Alan Atkinson observes, 'All the Macarthurs shared a secure faith in the grandeur of their own ambitions, and with it a belief that such virtue as theirs must someday receive a stamp of approval which would be binding for all time . . . Behind their proud and secretive manner was an ambition to one day publish all, and so to win crowns of glory from an all-knowing posterity . . . The family letters were kept with a perfect confidence that no Macarthur had anything to hide, at least from the future . . . Any warts in the final picture would only add to its dramatic effect, and its truth, so ensuring its power to last.'[42]

Later descendants would bring these records to the public's attention, securing the family's place in history. They would also continue the tradition of 'never throwing anything away', so that the Macarthur papers on the public record continue well into the twentieth century.[43] Indeed, few family stories have been so well documented as that of the early Macarthurs. But despite the wealth of evidence, argues Alan Atkinson, no Macarthur ever felt the need to justify or explain their actions. Their writings contained little, if any, introspection or reflection, simply a recounting of events which were left to speak for themselves. As a result the family's motivations and the future it envisaged for itself in the colony remain open to speculation, not least because of an apparent ambivalence on the part of the individuals themselves.

Certainly the second generation of Macarthurs saw themselves as leaders of a new meritocracy; but after this, things get muddy. James would consistently oppose the popular demand for representative government based on wide suffrage, but by the 1840s concluded that self-government for New South Wales was inevitable. He would then seek to make the parliament as conservative an institution as possible, even supporting William Charles Wentworth's proposal for a local House of Lords made up of an hereditary colonial peerage that included both families in its ranks—a suggestion that was abandoned only after some of the largest popular demonstrations ever seen at Circular Quay. He would later express dismay at the increasingly populist direction of colonial government as influenced by a growing and increasingly assertive lower middle class born of the gold rushes. And yet James would also refuse the offer of imperial honours (unlike William who was knighted for services to agriculture) despite returning to England on his retirement, having made the claim that, with the exception of Camden Park, he felt like ridding himself of all his colonial assets. One can only assume that the lure of the family seat eventually grew too strong to resist, for he left England after four years, settling back at Camden Park until his death in 1867.

James's heir became the sole descendant of the Macarthur male line for, of all John and Elizabeth's four sons, only James had children. This lack of interest in securing an heir seems all the more perplexing when viewed against the family's historic aspirations in the colony. One explanation may be that the focus, even at this early stage, had shifted to upholding the family's accomplishments thus far. Perhaps, to borrow from William, the boys (at least) saw themselves as too much their father's instruments to emerge as patriarchs in their own right.

Or perhaps, as Elizabeth's biographer Beverley Kingston would have it, the fault lies with a 'dominating and possessive mother'[44] who, in keeping with the emphasis she placed on breeding, felt that none in the colony were good enough for her children.

Elizabeth Macarthur would long survive her husband and until her death in 1849 continued to take a keen interest in colonial politics, the family and the business, complaining about the cost of servants and doing her best to economise through the depression of the 1840s. (The only portrait of her with provenance dates from this time, and however shy she may have claimed to have been, there is no mistaking the strength of purpose on her handsome, almost masculine features.) Of her three daughters, the eldest, having rejected William Wentworth's proposal, would never marry, while the youngest would wed late in life, against her mother's initial reservations. Only James of all her sons married during Elizabeth's lifetime.

James found his wife not in the colonies but on a trip to England in the late 1830s. This 'unromantic but most useful marriage to Emily Stone, daughter of a Lombard banker', notes one historian rather cuttingly, was 'the most spectacular feat of his visit'.[45] James and Emily's descendants, however, insist their union was a love match, for what else could have persuaded Emily (even as a spinster in her thirties) to abandon family and friends in London for the distant primitive society of New South Wales? There is no doubting, however, that the alliance brought James a decisive material advantage, even though her family may not have warranted a mention in the social lists of the day. Through his wife's banking connections, James was able to secure himself a greatly increased overdraft and, as the prosperity of the 1830s slid into drought and depression, he was able to lend money profitably at high interest and to continue consolidating the Camden estates.[46]

The marriage produced a daughter, named Elizabeth after her grandmother, who was born in May 1840. This only daughter would, by default, become the progenitor of the dynastic line—John had died a bachelor, as would William;

and Edward, though marrying late, had no children. Elizabeth the Second, as the family have since regarded her, would marry a naval officer, Arthur Onslow, the unremarkable grandson of Alexander McLeay, a gentleman contemporary of her grandfather's. (Elizabeth was twenty-seven and her new husband had arrived in New South Wales only three years earlier, suggesting once again the scarcity of partners considered suitable among the upper echelons of the colony.) Even after their marriage, Elizabeth and her husband would continue to live at Camden Park—her husband becoming the parliamentary representative for the district—and in 1882 she inherited the family estate on the death of her uncle William who, like his brother (her father) before him, had made his niece his sole heir.

Despite unprepossessing parents—for Emily was as plain-featured as her husband—the second Elizabeth was a striking young woman. Her obsidian eyes stare penetratingly out of her uncle's photographs, her long dark hair austerely fashioned in two smooth wings on either side of a classically oval face. By the time she inherited Camden Park, however, Elizabeth was middle-aged and plump, the mother of seven children and a widow, for her husband had died that same year. Ten years later, in 1892, Elizabeth would change her name to Macarthur-Onslow to ensure the continuity of the Macarthur line. (Her husband's contribution, other than bringing the Onslow name into play and consolidating the family's position among a small and increasingly interrelated elite, may be rather brutally summed up by his will, in which he left goods valued at under £500.)

The widowed Elizabeth briefly considered selling up and returning to England where her mother's family assured a warm welcome and comfortable retirement. In the end, however, her links to the legacy of a beloved father and uncle proved too strong to sever. Instead, in 1887, Elizabeth would embark with her children on an agricultural study tour of Europe, leaving a distant cousin to manage the estate in her absence. Having determined not to take the money and run—the prerogative, we are told, not only of widows, but of the third generation per se—Elizabeth proved a far-from-passive beneficiary. For the next two years, she taught herself dairy farming and, on her return, transformed Camden Park into a model dairy. In doing so she would ensure the estate's survival by successfully negotiating its transition through the economic crash of the 1890s, which culled all but the hardiest of the colony's pastoral elite.

In bringing the family enterprise firmly into the next century, Elizabeth sought to confirm the achievements of generations past. One imagines she was brought up to fully share in her father's admiration of his illustrious patriarch, and to appreciate the brilliance of his endeavours. In keeping with this belief, Elizabeth devoted her attention to editing a volume of the family's earliest private papers, which her father had selected. Completion of this task later fell to her own daughter, Sibella, who published *Some Early Records of the Macarthurs of Camden* in 1914, three years after her mother's death.[47]

Sibella also inherited the family home at Camden Park—the first but not the last time a woman would be so favoured by choice rather than necessity. That Elizabeth had bequeathed the house to her only surviving daughter was, as Sibella's biographer makes clear, 'a great compliment to her capabilities over those of the heir, her brother'.[48] Sibella, who never married, proved a model custodian, despite at times becoming 'very excitable'. She would take her place at the forefront of society, which in keeping with the custom of the day entailed taking charge of various clubs and charities.[49] However, as her biographer notes approvingly, 'Camden Park was her life: there, Sibella entertained such distinguished visitors as the Duke and Duchess of York.'[50]

The running of the family estate, however, passed more conventionally to Sibella's eldest brother, James—confirming the inherently patriarchal nature of dynasties and suggesting that Elizabeth, his mother, was only able to make the contribution she did in the absence of any male heirs. James became chairman of the private company his mother had founded to manage the Macarthur pastoral enterprise, now focused on some 8000 hectares at Camden Park, which included twelve cooperative farms and forty leased holdings serving nine model dairies.[51] But the Camden Park estate was much more than a business. It was its own small community, made up of the hundreds of loyal farm workers and tenants who lived on the property, many descended from the family's convict servants or assisted settlers. This community lived, died and intermarried on the estate; they bought their provisions from the estate store, attended the family church and sent their children to the estate school. If Sibella, living as she did in the mansion itself, was its virgin queen, then James Macarthur-Onslow was its commander, closely flanked by his two surviving brothers, for Elizabeth had made all her children—male and female—shareholders in the family enterprise. This thoroughly contemporary gesture (at odds with the feudal nature of the estate itself) would sow the seeds for Camden Park's eventual disintegration as, over the next two generations, the family assets were rapidly dispersed among a growing number of stakeholders.

The slow erosion of the family's dynastic capital would take place, however, behind a veil of grandiosity. Already by this fourth generation, the family's position, as one of the oldest in the colony, had become 'as good a claim to respect as having come over with the Conqueror'.[52] In a society that was still overwhelmingly British in composition and that still mimicked its colonial parent, Elizabeth's children were at the very apogee of a colonial upper class. Educated in the manner of their English peers at Oxford or Cambridge, the Macarthur-Onslow males fulfilled their duty to empire in the army, becoming officers. They would also assume leadership in local or regional government where, as one might expect, they proved bastions of conservatism. James Macarthur-Onslow, who followed his father into the Legislative Assembly, opposed socialism, the Saturday half-holiday and the abolition of capital punishment. Dominating the social pages and honoured for their service to community—although James, as his biographer confesses, was 'usually inactive or on leave'[53]—the Macarthurs represented a social position to which others aspired. They were among a small handful of families upon whom all eyes were focused— and the first names on the guest list of an elegant society party that lasted from the 1920s until the 1960s.

Of course, the best place to congregate was probably Camden Park itself, and one can only imagine the various glittering country house gatherings that would have marked the social calendar. The house continued to pay host to royalty—including the future Queen Mother as a young bride who, in a warm letter of thanks, remarked how nice it was to gaze upon horses after all the faces surrounding her on her tour. This was Sibella's last brush with the British monarchy. Aware of her mother's wishes that Camden Park remain in the family in perpetuity, Sibella dutifully exchanged houses with her eldest brother in 1931 (twelve years before her death), moving to another family property, the nearby Gilbulla.

James's residency at Camden Park was marked by equal aplomb. A staff of twenty-five (divided between the house and garden) maintained the property along the lines of a grand English manor house. 'It was all so sort of picked up and smart,' recalls his grandson Quentin, who stayed at the house during childhood visits to the ancestral estate. 'All the paths were swept. It was very different-looking.' He still remembers his delight as a young boy on coming down to breakfast in the grand dining room and discovering the long mahogany table laden with kippers, sausages and eggs, as if conjured for his enjoyment. After eating his fill, he was then free to disappear for the day, roaming the property in his pony-and-trap.

Reminiscences such as these bring an understanding of the enduring appeal of Camden Park to generations past and present, for they describe privileged childhood freedoms most could only dream of.

James married a distant cousin, Enid Emma Macarthur—the granddaughter of a nephew of John Macarthur's who had followed his uncle to New South Wales but who had been bankrupted by the depression of the 1840s. The couple had three children, but James's grandson Quentin did not grow up at Camden Park. He spent his childhood in England, where his mother, James's eldest daughter Helen, now lived. Like many of the women in her family, Helen Macarthur-Onslow had married a military man and an expatriate. An Englishman, Sir Reginald Stanham had served briefly in Australia as aide-de-camp to the governor of New South Wales and later became paymaster-general in the British army during World War II. Quentin, too, would fight for Britain in the war, and it was not until 1946 with the death of his grandfather James that the family's Australian future was confirmed.

In a scandal that rocked Camden for years after, James Macarthur-Onslow followed his mother's example and made his daughter, Helen heir to Camden Park, bypassing his oldest son and namesake. This fifth-generation James—or Jimmy, as he was known—had been bankrupted twice, and his father clearly sought to place the dynastic legacy in steadier hands. James bequeathed his son only a small shareholding in the family estate—now under the management of a cousin, Sir Denzil Macarthur-Onslow—and a property in Muswellbrook. The result of this decision was enduring bitterness between Jimmy and his siblings.[54] Jimmy, if family gossip is to be believed, never spoke to his sister again. It was the first schism in a family that, for more than four generations, had been remarkable for its loyalty and cohesion. (Even Edward's decision in the second generation to sever his financial ties had been a relatively amicable one.) And it is telling perhaps that this breakdown preceded the irrevocable collapse of the family enterprise, leaving a dynasty bound by its ties to history alone.

Helen returned to Australia in 1948, two years after her father's death, to take possession of Camden Park. She was by then in late middle age, and accompanied by her now retired husband, their son and his family. As his mother's only child and heir, Quentin would eventually come to manage the estate and, at his mother's request, would change his name by deed poll to Macarthur-Stanham to continue the dynastic line. (He insisted, however, on dropping Onslow from the equation.) Quentin was twenty-seven when he came to live at Camden Park, with a wife and son of his own. One-year-old Mark had been born at his grandparents' home in Surrey, where his parents had wanted to call him John. However, as Mark's mother ruefully notes in her memoirs, 'my mother-in-law forbade it, saying it was an unlucky name in the family'.[55] A daughter, Anne, was born soon after the family's arrival.

Also emigrating was the Stanhams' long-time retainer, Marion Millwood, whose first vivid impressions of Camden Park are of opening gate after gate before the entourage arrived at the house itself. While her first sight of Camden Park, with all the staff lined up to greet them, struck Marion dumb, her employer's attention was drawn to the British flag flying at full mast. Was it to honour her or the royal heir, Prince Charles, who had been born the previous day? Helen inquired—to be duly reassured that it was both.

Marion had joined the Stanham household at the age of seventeen and had long considered herself part of the family. However, her relationship with Helen became far more formal and hierarchical when 'Milady' (as she became known) assumed the mantle of the *grande dame* of Camden Park. 'She was very proud of her heritage—a Macarthur to her fingertips. She was head of Camden Park, and extremely proud of it.'[56] While her employer insisted on a strict pecking order—and bristled at suggestions that Marion was more her companion than servant— Marion insists that theirs remained an intimate, if often volatile relationship, largely because of the Macarthur temperament. 'There are traits that have run right the way through,' she insists, recollecting the enormous rows that would flare up between them when she was perceived to step out of line. 'The temper is one. I think, too, there's a lot of sunshine about them. Lady Stanham could be very autocratic, but she could also be a lady of pure sunshine. She had the most marvellous smile when she was happy.'

Nothing of that smile shows on Milady's face in a black-and-white portrait captured by the camera just before her first Buckingham Palace garden party after the war. Instead, handsome features and a steely gaze make their impression through the netted veil of a hat that seems too frivolous for its owner. 'I hero-worshipped my mother,' says her son Quentin. 'When she was being brought up, she had virtually no education. She was brought up by a series of governesses, and she had far too strong a character to be controlled by governesses. As a result, she learnt nothing and spent her time riding all over the place and enjoying herself. However, she had a love of Camden Park, which I inherited, and she was a person of great ability. She could barely read or write, or do arithmetic, but during the war she became head of the southern England women's voluntary services and ran this huge organisation, counting on her fingers. She was a woman of great personality and determination.'

That personality and determination found its focus in shoring up the Macarthur presence at Camden Park, for the inherited grandeur was fading fast. The house was in need of considerable modernisation, and had been neglected during the war. 'The first job we did was to totally rewire the house, and that took a period of two years. The next job was the plumbing; all the plumbing was cast iron so we had to replace all of that.'

From this point on, acknowledges Quentin, Camden Park would come to represent a significant drain on the family's resources at a time when its fortunes were being challenged as never before. Over the next two decades, as agribusiness became more competitive, the family enterprise became steadily less profitable, and Sir Reginald's pension was modest compared to the upkeep of such a large house and grounds. At the same time outlooks were changing and Sir Reginald would complain to Marion of the difficulties in finding good staff and meeting their escalating demands for better pay and conditions, including regular days off. Marion herself would work for the Macarthurs until her mid-fifties, when she left to marry a podiatrist—a widower who had treated both Milady and Marion and who insisted (quite accurately) that, after a lifetime in service, Marion's feet needed his full-time care.

For much of the 1950s, however, life at Camden Park under Helen's stewardship continued very much as it had before. While Milady and her husband took up residence in the main house, Quentin and his family made their home in the former 'convict wing', across the courtyard from the kitchen where Marion Millwood worked. As Mark, Quentin's eldest son, recalls, 'We lived in a wing of Camden Park, and there were certain doors and certain areas in the garden that we did not walk past, unless we were specifically asked for Sunday lunch.'[57] Agrees his sister, Anne, 'We were cordially invited for Sunday lunch and off we'd go up to the other end, and sit down at the polished table with all the crystal and the china and what have you. So we learnt very early on how one was supposed to behave—and some of the behaviour that goes on round dining tables these days was very much frowned on.'[58]

Marion was one of the few people—other than Milady and Sir Reginald themselves—who was free to move about Camden Park at her discretion. (Frances Warner, the current housekeeper, recalls as a young laundrymaid coming to the back door to collect her weekly wages, never daring to step a foot inside.) But even Marion was expected to change into a clean uniform when called to an audience with her employers. 'In those days, the house staff didn't wear their own clothes,' says Anne. 'My grandmother had brought back fabric [from England] that was suitable for staff uniforms, and had a whole lot made up by her dressmaker. The staff had pink and blue uniforms for morning and afternoon wear, and a black one for entertaining, with a little white apron—you know, terribly English.'

The changes wrought by the war—the ascendancy of American free enterprise and multiculturalism—had yet to make their full impact, and the Macarthur family was still very much at the top of an Anglocentric social tree. Camden Park still played host to large house parties for friends from the Sydney establishment, as well as visiting dignitaries from Britain.

Neighbours in the district included Sir Warwick Fairfax, scion of Australia's oldest newspaper dynasty, whose eldest son James would become godfather to Quentin's youngest daughter. However tight finances may have been, Quentin and his father built a croquet lawn on the front lawns and later established cricket grounds—the scene of an annual tournament among a select circle of landowning families.

The outsider in all of this was Quentin's English wife, Andalusia, despite being from minor gentry herself (albeit only from Jersey). 'It's interesting that Sydney society in the 1950s was so cliquey and snobbish,' reflects her daughter Anne today, 'because when my mother came out from England, she had a lot of trouble fitting in.' Nor would Andalusia enjoy living in the shadow of her imperious mother-in-law—although her children adored their grandmother. 'As a child, I certainly didn't notice my grandmother being formidable at all,' says Anne. 'She was just wonderful. But now, as an adult, I look back and I think, "Oh, she must have been terrifying for some people." You know, if you're on the wrong side of her—and every now and again, I can see myself doing the same thing, which is a bit scary.'

Increasingly, Mark and Anne came alone to Sunday lunch. At the appointed hour, Marion Millwood would meet them at the back door and escort them in to join their grandparents. 'One of the prettiest pictures I remember is of Mark and Anne walking up from the wing. And Anne was in a little green velvet skirt with a red-and-white shirt, and Mark was in green velvet pants and a red-and-white shirt. And they were coming up, hand in hand, and they were gorgeous. I will never forget; it just made me want to cry. That's how close those two are. I don't know what would have become of Mark if he hadn't had Anne. I think she was his lifesaver as much as anything.'

Brother and sister would be thrown together even more when, shortly after the birth of their youngest sister, their parents' marriage disintegrated. Andalusia, or 'Miss Andy' as she was known by the staff, returned to England, leaving her two eldest children behind. 'Full marks for my mother for just quietly gathering herself up and saying, "This isn't going to work" and removing herself,' says her eldest daughter today. 'It must have been an extremely difficult thing for her to do, particularly at that time.' Although determined that her son would grow up among his heritage at Camden Park, Andalusia had initially wanted to keep both her daughters with her, but was prevailed upon to leave Anne with Mark. The two have remained close ever since. (They have also stayed in touch with their mother and sister—although they did not see each other again for several years.)

Of the two children, it was Anne who found the separation the less traumatic. She was only three at the time, and says her mother's departure was a relatively smooth transition. Looked after by a succession of nannies, the children's life continued very much as before in which, in keeping with an upper-class English formality, her mother had been a somewhat distant presence. Mark, who was six, however, never recovered from the separation from his mother, although he claims he has no regrets at being left behind. 'Poor old Mark,' says Marion, who cherishes her memories of the little boy he once was. 'He has had to build up a shell. In the middle, he is just so soft and easily hurt. I had to put him to bed a couple of nights, fairly early on in his life. I bent down to kiss him good night, and he put his arms up round my neck, and he hung on so closely.'

But no number of caring adults, including Marion and other household staff, could take the place of Miss Andy in her son's life. Nor, says Mark, who is himself separated with a son—named Andy after his mother—could others make up for his distant relationship with his remaining parent. 'I don't remember the sort of closeness with my father that I think I've got with my son Andy. I try and read him a story before bed to settle him down. I don't remember Dad reading to me—that sort of thing. Maybe it's just a sign of the times. He was the only child of a very Victorian mother.'

Quentin, caught in a flurry of work, social and sporting engagements, was, many agree, a hands-off dad. Nonetheless, Mark insists that as a child he idolised his father. At the same time, he clearly carries with him an enduring sense of having been wronged—not least by his grandmother's decision to send him (and later his sister) to boarding school at the tender age of eight, in the belief that as Macarthurs they should not attend the local public school. (It was, says Marion, a tough awakening for the little boy who up to then had been brought up as a little English gentleman; and who was, she is sure, teased about his accent and old-world manners.)

Four years after his divorce Quentin remarried. His new wife, Antonia Blaxland, had both the lineage and experience to take becoming a Macarthur in her stride. She too could claim to be among Sydney's founding families, as she was a descendant of Gregory Blaxland, a contemporary of John Macarthur's who, with William Wentworth, had pioneered the trail through the Blue Mountains. Moreover her mother, Dame Helen Blaxland, was a leading establishment figure, and as autocratic and confident as her new mother-in-law. A portrait photographer, Antonia had taken photographs of the Macarthur children before her marriage and continued to document life at Camden Park. It was in many respects a perfect match—in all but one pair of eyes. 'We all thought Mark was happy when Quentin and Antonia married,' reflects Marion. 'We didn't realise—I didn't realise even when I lived there—that he didn't like it. But as their relationship [between father and son] deteriorated, Antonia was the biggest mediator between the two.'

For Quentin, this second marriage was a happy one and he and his new wife had two children. The eldest, a son, was named John—family superstitions either forgotten or rebutted—and the youngest, a daughter, Jane. Despite Antonia's illustrious forebears, 'Miss Toni', as the staff called her, was a down-to-earth, informal and more contemporary presence at Camden Park. She would set up tent and camp with the children on the lawn, and would resist some of the formal hierarchies that had previously governed life on the estate. 'Toni was incredibly fair; even if you were wrong, she had a way of telling you that wasn't a put-down. She was the sort of person who would have been quite happy in a tiny little cottage somewhere with Dad and her two children,' says Anne of her stepmother. 'But also she had my grandmother breathing down her neck and saying, you will do this and you will do that. And she had to accommodate that for us. But she put her foot down on what she believed was right when it came to John and Jane—and I thought that was quite good. That's why they went to the local public school and we didn't.'

John's and Jane's relationship to Camden Park was thus quite different to that of their half-brother and sister. For them, Camden Park would become first and foremost a family home—particularly following the death of their grandmother in 1968 when they moved into the main house. Anne and Mark were already ensconced at boarding school by this time and, during his vacations, Mark would increasingly find his companionship among the estate workers, who became his 'unpaid babysitters'. 'From the moment I got home, I'd be into some working clothes and off down to see what I could do on the farm,' he recalls.[59] The house had been his grandmother's domain and was now his stepmother's, but had never really been his. In contrast, his half-brother's love affair with the house began as a child. 'Growing up in Camden Park is just an absolute treat for a kid,' recollects John Macarthur-Stanham with a broad smile of pleasure. 'It's just a lovely place to grow up, and now I have three children of my own that's the nicest thing. It's a lovely environment to have an old house, with 80-odd rooms to run around in, and have a fantastic garden to explore. There are so many places to play hide-and-seek. It's a lovely place to race up and down the corridors. Our kids still do it. Every now and then something gets broken, but that's life in a house. You couldn't find a better place to grow up as a child than Camden Park. I think it gets better as you become an adult, but there's a bit more work then.'

Unlike Mark, John would spend relatively little time working on the farm, taking a greater interest as a teenager in the house and its history. Mark, meanwhile, had become the first Macarthur to graduate with a degree in agriculture. He looked forward to taking over from his father as manager of the family's agricultural enterprises. But Camden Park's model dairies were no longer industry leaders. Instead, other smaller farmers were lobbying for their share of dairy quotas, and profits were steadily diminishing. Moreover, by Quentin's generation the family shareholdings were spread increasingly thin. By 1973, certain family members, including Quentin's first cousin whose father Jimmy had been disinherited, began to feel that their investments might be better placed elsewhere. When a development company expressed interest in buying Camden Park's farmland for urban housing, they leapt at the chance to exchange their share of the family's pastoral assets for cash.

'I personally was under tremendous pressure to sell out, and I resisted it very strongly,' says Quentin, who still regrets the loss of the family estate. 'But eventually, there was, I think, something like 54 per cent of the family that wanted to sell.' It was a majority vote. Much of Camden Park estate was sold, with Quentin retaining only the house and 400 hectares surrounding it. In retrospect he regrets not going into debt to buy out those family members who wanted to sell, but with a young family to support says he lacked the courage of his convictions in the face of the risks entailed. As it was the developers went bankrupt, the family did not receive all the money owed it and much of the land was bought by the state government, which preserved its heritage value by establishing the Elizabeth Macarthur Agricultural Institute.

For Mark Macarthur-Stanham, who had just graduated in agriculture and who had been informed of the sale by mail while on his 'grand tour' of Europe, the loss of the extended family enterprise was a 'tragedy of short-sightedness and bloody-mindedness'. But he was determined to make a go of his family's remaining farmland and dairy, which he and a partner leased from his father. It was an increasingly fraught relationship as the enterprise struggled and Mark's management steadily lost Quentin's support. By 1981 Mark was spending less and less time running the property. However, he insists his absences simply reflected his deteriorating relationship with his father, who in his view never appreciated his commitment. 'I remember being devastated when he said to me, "You've got no interest in Camden Park, and the house and the farm." I looked at him and I thought, "What are you talking about?" I had never considered the main part of Camden Park my home. But the farm was different. And this was after I had been involved with a various number of open days.'

Two years later Mark and his father parted ways. 'All I can tell you,' says Marion Millwood, 'is that my matron of honour rang me up and she said, "Oh Mark's been cut out of Camden Park." And I said, "Oh, why?" And she said, "Oh, it's a big, big thing!" But she didn't tell me any more. Apparently all of Camden knew it—because it was a big thing. Mark was the oldest son, and it was believed he would inherit.'

Perhaps no one outside the immediate family will ever really know what happened between father and son. Quentin refuses to discuss his eldest son—except to say that he has since financed him in setting up a haulage company of his own. Mark, while admitting he has not fared well in business ventures since, insists his management of the family farm was plagued by bad luck, drought, flood and increasingly restrictive dairy quotas. But he says he cannot remember the full details of his disinheritance, only the fact that he was cut out of the family trust that oversaw Camden Park. 'The words that are written into this discretionary trust are: "The power of discretion shall go from Quentin Macarthur-Stanham to his wife, Antonia, to his son, John, failing John to Anne. But under no circumstances shall the power of discretion go to my eldest son, Mark". And those words ring in my ears, day in, day out.'

Father and son's falling-out would be the first step towards a radical solution to safeguarding the family's dynastic inheritance.

Having presided over the break-up of the family estate, Quentin by now had come to believe he had no choice but to leave what remained of Camden Park to just one heir. It was, he concedes, a difficult decision, but one he would make again.

'In this day and age, the place is quite unable to generate enough money to maintain a family—as I had—of five children. So therefore I went back to the old English system of primogeniture and chose one member of the family as being the person who should continue on. I've explained to the other children that, unlike the normal situation in Australia, where one's estate is divided equally between one's family, I believed that to preserve Camden Park, I should hand it over to only one. I chose John out of my family of five, as being the most able to succeed in carrying out what is and was a very difficult job of maintaining this house and lands. The rest of my family has been looked after in other ways in my lifetime, and I've tried to compensate them by handing over as much in the assets that I had control over as I could. So John, hopefully, when I die, will be unencumbered in managing and running this place. That is how I saw the only possible way of being able to maintain Camden Park into the foreseeable future.'

It is tempting to see Quentin's choice as reflecting his obvious affection for this untroubled second son from a happy marriage. But many in the family acknowledge John's strong sense of responsibility to Camden Park from an early age. In John, concurs Quentin, he found someone who shared his passion for the house and its place in the family's dynastic history. Ironically, Mark had never considered his half-brother a rival in the succession, simply because John had never shown much interest in the family's pastoral pursuits. In his view, John was a financier, interested in dollars and cents, while Mark was the practical agriculturalist who wanted to continue the family traditions. But for Quentin, who had struggled in several new agricultural ventures (including rabbit farming), this was precisely his younger son's appeal. 'I do not think it is possible in this day and age to preserve and make enough money to maintain a house of this size and a garden by farming alone,' insists Quentin. 'John, I think, has shown exceptional ability in the big smoke and therefore is not entirely dependent on what the farm can produce. And I think if you look at it financially, why would anybody want a house of this size and awkwardness to run? At the same time, there is an immense satisfaction in doing it.'

In many ways Mark never expected to outdo his brother in his father's eyes—but nor did he expect to be ousted from his place in the family hierarchy. For him the great loss, clearly, is the opportunity to continue the family's pastoral enterprise rather than the house itself. Why, he asks, couldn't he have continued to manage the farm while John administered the house and its assets? 'It was always my feeling that John and I could work together, but that wasn't to be. I think if you look at Father's five children there's an incredible diversity of talent and ability there, and if it was to be teamed it could have been quite formidable. But I think that Father, going on previous generations' experience where they fought like cats and dogs, set things up so that it didn't threaten the stability of what was left, rather than setting it up as Elizabeth Macarthur-Onslow did, which was more family-inclusive.'

In contrast John, like his father, believes the days of a Macarthur family enterprise are over. All that remains, he believes, is the 'great affinity many members of the family, both close and distant, have with Camden Park'. With the assistance of a manager John has made the farm a moderate success, continuing a small dairy enterprise and raising chickens. But the farm, from his perspective, exists as an adjunct to the house and its heritage. 'I think farming is very important for this property to keep its historical integrity. I certainly don't want to get heavily into tourism and things like that. I think it would destroy the atmosphere of the place. So it's important to keep farming for that sake. It's still viable. It's not hugely profitable, but we're happy being financial mugs in that sense.'

John looks to his own paid employment in the city for his income. The house itself is maintained by a charitable trust, the

Camden Park Preservation Committee, which Quentin set up in the early 1970s. With a majority of non-family members, the committee works to preserve the house and gardens in perpetuity, and keep it in the Macarthur family. Its primary source of income is the annual Open Weekend, the proceeds of which—together with any revenue derived from filming or advertising companies and other commercial uses, as well as private donations—are tax free. Certainly, Camden Park is no longer the grand manor house it once was. By the time John and his family took up residence in 1990, following his mother's death from cancer, the house and its grounds were in need of considerable restoration. The days of uniformed house and ground staff had long gone. Only Frances Warner has stayed on as the family's housekeeper. John's wife, Edwina, does her own cooking in a modern kitchen installed in the main house. The original kitchen, which was once Marion's domain, has been preserved. Nor does John feel any obligation to follow in the footsteps of his illustrious ancestors. He is a businessman with a passion for his family history—but with no intention of living up to its past agricultural, entrepreneurial, military or social glories.

'I don't think there is such a big deal about being a Macarthur, personally,' he insists. 'Historically, it's an interest, you might say, but it's not of particular significance in this day and age. And I'm grateful for that. The Macarthur golden era was some generations back—it is not here and now. I don't feel like I'm in anybody's shadow. All my family is very much their own person, and march to the beat of their own drum. I don't feel overshadowed by history, and therefore there is no need to get away from it.' The only issue that brings discomfort is the question of inheritance—an issue that John steadfastly rejects, preferring to describe his position at Camden Park as custodial. This may reflect a small measure of survivor's guilt, but also a sense of obligation to his anointed role in preserving the family's historic legacy.

While insisting that Camden Park is first and foremost his family's home, John sees it as his duty to facilitate a continuing interest in the house and its history. For his wife Edwina, who was not born to the task, this has meant unanticipated intrusions. 'You don't realise how many people will ring up and want to know bits of information. "My son is doing a project on John Macarthur— have you got any information?" "My grandfather was a butler at Camden Park in 1920." You have a nice conversation, and that's very interesting. But people drop in, not realising it is your family home, and that you didn't really want them to just drive in and say hello. But you have got to appreciate that people admire the house and want to see it, so you can't be rude.'[60]

Even more significant is John's commitment to maintaining Camden Park's primacy within the family at large—although he admits that this too can be a double-edged sword. 'It's very important that all the family feels welcome here, and they do. I think Edwina feels there are times when her home is not her own, and that's on occasion a little difficult. I mean, the nature of Camden Park is that you've always got various members of the family saying, "Can I bring such-and-such to visit the place?" or "Can we come and stay?" or [my younger sister] Jane will say, "Can we have a dinner party here?" It's very difficult to say no. You'd feel the biggest heel in the world if you did, because you've got an obligation to share with others. But every now and then, you think, "Oh God, just give us a little more peace and quiet".'

These custodial obligations at the cost of the family's own privacy reflect an attitude (and diplomacy) much appreciated by most of John's siblings. Half-sister Anne is enthusiastic in her praise of the welcome she receives on her visits back to the family home. Like Mark, she has a designated bedroom in the old 'servant wing' at Camden Park, while the 'convict wing' has been reserved as half-sister Jane's weekender. (An architect living in Sydney, Jane sits on the Camden Park Preservation Committee and has a more engaged, perhaps proprietary, interest in its future.)

Anne's visits are rarer, in part because she lives in Cowra near her eldest brother Mark, where she and her husband have begun a vineyard with her father's support. (She will use the family name on her labels, making a connection between her wines and the first vintages produced in Australia at Camden Park by her second-generation ancestor, William Macarthur.) Her appreciation of Camden Park, while deeply felt, is not such a significant force in her life—perhaps because as a girl she was always encouraged to see her future elsewhere.

'I can remember—I think I was about twelve at the time— and my stepmother said to me, "Oh, you'll get married and go off and live with somebody else." And I said, "No, no, no. I want to live here all the time." And she said, "No, you won't." And, of course, as a twelve-year-old I thought that was quite inaccurate. I knew we had lots of cottages on the place, and I thought I could live in one of those. And of course as daughters do, I got married to somebody and moved miles away, and I don't go home very often, in fact.'

There is no sense that Anne believes she was cheated either of a home life or a heritage—only that she has grown to appreciate how extraordinary her childhood at Camden Park was. She has, in a sense, long accepted her place on the fringes of the dynastic narrative. As her father points out, 'I think that the important people as far as the Macarthur family are concerned are the people who have lived in this house. The people who have been born here and gone out and made their own way of life elsewhere, I don't think are particularly important to this house. They're members of the family.'

John too, for all his contemporary sensibilities, understands and is quite comfortable with his place in this history. Two voluntary archivists from the Camden Historical Society spend one day a week at the house 'just sifting through all our boxes and bits and pieces, and collating things, which is great'. The two men have their own archive room in the house where they index and store the family memorabilia. While still uncovering historic material, they are also keeping a record of dynastic history in the making for, on the shelves above their heads, are storage boxes of personal records and correspondence for the current generation, particularly John and Edwina. It is a considerable step up from keeping a family photograph album—evidence of the dynasty's ongoing obligation to its rightful place in history.

While Mark also has his own file, he must live with the knowledge that the main thread of family history has passed him by. Camden Park, he says, still 'cries out' to him and for many years he refused to speak to his younger brother. He has since come to consider John an equal 'victim of circumstance' and the two have arrived at an unspoken reconciliation. While one suspects that they have little in common and are not close, they are at pains to get on. Mark and his son Andy are regular visitors to Camden Park, and Andy, says his doting father, simply 'loves going down to see his cousins and playing with them. So, hopefully, you know, we're starting to learn to live together, which is something that certainly my grandparents' generation weren't real good at.'

For all the pain it has caused him, Mark is determined that Andy will grow up with a strong sense of his dynastic heritage. As someone who believes he missed out on an intimate sense of family (until he became a father himself) the importance of his Macarthur heritage has loomed almost painfully large. Far more than his younger half-brother, Mark sees an ongoing significance in the family's agricultural and military connections, as well as its sense of public service. He still feels the loss of his place in the dynastic hierarchy—a validation that remains keenly important to him.

After several tumultuous generations, most of the wider Macarthur family looks upon John's presence at Camden Park with relief. There is every hope among the family and its supporters that he will be the person who enables the dynasty to hang onto Camden Park, if only for one generation more. 'I have thought a lot about it, because I adore Mark—he could be my child, I love him dearly—but I can also see that John is the right person, and he is married to the right wife,' says Marion Millwood, from her distant armchair in a Sydney retirement home. For her, as for the family itself, what ultimately matters most is that the Macarthurs' dynastic line at Camden Park is unbroken. 'And so therefore it continues on,' observes Marion. 'John and Edwina's eldest son William is a Macarthur, so it will still go through and stay in the one name, which is unique. There isn't another house that was built in the 1800s in Australia that is still in the same family and never has been anybody else's.'

While family history has shown us that it is not the first-born son who necessarily inherits, traditional expectations clearly persist. As with his father before him, John's eldest son William has gone from public school in Camden to the private and exclusive prepatory college Tudor House. It seems somewhat ironic, however, that it was only once the Macarthur dynasty had lost all claim to land-holdings of aristocratic proportions that it reverted to the feudal tradition of leaving everything to just one heir. Primogeniture, had it been invoked earlier, may have once served to secure the fortunes of Australia's great pastoral families, for most, like the Macarthurs, have seen their land and assets gradually whittled away, divided time and again by subsequent generations. Had primogeniture been introduced two centuries ago, Australian society today could have been a far different place, with perhaps a true colonial aristocracy. Instead, most historic properties have passed to new entrepreneurs and their families, and there is an expectation that fortunes are, for the most part, cyclical. Land is no longer seen as the great source of wealth and status it once was, and the old landholding elites of the colony, while still known to each other, are an increasingly minor part of Australian society. The Macarthurs are among the last, and certainly the oldest, remaining on their dynastic estate, but their new-found adaptation of primogeniture is, in contemporary Australian terms, an extraordinary and potentially divisive solution.

Nonetheless, Camden Park is still looked upon as the Macarthur family's unifying thread, despite having demonstrated the capacity to tear generations of kin apart. Managing one's dynastic legacy is clearly no easy thing—perhaps as demanding in its way as creating one, albeit requiring very different qualities and ambitions. To the present-day John Macarthur-Stanham will fall the difficult task of reconciling the future of the dynastic seat with his commitments to his own two sons and daughter. How will he resolve the problems that beset his father? There are no answers or certainties. Instead, he is well aware of the burden he carries—and the potential for passing it on unwelcome (and indeed amplified) to the eighth generation.

'I dearly love the place and I feel I have an obligation to pass it on to my children. It would be nice if one of my children felt a desire to continue living here. But at some stage, it may all become too much and that's a decision they will make. Yes, I have a responsibility to pass it on to them. No, they don't have a responsibility to take it up.'

THE DURACK FAMILY

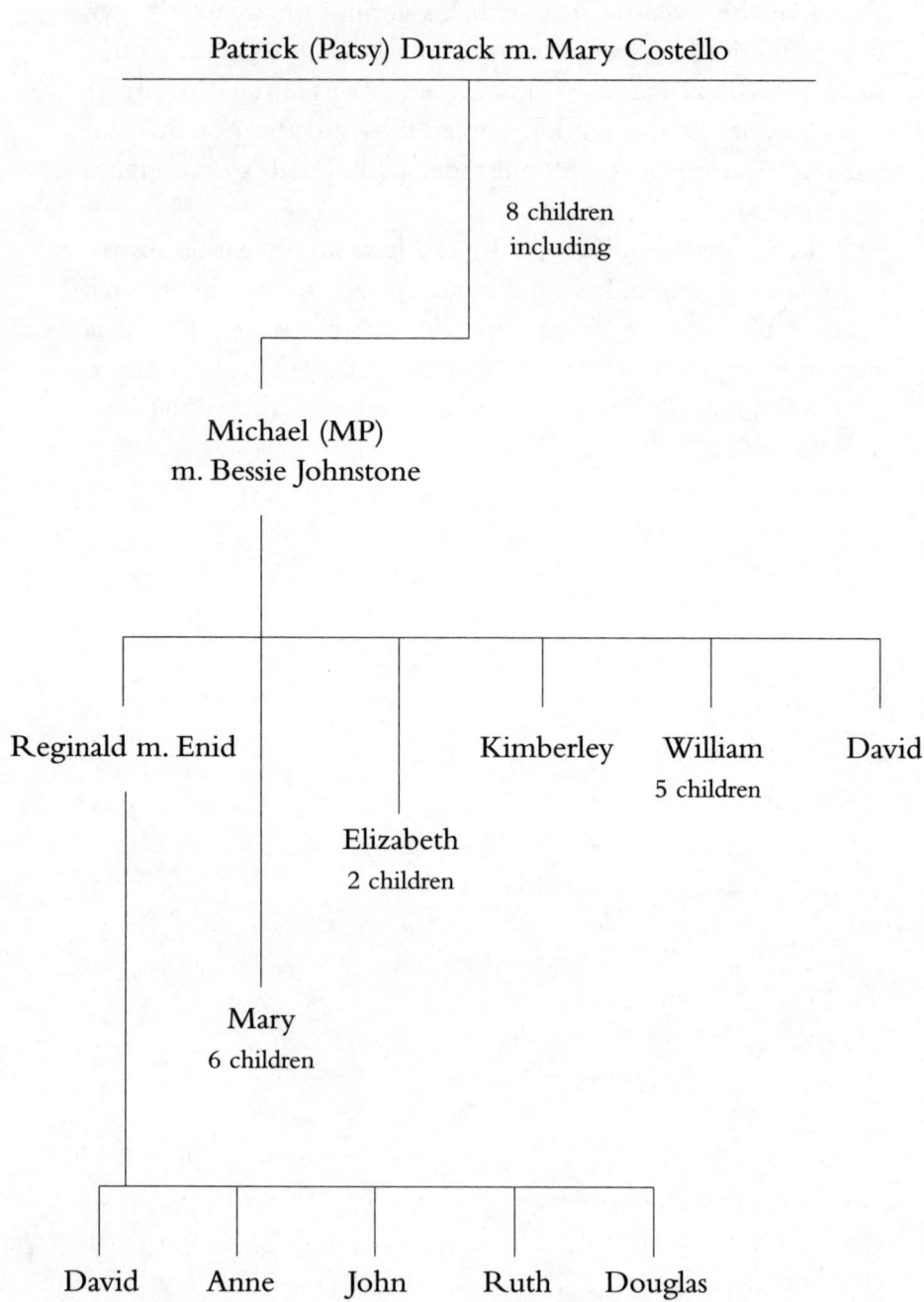

Patrick (Patsy) Durack m. Mary Costello

8 children
including

Michael (MP)
m. Bessie Johnstone

Reginald m. Enid

Kimberley   William   David
5 children

Elizabeth
2 children

Mary
6 children

David   Anne   John   Ruth   Douglas

TRAVEL HOPEFULLY

———— ▬ ————

THE DURACKS

. . . [A] colony in quicksand . . . black men wandering and white men riding in a world without time where sons do not inherit and money goes mouldy in the pocket, where ambition is wax melted in the sun, and those who sow, may not reap . . . the Northern Territory of Australia . . . land of an ever shadowed past and an ever shining future, of eternal promise that never comes true . . .[1]

THE LIGHT aircraft raises a puff of red as it touches down on a tiny dirt strip. It's almost lost from sight among the thick pandanus grasses standing more than two metres—the result of a good Wet season. The Wet is all but over, but access by plane is still the only guarantee of reaching this remote station in the Northern Territory. The pilot climbs out. His skin, slightly sweaty, is adjusting to the oven-like heat. This pale, thin man with milky blue eyes looks strangely out of place in a country where the sun beats down so relentlessly. A small black cloud of flies immediately descends around him.

The pilot is John Durack. He is a Perth solicitor, but thirty years ago he was heir to this property. He grew up here, part of the fourth generation of Duracks to manage this land. Now it's an Aboriginal station: Amanbidji. The dispossessed Ngarinman people, who were once the Durack station workers, have had their traditional land returned to them.

In the 1880s the Duracks were among the first white settlers in the East Kimberley region. Taking two years to move themselves and their cattle across from the east coast, these overlanders opened up vast acreage to the cattle industry. At their height the family ran a string of cattle stations with a total land area roughly the size of Belgium. The dynastic patriarch, Patsy Durack, likened these extensive holdings to a European principality, and for the first two generations the Duracks ran their secluded leasehold as latter-day feudal lords.

Amanbidji, or Kildurk as it was called by the Duracks, is a fraction of the original leasehold, but still amounts to 283 000 hectares. Between sixty and eighty people live here now. It's a difficult place for intensive agriculture: the ancient soil is generally poor and friable, the community isolated and the pastoral industry of less intrinsic value to the Amanbidji community than to the settlers who first brought cattle here.

As John Durack walks around his old station, waving away the flies, he is met by two Amanbidji elders, Annie Packsaddle and Eileen Humbert. They know John—they know all the Durack mob. Who could forget the old benevolent white-fella bosses? To Eileen and Annie, the Duracks are always welcome. They walk into the small wooden homestead—galvanised iron above, dirt floor below. Eileen and Annie can remember better than John the former layout of the old house—who slept where, the location of the stove and the office. Annie points to the rusting bread oven standing outside the house, an ageing testimony to the long-gone days when John's mother and Amanbidji women would bake loaf after loaf for hungry cattlemen. Their memories brim with intricate detail. As the writer Mary Durack, John's aunt, once said: '. . . perhaps typical of a people whose culture has been perpetuated from time immemorial by the spoken word'.[2]

This skeleton of a house is used as a storeroom. It was never luxurious; a rudimentary home built by John's tenacious father

Reg and a band of ringers. A house built because Reg was determined to stay on the land his father and grandfather had occupied, despite the odds. Annie tells John they'd like to keep the house and the rusting ovens as monuments to 'old man Reg Durack'. Thousands of kilometres away in the city of Perth and on the east coast, the Duracks were once regarded as part of the pastoral elite, but this perception was never reflected in the lives of Reg's family: tough, spartan and raw.

John picks up a saddle lying forlornly in a corner of the room. Annie and Eileen think it might be his old saddle, still functional after thirty years. John doesn't want to stay at the old homestead for too long. It's no longer his home. The station looks tatty, the grass is long, no cattle can be seen, a few mangy horses stand in the paddocks. The army is expected to arrive any day now to clean up the debris caused by the Wet.

The Duracks are always welcome, but now they're mere visitors. They can only dream about the land they once occupied. And they do dream of this place. John's sister Anne says her dozing visions are full of the things on the station that once lulled her to sleep as a child: 'The sound of the didgeridoo and the clicking sticks and the lovely monotonous song, that lilting, droning song that the women used to sing.'[3] For the Duracks life on the station was wonderful.

The Durack pastoral dynasty was established by John's Irish Catholic great-grandfather, Patrick (Patsy) Durack. Ireland, in the 1850s, was racked by famine—any who could escape leapt at the chance. When news arrived that gold had been discovered in Victoria and NSW, the Duracks, along with thousands of others, decided to act. In 1853 the family landed in Australia with nothing. When his father was killed a few weeks after the family's arrival in the colony, Patsy, the eldest boy, became the main breadwinner. At eighteen, Patsy was a slim, dark-haired youth with blue eyes and fair Irish skin that constantly burnt and peeled under the harsh Australian sun. He was a determined young man with an eye for the main game, he made his first fortune after eighteen months on the Victorian goldfields. This windfall bought the family's first property in Goulburn in New South Wales. The 1850s was a time of speculative land grabs, and the Durack brothers were keen to take the risks and reap the rewards. Patsy's mother, amazed at her son's frenetic pace, once commented that he worked as though he had 'the devil on his tail'. 'And so I have,' he said, 'but he'll not be catching up with me this side of tomorrow.'

He encouraged many other friends and relatives in Ireland to follow them. In a letter filled with the spelling mistakes of a man who had little formal education he wrote:

> *Dear John,*
>
> *I sed I would let you know when it was a good time to come out, well no time is to good if ye look at it from the shady side but this will be as good as eny time and I have a smawl block taken up forty acres about thirty miles from Goulburn.*[4]

Relatives did join the Duracks, but Patsy soon tired of the steady life in Goulburn. In 1863 he set out with a group that included his brother 'Stumpy Michael' and brother-in-law, John, to find more rugged land in south-west Queensland. The trip was a disaster. The party took over two and a half months to reach the tiny outpost of Bourke. From here the arduous trek became life-threatening. The men rode the southern reaches of Queensland, through dusty mulga and brigalow scrub and eventually onto arid plains. With their tongues blackening from thirst, they desperately sought water. Only two years previously the explorer Robert Burke had died in similar terrain. When the party eventually neared the Bulloo River, the 400 head of cattle smelt the moisture and stampeded towards its source. Half the herd drowned and the remainder got bogged after the desperate cattle and horses drank the river dry. The flagging beasts had to be shot. Despite the loss of their herd and most of the horses, the men determined to go on. Patsy believed in miracles and perhaps he thought what happened next was proof of his beliefs. Patsy's life was saved, not by rain falling, but by a group of Aborigines. They revealed a secret well of stagnant water hidden by brushwood and stones and fed the white men roasted goanna and grubs.

Disregarding the calamities, the indomitable Patsy endeavoured to keep moving north. But even he had to give up when it was made clear the Aborigines would only help if the party returned south. The indigenous men showed them hidden waterholes *en route* until they reached less drought-afflicted country. Perhaps if the Aborigines had known the Duracks would soon return to claim traditional lands, they might have withheld their expertise and kindness.

Patsy's stubborn determination was never more evident than when, despite the ill-fated nature of this expedition, he decided to move his family to south-west Queensland. He, his wife Mary and their family returned in 1868 and established Thylungra station on a tributary of Cooper Creek. Not content with this prize, Patsy and brother-in-law John rode approximately 25 000 square kilometres, laying claim to land between Kyabra Creek and the Diamantina River. These were later sold off in parcels, most often to Irish friends and relatives.

It was at Thylungra that Patsy met and began working with a local Aboriginal man. The young man introduced himself as Burrakin; Patsy called him 'Pumpkin'. Patsy and Pumpkin, as Burrakin soon renamed himself, would work together for thirty years. Mary Durack writes that Pumpkin was the only man ever to question Patsy's management decisions, and Patsy believed Pumpkin was a key to the initial success of the family enterprise.[5] At Thylungra the Duracks prospered, but the ever-acquisitive Patsy was thirsty for more—he longed to find land free of the twin curses of drought and flood.

Patsy's colonising ambitions were given a new focus when Alexander Forrest returned from his exploration of the East Kimberley in Western Australia. Forrest claimed to have discovered some 12 million hectares of land capable of sustaining sheep and cattle. Patsy thought this was an opportunity too good to miss. Though there was no market for cattle, Patsy and a business partner began organising the finance for his brother to lead an expedition to examine this little-known region more closely. This expedition, which included two Queensland Aboriginal stockmen, took six months to reach the Kimberley via the coast, but it was worth the journey: the land possessed magnificent ridges, waterways and lush grasses that were swarming with emus, pelicans and dingoes and its rivers were home to large and plentiful barramundi.

It struck these hopeful if naive pioneers as a dream come true. They arrived in the Dry and with satisfaction the party cast their eyes over the grassy plains and crystal-clear creeks. Patsy's dream to escape flood and drought seemed realisable. Grasses and brushwoods indicated the high-water level reached when tropical rains swept down the channels, 'but there was no evidence of inundation on the plains above and the vegetation was nowhere that of a country subject to long, rainless periods. Here the trees spread broad trunks and luxuriant foliage in marked contrast to western Queensland's stunted mulga scrub.'[6]

As the group made their camp under the spread of wild figs and Leichhardt pines they imagined an exciting future. In their enthusiasm they couldn't foresee the swollen creeks, soil degradation, swarms of malarial mosquitoes or the cattle ticks that would nearly destroy the East Kimberley cattle industry. For these optimists, only the remoteness of the Kimberley counted against it. However, Stumpy Michael reasoned that where one man dared, others were not slow to follow, and with the rumours of gold on everyone's lips the Kimberley would certainly soon have a burgeoning white population.

Stumpy telegraphed his brother with the good news. Patsy quickly secured the leaseholdings on hectares of wilderness and set about moving the family and eight thousand head of cattle to this remote region. He dreamed of a Durack dynasty living forever on the fat of this new land. His ambition outweighed his pragmatism.

In May 1883 the Duracks' treacherous journey began. From the safety of his Queensland properties, Patsy directed these proceedings. The group trekked 3000 kilometres overland from

Cooper Creek to the Ord River. It was one of the world's longest cattle treks. It took more than two years and half the cattle died in transit. The party faced disease, a ruthless climate and hostility from squatters and Aborigines. Finally, in September 1885, they reached their destination.

As 'first-footers', the name given to the area's first white occupants, the Duracks would ultimately lay claim to a tract stretching from the mouth of the Ord River in the East Kimberley of Western Australia across into the Northern Territory. For the next sixty-five years they leased and managed almost 3 million hectares of land. On this vast acreage there were several stations, the most important being Argyle (on the banks of the Behn), Ivanhoe (the station closest to Wyndham Port) and later Auvergne (stretching into the Northern Territory). The Auvergne station was added after the Duracks established a business partnership with two other Irish fortune-seekers, Francis Connor and Dennis Doherty.

The nomadic Aboriginal communities must have watched the arrival of these white intruders with alarm. The Duracks were squatting on land these people had always inhabited, and had used since the Dreamtime for hunting, fishing, gathering food, trading and ceremonies. If they couldn't roam over their traditional land they faced disease and hunger. As the first-footers built their homes, Aboriginal tribesmen tried retaliating, mostly by spearing the hoofed beasts the whites had brought with them. Almost a third of the cattle were killed—and two of the Durack men suffered the same fate. The first-footers made no attempt to come to any understanding or even establish friendly terms with the indigenous communities. With unconscious arrogance they settled on the fertile banks of the Ord River and waited until the Aboriginal people realised they had only two choices: either to work for the cattlemen or to keep out of their way.

It would take ten years before the Duracks could feel settled and relatively safe as many Aboriginal people yielded to the awful inevitability of their situation. Patsy had fled a country where Protestant Irish had taken possession of the land occupied by his Catholic countrymen, and perhaps he felt justified in now taking possession of someone else's soil.

The Durack family established their mudbrick, dirt-floored homes by the long, clear course of the Ord River, its banks fringed with trees, bamboo and pandanus palms and framed by the mighty red ridges in the background. Initially Patsy was kept informed of his new stations via letter and hoped the next generation, his six living children, would play their part in his new enterprise. In particular, he wanted his eldest son, Michael Patrick, to succeed him. In 1886 Patsy ordered his two eldest sons, fresh out of a genteel NSW boarding school, to Western Australia. The two young men, Michael Patrick (MP) and John, were reluctant but were impelled to follow their father's directive. Shortly after, Patsy assigned his Kimberley interests to his four sons. MP and John arrived at the head station at Argyle Downs just in time for the Halls Creek gold rush. With the discovery of gold the Duracks had a swelling local market for their beef. On his twenty-first birthday MP Durack weighed out £1200 in raw Kimberley nuggets. His bullocks sold at £17 a head. The autocratic Patsy considered this additional wealth ample justification for the risks he had taken.

By 1886 Patsy was a prosperous and influential Queensland businessman, but couldn't settle into a staid middle-age. The following year, with the trusty Pumpkin, the spirited Patsy made the difficult journey to Argyle. On his arrival Patsy admonished his sons for their shoddy building skills. Then he and Pumpkin set about mustering and branding cattle and building yards, seemingly oblivious to the stifling heat of the Kimberley.

But the Kimberley gold years were shortlived and Patsy's optimistic spirit was dealt several blows. In 1889 Patsy was at Argyle when he received a letter telling him to return to Queensland post-haste. The patriarch's fortune had come to grief in the regular boom-and-bust cycle of the Australian economy. He had lost the Queensland business.

The 1890s depression bankrupted thousands of landholders.

But by assigning his Kimberley interests to his sons, Patsy had stayed one step ahead of complete disaster. Left with only household possessions, Patsy brought his wife Mary to live in the wilds of the Kimberley. A few years later, at the age of fifty-one, Mary died—as did so many—of malaria. To add to his grief, Patsy found himself sidelined by his sons who, perhaps because of their father's own business failure, were not highly receptive to his financial advice. Patsy was never to see his fortune secure, and ended his life a lonely and rather cantankerous man. He understood the tenuous nature of Durack money and assets, and once described the family as 'kings in grass castles, that may be blown away upon a puff of wind'.

After the death of his wife in 1893, Patsy's closest companion was Pumpkin. Patsy thought Pumpkin unusual among Aboriginal people—a 'better sort of black'. Pumpkin served his white 'lord' with devotion, insisting on leaving his traditional home at Cooper Creek to settle way up north with Patsy. He was the old man's final confidant.

Patsy died in 1898, his ill-starred and problematic legacy passing to his sons. Patsy's eldest son MP heard of his father's death while riding in the Northern Territory. The news brought back into his mind a letter Patsy had written to him sixteen years earlier: 'One day I will be leaving ye in the saddle, so to speak, and I hope in God ye will know enough to take the right direction when that time comes.'[7]

Taking the right direction was a task that would haunt the new patriarch of the Duracks for the rest of his life. MP, now thirty-three, had been 'saddled' with a vast acreage in an alien land. This prince regent would have preferred an urban principality to a huge rural estate. His daughter, the noted writer Mary Durack, described her father as a 'man of considerable versatility, at home in stock camps and salons, experienced in the handling and judging of stock, an able company director and for some years a conscientious politician'.[8] But in his heart MP was a scholar, not a natural cattleman; only his loyalty to his father's dream and a belief the stations would inevitably reap consistent rewards bound him to the dynastic vision. MP remained uneasy on the land his father had claimed. He dreamed of an academic life in the ivory tower of a city university. Instead he battled the locusts, mosquitoes, heat and rain.

Family photographs show MP as an upright Edwardian gentleman. His neatly trimmed red beard, immaculate cream suits and straight-backed posture, even on horseback, gave him a regal bearing. The long days riding the rugged land he found mundane and tedious. He envied his brother Jeremiah who had been able, as the youngest son, to pursue an academic career. But MP felt it his filial duty to carry on the dynastic inheritance, no matter that it was in a country where brute survival was the standard.

It was the Aboriginal communities, however, who bore the brunt of much of this brutality. The punishment for spearing cattle or white settlers was swift. It became common to see Aboriginal people chained neck to neck as they walked to the Wyndham lockup. Indigenous life was torn apart; the people had lost land and they faced starvation and violence from police and pastoralists. In those early years no Aboriginal person brought to trial was acquitted and no white man charged with mistreatment or murder of Aborigines was convicted.[9] Neither MP nor his father before him took part in the cruel maltreatment of Kimberley Aboriginal people, but they did hold with the prevailing white viewpoint that Aboriginal people were inherently inferior to Europeans. MP also found the appearance of 'half-caste' workers alarming as 'it being common-knowledge that the half-breed inherits the worst characteristics of both races'.[10] In the year of his father's death, MP wrote in his diary that he 'shot a beast today for bush niggers hanging about the station—the most wretched, haggard looking lot of 38 individuals I ever saw together—all suffering from sore eyes, sickly and hopeless looking'. But like his father, MP didn't criticise the source of Aboriginal misery: the squatters.

With the loss of their land for hunting and the threat of draconian punishment for spearing cattle, many communities knew their safest option was to resign themselves to the takeover and seek work with the white bosses. With the end of the gold rush and the resultant loss of European labourers, the Kimberley pastoralists found they needed a black workforce. The pastoralists needed the skills of the Aboriginal people, their physical work, their understanding of natural cycles. They could read the bush, they knew how everything worked. And then the Aboriginal people needed settlers' food and clothing and at times their medicines. With the Aboriginal world turned upside down and the gold rush over, white cattle barons and black communities forged an uneasy interdependence. MP Durack's second daughter, Elizabeth, coined the phrase 'mutual exploitation' to describe how she saw this fragile alliance. The Duracks were regarded by their Aboriginal workers as 'better than average' bosses.[11]

From the turn of the century, life on the Durack cattle stations was built round predictable cycles of time and season. During the Dry there was constant mustering, branding and driving the stock to Wyndham abattoir. The long working day began at sunrise and finished at sunset. Sunday was a day for going to the races or polishing saddles and boots for the following week. At Argyle station alone there were around 25 000 head of cattle roaming the cracked plains. The majority of the ringers were young Aboriginal men. As one white stockman described in a letter to his family:

> There are twelve of us in this camp—(three white men)—the rest blacks. Boxer the oldest boy, is about 30 years old. He came from Queensland and has been with the Duracks for over 20 years. He is a fine all-round fellow . . . The other stock boys are also good sorts, pretty good horsemen and generally a big help to the pastoralists. The same cannot be said of the outside blacks who are a constant menace to both cattle and horses.[12]

Kimberley women were put to work in the homesteads—sweeping, cleaning, making bread. There was also a cook who would do what he could with the limited food stock. Meat, flour, jam and tea were the staple provisions. When schools of resplendent silver barramundi were spotted, ringers would grab their spears and provide bonus fare. During the four-month Wet, station work almost ground to a halt. The swollen rivers transformed the dry plains into bogs, drenching the ground and making mustering impossible. From December to March, life centred on sedentary work: repairing saddles, packs and boots, drawing up inventories and reading. For the black station workers it was the season to meet with their tribal group and conduct community business. Where once the passing on of sacred rites and tribal traditions had been a year-round activity, it was now confined to the Wet. Much later in a poignant short story, Mary Durack wrote of the gradual loss of Dreamtime knowledge:

> The old people had gone now, and the children were scattered around the stations, the missions and the bush towns. Some of the younger men had been through two stages of initiation. They knew something of their past but had given no more than half their hearts to it, and only a whole heart could be entrusted with the last and greatest secrets, the powers and the magic.[13]

Unlike his daughter Mary, MP Durack had no interest in the loss of tribal knowledge among his station workers. He wanted to extend the family business and dreamed of finding riches under the soil that would far exceed those upon it. He was convinced that oil worthy of the Texan fields lay under the Kimberley rock and spent many years trying to create government interest in exploration, but it proved fruitless. MP never envisaged what actually did lie underfoot—diamonds. By the time the now world-renowned Argyle diamonds were discovered, the Duracks had long left Argyle.

MP felt little affinity with the locust- and crocodile-infested Kimberley. More at home in the city than the bush, he gladly fled his remote stations before the torrential rains marked the start of the Wet. The sedate city of Perth was where MP conducted much of his business. His significant landholdings ensured an immediate entree into Western Australia's small, elite business and political circles. He settled his wife Bess and six children in a mansion in central Perth. As befitted the now established squatter, he offered his offspring a genteel and educated city life. But come the Dry season, the dynastic responsibilities beckoned—and MP would wearily venture north to manage the family enterprise.

For thirty years this cattle empire generated a fluctuating but generally solid income. The Duracks rolled with the punches: cattle ticks, drought and flood. However, the biggest blow would come in the late 1920s—a crisis generated by a combination of factors. When the first whites arrived in the Kimberley, they had found a land rich with verdant grasses. But underneath, the soil was poor—deficient in nutrients and the grasses unable to sustain the assault of hundreds of thousands of introduced hoofed animals. Within thirty years the river frontages were eaten out and the country was beginning to suffer devastating erosion. Compounding the natural decline, beef prices were falling disastrously. By 1930 Australia was in the middle of the Great Depression—and MP Durack was deeply in debt.

MP had long hoped his prodigiously talented children would escape the burden of the North, but found he needed them on the stations. His first child, Reg, had reached adulthood. Born in 1911, Reg had inherited MP's scholarly intellect and ambitions; however, Durack duty once again thwarted academic aspirations for the more pressing demands of life in the saddle. By the 1930s Reg was managing the family's most problematic property, Auvergne, having been told the family could no longer support his university studies. Then in 1933 MP's daughters Mary and Elizabeth put themselves in charge of Ivanhoe station.

Unlike their father, and despite their upbringing in Perth, MP's children felt gripped by the Kimberley. It was a visceral connection. Mary and Elizabeth came to understand it as their spirit country. For the young writer Mary, her first memories were of Ivanhoe, around 1916, and a Mirriwung woman named Dinah who carried the toddler around with her as she cleaned the house or waded in the billabongs. The now twenty-year-old Mary was ecstatic at the prospect of returning to the home nestled between a river teeming with fish and imposing red ridges.

Instead of attending debutante balls, MP's vivacious daughters rolled up their sleeves to manage the 400 000 hectare property. They had no phone or radio. They cooked and organised the stores and the musters. They were paid £3 a week between them, but added to their income with their illustrated stories and articles on station life which were regularly published in the *West Australian* and *Western Mail*. Station life fuelled Mary's writing and Elizabeth's art, and would enliven their creative work for the rest of their long lives.

Their father would occasionally visit as he travelled between the stations—and it was testament to the absolute trust he placed in the Aboriginal community that he would leave his daughters in their care. There were about sixty Aboriginal people living in camps on the waterfront 30 metres from the main Ivanhoe homestead. Mary and Elizabeth lived alongside them. The Durack girls would often go walking with the accommodating Mirriwung women. They would head along the river tributary, scouring it for bush tucker. Sometimes during the Wet the station community would be gone for days, walking to the waterfalls hidden in the hills to meet with other communities to discuss business and perform ancient ceremonies. The sisters found they were welcome at all but the secret ceremonies and corroborees. Mary and Elizabeth wondered if the Mirriwung pitied them for being without their family. Whatever the reason, they treated the writer and artist as family—accepted them as sisters to the women and mothers to the children.

The Wet season was a time for both traditional Aboriginal business and Christian festivity. At Christmas Mary and Elizabeth, like most Kimberley squatters, rustled up the expected fare for Christmas Day. Even in the intense heat paper chases, treasure hunts and races were the order of the day and under a corrugated iron roof a roasted Yuletide feast was devoured.

But the power of the elements could always override ritual. Mary wrote of Ivanhoe festivities coming to an abrupt halt with the force of the Wet. 'Storm clouds darkened in the afternoon and under the rumble of thunder we heard the unmistakable roar of the river coming into flood. We hurried through the steaming heat to watch it swirling, brown and turgid, from bank to bank with its load of debris bound for Cambridge Gulf.'[14] The rest of Christmas Day was spent catching giant barramundi and watching the tumultuous river.

For MP's children and even for some station workers, the 1930s were a golden decade. Despite Aboriginal people receiving no wages, no education and no proper medical facilities, at least the whole community could live on the station; they had food and could maintain a hold on what remained of their traditions. Importantly, in the case of the Duracks, these white fella bosses were all right. Here the benevolently paternalistic working relationship was working as well as it could.

In contrast to his father, Reginald enjoyed managing the family's most remote property a few hundred kilometres from his sisters. Something of a Renaissance man, Reg was a Latin and Greek scholar and a hands-on pastoralist who enjoyed the continual challenges the Kimberley threw at him. Unlike his unorthodox sisters with their capacity for mischief, Reg brought a certain gravitas to his own life and those around him. When he mustered the cattle or drove them to the Wyndham abattoir, a battered book of poetry or a well-thumbed Greek history text was inevitably part of his swag. He could build houses or mend the yard fences while reciting ancient Greek verse.

An effective manager, Reg had given up his studies to work on the family stations and had grown to love the life and the breathtaking country. He believed his generation, Patsy's grandchildren, should sustain the pastoral tradition. As the responsible eldest son he embraced the dynastic legacy that had so troubled his father. MP had spent his adult life trying to adapt to a land he found alien and to Patsy's ambitions. He wanted to leave a heritage more sustainable than the one Patsy had left him. But with the Depression, erosion, isolation and no oil or gold, he was not able to let go of the Durack land. Until the economic tide turned, an unenthusiastic MP was forced to allow Reg to assume control.

With Reg settled in the Kimberley, MP and his wife Bess decided that at the very least their eldest son had to marry a city girl. They feared their heir would lose the civilising effects of urban life. The possibility that Reg, whose only company now was the station workers, would form sexual relationships with Aboriginal women must have preyed on their minds. Reg's parents set about finding what they regarded as a more suitable wife for their eldest boy—and they didn't have to look far. According to family legend, in 1943 when Reg (then a man in his thirties) was visiting his family in Perth, his mother told him that when he returned to the Kimberley he would have to be married. As he didn't know anyone in the city, his mother suggested the girl next door. He replied simply, 'She'll do.'

And she did. The twenty-eight-year-old daughter of a Presbyterian minister, Enid was charmed by this Catholic pastoralist who could recount intricate details of ancient Athenian history and manage a remote cattle station. Six weeks later the couple was married. Enid had little idea what sort of man she was marrying, or what sort of life she was about to enter. But she never regretted her decision. Enid Durack, now in her late eighties, laughs as she remembers the first few days of married life: 'We were married on the Tuesday, at the end of that week we'd left in a truck. I'd never sat in a truck before. It was really a bit of a shock, a culture shock, but it didn't matter . . . because it was with Reg. It took us twenty-eight days to get there. I said, "Reg, that was our honeymoon, twenty-eight days of camping out under the stars." And he'd just say, "Oh, not many people get a twenty-eight day honeymoon." He loved it all the way . . . it was his life. It certainly wasn't mine then. And when I got there, home was just a big shed. I couldn't believe it . . . I'd look at this place and think, "That's my home, my first home." It was pretty terrible.'[15]

Enid's new home was the very basic Auvergne homestead, with its dirt floor and rusting iron roof. It was far removed from the quiet gentility of Perth, with its elaborate Italianate mansions and wide tree-lined streets. Enid realised her much enjoyed weekend tennis games were now a thing of the past (although her husband did attempt to build her a court). She stared despondently at the red-mud, fast-flowing streams and absorbed Auvergne's unforgiving splendour. Now Saturdays would be spent in the same way as every other day: the men mustering cattle, the women baking bread, cooking and sewing. As she digested her new surroundings Enid wondered how she would ever love this life. She never did quite love it— but she adored her eccentric, bookish husband and determined never to complain about this untamed vastness she had been brought to.

Enid married her decidedly unromantic prince as the sun began to set on the Durack empire. For close to seventy years the family had battled the natural and economic elements. MP's children believed that after the Depression, and particularly after World War II, the Duracks had some prospect of making their land self-sustaining and successful—communications were improving and the North was ready to start a new era. Their father, however, was moving in the opposite direction. For him the time had come to move on. MP wouldn't listen to his children's protestations. He reminded his recalcitrant offspring of his motto: 'Travel hopefully'.

MP had hoped to sell the properties in 1938 to an American Zionist group who wanted to buy a Jewish homeland for 75 000 families. (This plan was thwarted by the Curtin government.) Now, in 1950, as he neared his eighty-fifth year, MP told his children he had finally secured a buyer for the leasehold titles. The younger Duracks argued fervently against the sale, but their father wouldn't be persuaded. Everything bar a small section was sold. The sale brought little financial security to the family. His exasperated daughter Mary described it as her father's 'final act of folly'.

Mary believed her father's decision to sell up was the product of exhaustion. He was the only one left of his company—his partners had died. He had survived two world wars and numerous depressions. And he would rather leave his children a tidy sum of money than a problematic parcel of land. He told his children that if running the place hadn't killed him, then selling it certainly wouldn't.

But three weeks later MP Durack died. On the day of his death the old Ivanhoe homestead burnt to the ground. The Durack dynastic dreaming was in ashes.

MP was a pragmatist with no sense of timing. He and his father Patsy had regarded the land as a piece of real estate; an investment to be sold when the time and the price were right. But no sale price could ever match the years of work and effort by several generations. Like his father, MP was ultimately defeated by a land ill-equipped for grand pastoral ambitions.

Despite wanting to provide security for his children, MP left them with substantial debts. By the time death duties and the stations' owings were paid, there was little left for MP's widow, Bess. The most enduring riches MP was to leave were cultural. For a man who dreamed of becoming a scholar rather than a farmer, it's not surprising that he hoarded letters, diaries, invoices and receipts—not just from his own life, but also from his father's. The dynastic chronicler, Mary, managed to salvage these, providing the central source material for her best-selling books, *Kings in Grass Castles* and *Sons in the Saddle*. In these epic tales Mary tells the family's pioneering history. The books contain rich detail and celebrate her family's endeavours. Mary was uneasy with this history as it had also brought devastation to indigenous communities, but she could never bring herself to write a truly impartial assessment of the dynastic legacy.

The Durack pastoral heritage didn't completely disappear with MP's death. The third generation, his children, already had the East Kimberley in their blood. The founder's impossible dream rose from the ashes—smaller in scale, but undiminished in passion and determination—through Patsy's grandson Reg.

When MP first told the family he was selling the leasehold, Reg dug in his heels. All six children had shares in the Durack properties and Reg wouldn't relinquish his. He tried to persuade MP to give him a slice of Argyle, the Duracks' most resource-rich station. MP refused, believing it would jeopardise the sale of the rest of the land. Ultimately the octogenarian father and recalcitrant son took to the saddle and rode for days before reaching the dusty outskirts of Auvergne station, well into the Northern Territory. Here they agreed to section off a substantial block for the determined Reg, who was grateful for the opportunity to stay and build his own castle.

This slice of land was the most isolated and difficult country under Durack management, considered so poor that buyers didn't regard it as an asset. But Reg knew the land better than these blow-ins. After all, he had spent his adult life working Auvergne, making the station as profitable as it could be. The landscape was crisscrossed with stony ridges where no grass could grow, but in between there were stretches of rich black soil growing some of the better Mitchell and Flinders cattle grasses.

The designated land was Reg's only resource. The new station had no homestead, no communications, no sound roads and, most importantly, no cattle. Reg and Enid would be starting with nothing. The odds against them were enormous but Reg, unheeding the family history, was buoyant. He was not only a stockman, he was a builder, a vet to his animals and a doctor to his children. And he had the good fortune to marry Enid, a steadfast woman who, despite the dangers this life posed to her children and its limitations, never dreamed of doing anything else but following her husband even further into the unknown.

They were to live many hundreds of kilometres from the nearest outback town. The closest station was a day's ride away and the family's only regular companions were the small community of station workers. Their new home was called Kildurk, in honour of the two families on the original overland trek, the Duracks and the

Kilfoyles. Before moving to the station, Enid insisted they were to have at least an airstrip and a Flying Doctor radio service. In her heart of hearts she was terrified of this isolation, but she duly packed their belongings and gritted her teeth.

In 1950, while most Australians keenly embraced the postwar boom with its technological advantages and consumerist ethos, Reg, Enid and their young family crammed a short-wheelbase Land Rover and a small trailer with pots and pans, rugs and books—all their worldly goods. Their young children were excited; it was a new adventure with their hero-like parents. And so the little party headed off across the vast expanse of red dirt.

Their new home was set up by a billabong. Built by Reg, the dwelling was a galvanised iron hut with a mud floor and a tent extension that would flap in the breeze. The oven was outside and each day Enid would stand at the stove cooking, an umbrella over her head to shield her from either burning sun or torrential rain. The children played with the Aboriginal children, had games of hide-and-seek in the erosion channels and swam in the billabong. During the heat of the day, the children would read or listen to the crackling 'Kindergarten of the Air', the dust flying up around them as they bopped exuberantly to the songs.

As the children danced, their parents discussed their first serious problem: drought. The dryness was apparent as soon as they arrived, and it continued. For two years the Wet season didn't reach Kildurk. Billabongs dried up and animals died. As the drought took hold, Reg had to ride further out on the property to fetch water for his family. This muddy water would be placed in ten-gallon drums by the house. In the cool of the evening Enid would throw in ashes or Condy's crystals to clear the water. In the morning the clearest one would be boiled. It tasted appalling, but at least they could drink it. Water also had to be fetched for the cattle and horses. Some cattle died and many horses, unable to find their usual grasses, ate young, green but toxic pea flowers—the resulting liver damage sent them mad and necessitated a merciful bullet.

The cattle the family were watering weren't even theirs. For two years the couple had to watch as the new owners of Auvergne station would muster and take the cattle off Kildurk. When rain finally fell after two years Reg could at last restock the land with his own cattle and begin to make some money from beef. His life was now far removed from the cattle-baron glory days his father and grandfather had enjoyed during those brief gold-rich years. The drought had forced the family to move 35 kilometres further into the property to what became known as Reg's Acropolis. Standing on a rocky outcrop, the new castle was built over the top of fresh clean bore water. This was a great improvement and for a time Reg felt like a king in his (tin, not grass) castle. New possibilities beckoned once more.

The soil surrounding the house was too poor to grow any fresh vegetables or fruit. The Duracks and the station workers lived on a monotonous diet of bread and beef. Twice a year, a plane would bring tonnes of flour, Bushells tea, jams, pickles, canned vegetables and fruit. Within weeks the luxuries would run out and only the bread and beef would remain. At Christmas they might kill a bush turkey for dinner. One Christmas a pig arrived by plane, an exotic treat for the Yuletide dinner table.

At times this isolation was life-threatening. When cyclones ripped through the region, the family could only hang on and hope the house would hold together—there was never any chance they would be airlifted out. When one cyclone threatened the family they all sheltered in Reg's study, the smallest children placed in the mailbags for warmth. This little room, filled with his precious books, was usually out of bounds to his brood. As the winds battered the house, six-year-old Anne, impervious to any danger from the cyclone, asked excitedly if they were now always allowed to come into Daddy's study? She was disappointed that once the storm had passed, her father's inner sanctum was once more firmly out of bounds.

The family had a radio system, but it didn't always bring help. Anne once suffered a terrible fever which raged for some days.

She was dehydrated and extremely weak. But this was the Wet—for days the Flying Doctor couldn't reach the station, and Anne lay sweating. Finally the doctor refused to fly in, saying that the child was so gravely ill she probably wouldn't survive the trip. He asked if Reg could find something in his medicine bag to at least halt the dehydration. Reg looked up his old medical books and rummaged to the bottom of his medicine kit. Eventually he found some obscure medication. Anne survived and recovered. Even crises like these never made the family think about moving to Perth and the security of city life. Reg was wedded to this land. It was his inheritance and perhaps he felt his harsh life was predestined. Anne remembers that the only persistent problem facing the family was water—either too much or too little. Great-grandfather Patsy had tried so desperately to escape the twin curses of drought and flood, but the family never escaped them.

The spartan isolation of Kildurk compelled Reg's children, this fourth generation of station Duracks, to find delight in the minutiae of life. Like the generation before them, they felt a sense of belonging to this country. There was excitement about storms, thunder and lightning; about the little bugs that flew inside the home, the praying mantises, the grasshoppers, the moths, the exotic birds. One year they kept baby crocodiles. They would search the barren and tough landscape looking for a few precious flowers. When a hibiscus or wild hop was found, the children would be absorbed by its vibrant colour and subtle perfume.

The children went on long walks and swims with the station children and women. Even as a mature woman, childhood memories can flood into Anne's mind. She vividly recalls the walks and stories and can, without thinking, drop into the voice and speech pattern of an Amanbidji woman:

'We'd go on walks with the women, with all these exotic ideas about coming home with pigeons and yams and potato and making a stew. I remember sitting with the women and telling stories. We'd sit to tell the stories and they'd have this piece of carefully worked-over dirt, lovely soft dirt, and they'd tell the story in the dirt. They'd draw a story like a little map to go with what they were telling us and then it would go for the next story . . . irreplaceable Aboriginal art. And they used to make little animal tracks and tell us "this one little wallapi come up to have a drink, you know that little wallapi, and this one snake and a big fella guana . . ." and they'd keep drawing patterns in the dirt. And we'd be laughing, perfectly comfortable with each other. And of course that terrible regret that we didn't hold onto it, that we didn't appreciate that for what it was. There was an interaction there that we didn't appreciate was not forever.'

Life on the station was generally slow and the routines didn't change. In the Dry season there was mustering and droving the cattle to the abattoir. The meat was then shipped and sold around the country. During the Wet, saddles would be mended, yards fixed, toys made for the children from bits of used material, and many books read. Then the property was totally inaccessible except by plane. Enid would sew and teach. Every other day she and the indigenous Amanbidji women would make thirty-two loaves of bread and on other days copious quantities of soap.

Reg's children, David, Anne, John, Ruth and Doug, all helped on the station. They would get up early to milk the cows, bed them in the yard at night, muster cattle, fix and build yards. Like their father, the children were scholarly. Reg and Enid soon decided that their eldest son, David, would be unlikely to work on the land (he was to go on to be a Rhodes scholar and medical researcher). It was their second son, John, who Reg hoped would continue the Durack pastoral tradition. John enjoyed the quiet, simple pleasures of station life, mustering the stock, the slow drive on horseback to the meatworks.

The children were Enid's main source of companionship during the day and she had no wish to part with them. The now poor Duracks couldn't afford preparatory boarding schools, so Enid herself was their teacher. She set up the first school in the region, not only for her five children but also for the Amanbidji offspring. As Enid describes it: 'I was doing our children by correspondence and there were three Aboriginal girls who would watch. So we invited them in. Reg cut an oval in three tea chests so their legs could fit underneath, they were the desks . . . and the chairs were four-gallon kerosene and petrol drums.

'One day we got a visit from the welfare department who asked if I could teach all the children in the camp. At one time there were sixteen: four Duracks and twelve Aboriginal. They loved it. I had a piano so we'd do lots of singing and a bit of country dancing. Reg put a shower down a tree, you'd fill it up and pull the chain. So the children would come up from the camp, have a shower and put on school clothes they left each evening at the shed school. Reg made a blackboard and there was a small amount of chalk.'

Enid says she 'hated' teaching. But despite her feelings and the limitations of their resources, Enid must have been an effective teacher—her children would all in time become city professionals. Enid reflected the pervasive attitudes of the time, and as such never expected such high achievements from her Aboriginal students. For most of these children, this was the only education they were to receive. But attendance rates were impressive (sometimes 100 per cent over a year), and the children enjoyed their basic introduction to white people's education.

Enid never felt entirely comfortable with the Aboriginal station workers. Sometimes when Reg was away she would hear sounds echoing in the night air and imagine intruders were breaking into the store. Her husband was completely at ease among the black workers and had a 'brotherhood' affinity with two Amanbidji men, Bingle and Ginger. For Reg's children, this was Home—and the indigenous community was part of their extended family.

The workers were given food and shelter on the property. Reg also set up a rudimentary banking system in the store. According to John Durack, station workers were paid a 'more than nominal' weekly wage, which was safeguarded in the store until the money was needed. Anne and John both remember the storeroom wages book into which workers would place their thumbprints. When money was wanted Reg and the station worker would add up how many thumbprints were in the book and therefore the amount of money owing. During the Wet season, when station workers left Kildurk for tribal business, they would often use this money to buy food and clothes from neighbouring stations. Once a year these wages were topped up for the August race day.

The fourth-generation Duracks believe they lived in harmony with the Aboriginal people and the land. Says Anne: 'There was no restriction of access, there was no feeling that there wasn't free movement for either us or for them. In fact they moved more freely than we did, with a lot more confidence, because they knew where they were going and what was happening. But we did share the billabongs, the fishing, the fun.'

But this paternalistic relationship reliant upon poorly paid Aboriginal labour was about to collapse. It was inevitable. Around the country, Aboriginal people were talking of their human rights—the right to own land, to be paid a proper wage, and to enjoy the same citizenship privileges as other Australians. An era had passed, and Australians no longer considered it acceptable for a small white elite to own vast tracts of land relying on the slave-like labour of dispossessed indigenous communities.

The Durack station workers hadn't been involved in the 1946 Kimberley stockmen's strike but now they felt the ripple of unrest from Wave Hill station, a few hundred kilometres from Kildurk. In 1966 Vincent Lingiari led his Gurindji tribe and other groups off Wave Hill cattle station, owned by the British Vesty group of companies. The treatment of workers there was notorious. One former station worker recalled: 'We lived in tin humpies you had to crawl in and out on your knees. There was no running water. The food was bad—just flour, tea, sugar and bits of beef like the head or feet of a bullock.'[16] The Wave Hill strike for better wages and living conditions quickly transformed into the beginnings of the Aboriginal land rights movement.

Life on outback cattle stations would never be the same. From the late 1960s, Aborigines were paid award wages. Communities no longer depended on the largesse of a station owner for housing, food, clothes and medicine. But award rates also meant enormous upheaval for station communities in the Northern Territory and the Kimberley. Under the new system, only the main stockmen and the women who worked in the house would be paid. The rest now drifted off the property. Some would find homes on the reserves set on the outskirts of newly established towns such as Halls Creek, Kununurra and Fitzroy Crossing.

For the Kildurk workers, who rarely used cash and whose cultural system gave money little value, it brought many complications. Enid would watch people pay for an item and not wait for their change. Whites could exploit Aboriginal people who hadn't been raised to know the 'value' of money. It also meant that for the first time Aboriginal people were allowed to, and could afford to, drink alcohol—with its often dire consequences. For three generations the Duracks had been able to make their landholdings economically sustainable thanks to a cheap and steady labour force. This now began to fall apart. Reg's son John remembers: 'People would go into town ... spend their money and quite often a lot of that went on alcohol ... and that process tended to make the families less stable; and I found in the latter part of the years I was up there that the stable families that we were quite used to ... were starting to break down.'[17]

His sister Anne concurs. She saw at close quarters the escalating problems of alcohol and alienation plunging Aboriginal people into despair and suicide. 'For however odd it might sound now,' says Anne, 'they had a place: they were Durack blacks or they were Kildurk Aborigines, they were our people and we knew it and they knew it. And I think that sense of belonging was one of the things that got lost.'

The Kildurk labour force probably saw it differently: despite new problems, there was no turning back to the days of unpaid work for white bosses. Reg and son John increasingly had to fly to the swelling towns and find ringers—a reliable and compliant labour force was no longer on tap.

As well as domestic social changes, Kildurk was also struggling with international upheavals. New international trade agreements were making it increasingly difficult for the resident pastoralist. For the Duracks, their dreams and aspirations for success as cattle kings—dreams that had driven the lives of four generations—had been dealt a deathblow. Reg was angry and bitter at the changes. For him, like so many Northern Territory pastoralists of his generation, it had seemed white and black were working well together—reconciled and living cooperatively. Equal pay, trade agreements and alcohol had combined to crush the optimism of even Reg, who began to bemoan the bleak future of station life. A third Durack patriarch had been beaten by the blows dealt by the unforgiving North.

Back in Reg's Acropolis he, John and Enid discussed the future. Since the age of seventeen, John Durack had been his father's apprentice, preparing to take up the reins when Reg retired. But John had been studying in the evenings and now chose a career as a city solicitor over the new uncertainties of station life. Reg the scholar, who had once dreamed of being a doctor and who sometimes appeared to love his books above all else, didn't stand in his son's way. For Enid, perhaps the strongest feeling was relief. For thirty years she had lived her life in this remote, alien and often physically dangerous place, not complaining because she was with the man she loved; however, she was eager to leave.

In 1973 the Duracks sold the last vestiges of their original kingdom. In a strange twist, the lease was bought by the newly elected Whitlam government, with its mandate to address Aboriginal aspirations for their traditional land. Reg and Enid were no supporters of land rights, but they were offered a good price and they desperately wanted out. That year, the station was the first pastoral lease in Australia to be handed to traditional owners, the Ngarinman. They called their station Amanbidji. (The Gurindji people won leasehold of Wave Hill station two years later in 1975.) The Ngarinman gained freehold title in 1994.

The one-time station workers celebrated their new tenure. The Canberra bureaucrats, however, gave little thought to how the Amanbidji community could uphold the cattle business, given their relatively recent experience with currency, their rudimentary education, and the fact that even a driven pastoralist like Reg Durack viewed the business as ultimately unsustainable.

Now Kildurk was gone, Reg Durack was rootless. He would later say that selling was the biggest mistake he ever made. He had lost his country, but the country still exerted its grip on him. For the next two decades, from 1973 to the mid-1990s, he and Enid moved back and forth between Perth, the East Kimberley and the Northern Territory searching for a new acropolis—but it couldn't be found. Ultimately ill health forced Reg back to Perth.

The frustration of dreams lost and hopes dashed was felt not only by Reg but also by his sisters, Mary and Elizabeth, and it ultimately drove a wedge through the family. By the 1990s all that remained of the Durack cattle dynasty was a cultural legacy—books, papers and pictures. There was no land, no money—only history. Even the ownership of these dynastic shreds became the subject of an extraordinary family battle.

Reg and his siblings had always been close, their experiences in the North creating firm bonds. Reg was proud of his two creative and now famous sisters. Mary's daughter Patsy says: 'It's difficult to realise how close these siblings were, bound to one another in a most unusual way—closer than [Mary was] to her children.'[18] Elizabeth was a successful artist, still painting the land and people of the Kimberley, and by the 1990s her art was distinctly 'indigenous' in its form.[19] Mary Durack was planning to write the third volume of the family's pastoral history.

For more than ten years Mary had kept in her possession MP

Durack's fifty-three detailed diaries, assorted notes, letters and receipts. It was the source material for *Sons in the Saddle* (published in 1983). Still holding onto this original material, she was now hoping to write the next book. As far as Mary was concerned, the papers were hers—however, her siblings and the Western Australian State Library felt differently.

In 1950, when the family sorted out MP's Perth office, Mary saved her father's and grandfather's papers from the rubbish tip. She painstakingly went through the earliest material which formed the basis for her four-hundred-page epic, *Kings in Grass Castles* (published in 1959). When this first volume was finished she deposited the family papers in the Battye Library in the Western Australian State Library, for safekeeping. These papers were catalogued and maintained by the Battye until Mary withdrew them again in the 1970s to write *Sons in the Saddle*. In the early 1990s the Battye asked Mary to return the papers. The library's administrators were concerned the papers might be lost to them after learning of an approach by the National Library asking Mary to consider placing the papers into their Canberra collection.

Mary turned down the National Library offer. She wanted to keep the papers in her possession. This alarmed Mary's siblings, who worried about who would inherit the documents after Mary's death. Reg, Elizabeth and younger brother Bill believed they should also supervise the papers' safekeeping. Reg in particular was adamant that Mary and her children had a moral obligation to the Battye: 'The simple fact is that the Battye owns [the papers], they have been borrowed out and not returned. Full stop. That's all that matters.' On the other side, Mary's children turned down financial offers of between $60 000 to $80 000 from the Battye Library and argued that it was Mary who had given the papers their value and it was she who should decide their fate.

The scale of the divisions caused by this undignified dispute is difficult to imagine or to understand. Here were Reg and Elizabeth at war with the children of Mary—whose failing health made the situation even more distressing. The last few months of Mary's life were marred by bitter public arguments between her beloved siblings and her children.

Mary Durack died in 1994, three months after being served a Supreme Court writ issued by the Library Board of Western Australia demanding the return of 'their' papers. After her death the dispute was mediated, but neither side would ever be completely happy with the results. The Battye Library has a collection, including photocopied papers, and Mary's daughter Patsy retains a substantial collection of original documents. Today the two sides of the family rarely speak to one another despite living in neighbouring riverside suburbs.

This bitter struggle was a blight on the last four years of Reg's life, too. Like his grandfather and father, Reg's early life was driven by passionate determination and tremendous ability, but at the end he felt worn down and broken. He had Enid and his children, but he was estranged from his sister's family, he had no land and the relationship with his Aboriginal stockmen was gone. No longer the king of his Acropolis, Reg was at odds with his world. Before he died, Reg filled in a questionnaire. As his daughter Anne describes:

'It was a funny little book, a sort of know-thyself book, where for some reason Dad had bothered to fill in pencil his little responses to the questions. One of them was along the lines of "Tonight you can dream whatever you want, you can have whatever you want, you can be wherever you want—what will your dream be?" And Dad had written "Branding calves on Kildurk".'

But those simple days in the outback were gone for good. Old Patsy Durack's dream of a permanent and concordant pastoral dynasty—founded on a fantasy of bounteous fertile land and free labour—had finally been reduced to a family feud over fragments of Durack history.

On the back of an old sepia photograph, one of the Duracks, possibly MP, has written 'Cockatoo Springs, beautiful shady camping ground'. Cockatoo Springs remains, lying between the old Argyle and Ivanhoe stations, a green oasis beside a cool shaded stream, where galahs and black cockatoos feed. A century ago ringers rested here, ate damper and beef and swam in the clear waters. Today the place is still beautiful and is home to a family who know the Duracks well. They regard Patsy's grand-daughters Mary and Elizabeth as 'Aunties'. When Elizabeth lived on Ivanhoe she often drew a little 'picaninny' boy, Jeff Chunuma. Jeff is now in his eighties and lives at Cockatoo Springs with his large family—including adopted son Ben Ward.

Jeff sits on an iron bedstead, Ben in a wheelchair—his paraly-sis the result of a recent car accident. As they talk, the children play, running noisily about. There is little in the house: stained mattresses on the floor, torn chairs. Despite the poverty the family are fairly happy with their situation. They can grow veg-etables in the garden and, most important of all, they are out of the township of Kununurra. They are Mirriwung people, but unlike the Amanbidji and Gurindji mob, the Mirriwung have not won rights to their traditional lands, remaining dispossessed.

Ben does most of the talking, mostly chatting about the old days. His parents have spoken much about the Duracks; they were 'nice people'. Ben feels that if his parents respected the Duracks, so should he. The Duracks were big names in the Kim-berley; still are. If you mention that one of the Duracks is coming to the area, people will start telling the old stories of the days at Argyle, Ivanhoe, even Kildurk. The Aboriginal station workers were known by which station they worked on: Jeff was 'Ivanhoe Jeff'.[20]

They always loved their country, beautiful and peaceful, always lots of fresh water. They have both been stockmen, mustering and driving cattle to the Wyndham abattoir. They would work six days, getting up early, looking after the cattle and the horses. On a Saturday afternoon they would clean the saddles. Ben is a great believer in a solid day's work. He worries about the changes that have happened since the Duracks left. Now Mirriwung people can't get jobs, no one in town employs blacks, and the community survives on social security. He believes that the biggest change for the Mirriwung came in the 1970s after the old Durack station, Argyle, was flooded by the newly created Ord Dam: 'See, when they started to flood Argyle, all they said to us was that they were going to put us down in the reserve, and that's what they did. They put us down in the reserve here in Kununurra and left us. That's when they started getting into the social security and things like that. That's what happened to most of these stockmen's lives.'

They're bush people, says Ben, and need to have some of their land back. He remembers being able to walk along the rivers and fish anywhere. He and Jeff agree that under the old pastoralists, the Mirriwung could at least walk several hundred kilometres over their traditional lands. During the Wet they were allowed to conduct their traditional business. Now those lands are fenced off.

For Ben the question of land rights is relatively recent and only arose in a practical sense when indigenous people were moved off the stations. The Mirriwung now have a land claim over a section of the old Ivanhoe station. It's not greed, say Ben and Jeff, just the ability to determine their own direction. When they left the stations they were put onto reserves and told how to live. 'Now,' urges Ben, 'let *us* make a choice on how *we* want to live.'

It is ironic that some of the dispossessed and the former pioneers who overran their land share a sense of loss for days gone by. Both yearn to recapture something of their former lives. Like Ben, Reg's daughter Anne dreams of being able to wander freely by the rivers. She yearns to be 'an eccentric old lady with a big straw hat and a broken-down ute and a little bower shed . . . perhaps out of Kildurk, somewhere down near Ginger Crossing—somewhere beautiful and impractical . . . It's my country, the few times I've gone back [there] is that feeling, that overwhelming feeling of coming home and feeling safe and of recognition of colours, and I feel the country's glad that I came home. There are bones there, there are ghosts there, there are happy times.'

Mirriwung and Durack, mutual affection still strong, dream of their spirit country: a land now broken by years of cattle trampling over its fragile skin. There is much that unites these diverse groups, but the indigenous peoples are still irrevocably tied to the land, whereas the Duracks can at least survive elsewhere. As Anne says, 'Nostalgia and dreams have their place but, in the tradition of hard-baked old Irish migrants, we move and the road takes many turnings . . . and this is where I remember my grandfather MP's motto "travel hopefully".'

On the afternoon Patsy's great-grandson John Durack leaves his old home, Kildurk, he doesn't look back. His small aircraft rises above the shabby station. The visit was bittersweet—and perhaps it is the last he will ever pay. The Duracks have to move on; dreaming is all that is left. An industry and dynasty begun by the passionate ambitions of one man has now, after four generations, been absorbed into the landscape he wanted to own.

THE DOWNER FAMILY

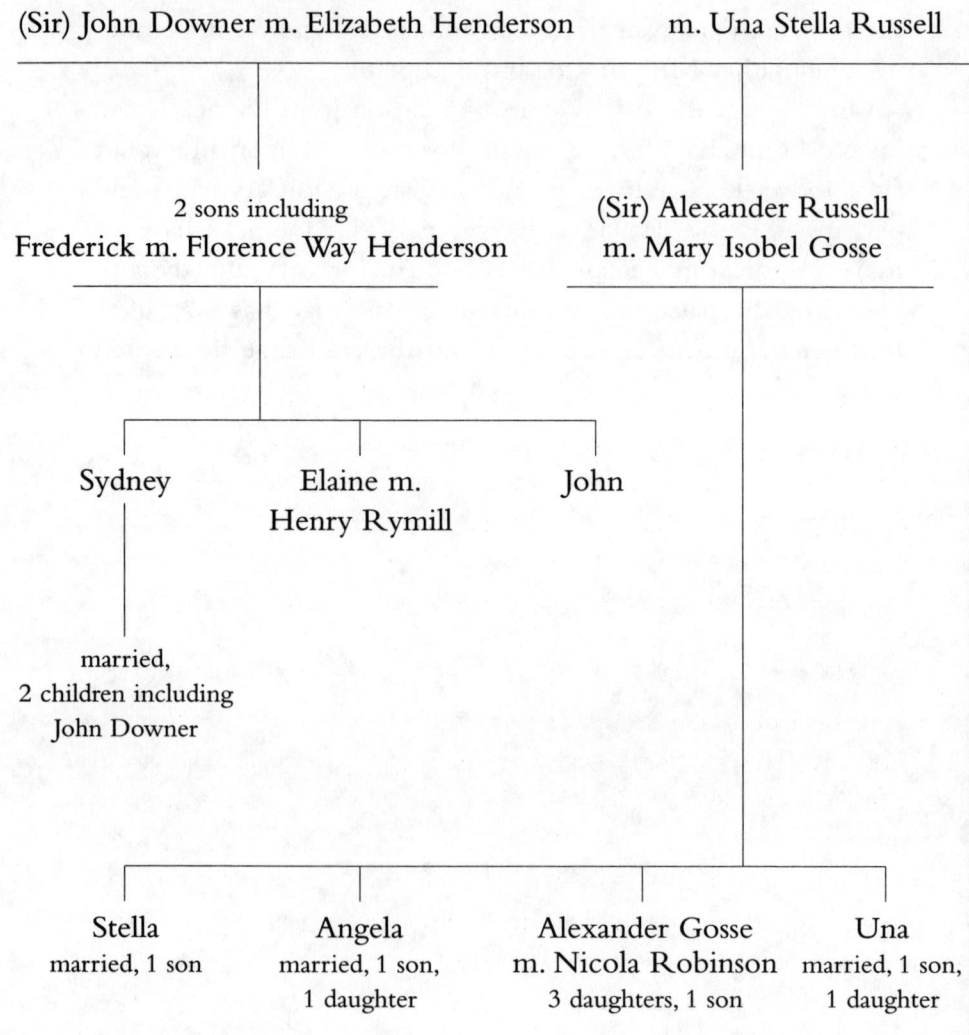

(Sir) John Downer m. Elizabeth Henderson   m. Una Stella Russell

2 sons including
Frederick m. Florence Way Henderson   **(Sir) Alexander Russell**
                                 m. Mary Isobel Gosse

Sydney   Elaine m.   John
              Henry Rymill

married,
2 children including
John Downer

Stella   Angela   Alexander Gosse   Una
married, 1 son   married, 1 son,   m. Nicola Robinson married, 1 son,
           1 daughter   3 daughters, 1 son   1 daughter

THE DOWNERS

TUCKED modestly away in the big end of town, the Melbourne Club is a subdued sandstone building, easily overlooked among the skyscrapers of Collins Street. But enter its small foyer, and wealth and power are immediately if discreetly evident in the nineteenth-century art and ornate furnishings. Sober-suited men leave their briefcases and mobile phones with the doorman, for this is a dedicated gentlemen's club. It is also the place where old money, business interests and conservative politics rub shoulders over dinner and drinks— long regarded as the epicentre of the Australian establishment. It is also the place Alexander Downer was summoned to on Thursday evening, 19 May 1994, for one of the most important meetings of his life.

The Liberal politician's star was in the ascendancy. In a party racked by internal dissension and adrift after ten years in opposition, he was being considered for the top job. Tony Staley, the party's president, wanted to see him in one of the many private rooms. Although the Melbourne Club's influence may have waned since the 1950s, its part in the anointing of Alexander Downer as leader of the Liberal Party would add to the public perception of the politician's blueblood heritage.

News of Alexander Downer's tête-à-tête with Staley tipped the balance in a party beset by leadership speculation.[1] Having suffered a resounding defeat at the polls the previous year, the Liberals were looking to replace their current leader, John Hewson, whom many felt had thrown away a sure-fire victory by force-feeding his stringent plans for economic reform to an uneasy electorate. Hewson was well aware that his leadership was being undermined—the question of who would challenge him now appeared to be answered. On hearing of Downer's meeting, the beleaguered incumbent called for a party-room ballot the following Monday in which would-be contenders for his job could 'put up or shut up'. Put up they did. Alexander Downer declared his candidacy and received the blessing of the party's royalty, including Malcolm Fraser and Andrew Peacock. Breaking with tradition—for past presidents had made a point of staying out of the political party's brawls—Tony Staley announced it was time for a change.

'I am born of the Liberal Party,' proclaimed Alexander Downer, after the party room duly voted him leader of the Opposition that Monday, 23 May 1994. 'I am a creature of the Liberal Party.'[2] Truer words had never been spoken. Alexander Downer's Liberal pedigree was impeccable. His father and namesake, Sir Alexander Downer, had been a minister in the Menzies government during the halcyon days of the party, and his grandfather, Sir John Downer, a conservative premier of South Australia. Now the third generation was taking the family's political fortunes to new heights.

But on becoming Opposition leader, Alexander Downer's political lineage was quickly overshadowed by his establishment credentials. Then Prime Minister Paul Keating branded his win 'a victory for the Melbourne Club', and attacked Alexander Downer's membership of the equally exclusive Adelaide Club— a club that, as Keating was quick to point out, admitted neither women nor Jews. Downer lashed back, labelling the prime minister 'a fast-money man'. Keating rejoined furiously, 'If it's not old money, it's fast, improper.' This heated exchange marked the beginning of a series of jibes, in which the prime minister would lambast the new Opposition leader as someone who had been 'born with a silver cutlery service in his mouth'. For this was also part of Alexander Downer's birthright. Not only was he heir to a political dynasty, but he was equally a scion of the South Australian establishment, linked by birth to three of the state's most illustrious founding families.

Indeed, in Alexander Downer politics and establishment are inextricably linked. His heritage brings with it both a sense of privilege and a feeling of public duty born out of that privilege. As observers will tell you, it takes more than money to make a family of the establishment in South Australia. Rather, it marks an exclusive set of historic families whose contribution over the generations carries with it 'the assumption that one has a duty to society and continues to have a role in its affairs, and will train one's children to that duty should the need arise'.[3] Accordingly, the guiding principle in the Downer household has always been 'if you are given a lot, a lot is expected of you, and you have to give that back to the community'.[4] As Alexander Downer says of his forebears: 'What was significant about them was that they had this rather traditional and conservative notion of public service. Since I can remember, I suppose, it's been ingrained into me, this notion of service.'[5]

In the Downer family, this public service ethic has, over three generations, found expression in political leadership and an expectation to achieve in this field. There is an understanding that the Downers have a place at the centre of politics—and it is no coincidence that in this family it is considered quite appropriate to fly the Australian flag in your garden. The result, says Dennis Grant, parliamentary correspondent and long-time observer of Alexander Downer's career, is a rather unusual breed of politician for Australia. 'When you think about the Downer family, they are very European. I don't mean that in any kind of disparaging sense. It's just that the weight of family history is not on most Australians, and I think it is on the Downers.

It's almost a sort of antipodean *noblesse oblige* . . . It's fascinating, and it's very rare around here.'[6]

But the Downer family's dynastic legacy is more than just a curious novelty. Instead, it reflects the development of a unique strand of colonial society and its place in a wider Australian history. The family's dynastic roots lie in the founding principles of South Australia, a colony that, unlike the eastern seaboard states, was established as 'one of the few genuine nineteenth-century utopias'.[7]

The story of South Australia's settlement is marvellous in itself, for it was conceived of by Edward Gibbon Wakefield during a three-year stay in London's Newgate prison. A Quaker who came from a long line of social activists, including Elizabeth Fry, the prison reformer, Wakefield had abducted a fifteen-year-old heiress from her school in March 1826, and absconded with her to Gretna Green where they were married. It was Wakefield's second such marriage—his first wife had been sixteen when they eloped and had died in childbirth, leaving her husband with a comfortable income for the remainder of his life. This time, however, despite his bride's compliance, Wakefield was brought to trial and the marriage annulled.

It was while serving out his prison sentence for statutory misdemeanour that Wakefield came into contact with convicts who had served time in New South Wales and Van Diemen's Land (as Tasmania was then known). Their recollections gave him a critical insight into colonial emigration to the antipodes; insights upon which he had plenty of time to reflect. He came to the conclusion that the colonies' development was suffering from a chaotic granting of free land, a shortage of labour and a consequent dependence on convicts. The solution lay in a scheme of systematic colonisation where land would be sold and the proceeds applied to the emigration of labourers, preferably young married couples, thereby giving 'maximum population relief to Britain'.[8] Encouraging couples would also address the 'great disproportion between sexes' in the colonies that had arisen through transportation, for as with all prison populations women were vastly underrepresented—in Wakefield's view the 'greatest evil of all'.[9] Wakefield was convinced his scheme would lead to a balanced, fruitful and prosperous colonial society, with the capacity and right to elect representatives to its own legislature, thus transplanting the best of British civilisation from an old to a new country for their mutual benefit.

On his release, Wakefield began promoting his theory by every means at his disposal, writing newspaper articles, pamphlets and books, holding public meetings, lobbying parliamentarians and lecturing friends and acquaintances. Supported by his first wife's inheritance, he became a colonial propagandist and a very charismatic one. As might be inferred from his private life Wakefield could be extremely persuasive. His ideas soon influenced several regulations for the disposal of crown land in New South Wales and Van Diemen's Land, including their sale by auction for a minimum price per hectare, with proceeds devoted to an immigration fund. Unimpressed by such a token salute, Wakefield began to plan the systematic colonisation of southern Australia.

His scheme found influential backers, notwithstanding the fact that the idea of a colony 'not for paupers or prisoners, but for the enterprising gentle classes with the dignity of self-government' was revolutionary in 1829.[10] The proposed colony's founding fathers 'looked on themselves as idealists of every sort, with a belief in human freedoms, social justice and religious tolerance, which they maintained had been the basis of British greatness but which their country seemed to have neglected somewhat. What they aimed at building was a better, more liberal and open Great Britain, a paradise of dissent.'[11] In late 1833 the South Australian Association was formed. A year later Wakefield helped draft a bill creating the British province of South Australia and providing for its colonisation and government. As soon as this was passed, he published a manual of advice and information for intending colonists—irrespective of the fact that he himself had never visited the continent. (By the following year, however, his attention had drifted to other colonies, including Canada and most notably New Zealand, where he eventually emigrated, living out his final years in relative obscurity.)

In 1836 the first boatload of settlers arrived in South Australia—fifteen ships would sail that year. Wakefield's proselytising had fallen on receptive ears, and the colony became the destination of choice for Britain's middle classes, whose hopes of upward mobility at home had been dashed by their lack of birthright, wealth or property. They dreamed of 'a balanced society. Not a utopian equal society but a utopian unequal society, in which a measured number of artisans and farmers, the lower castes of society, would be represented together with the rich and the affluent and the clever in a very city-planned and rural-planned environment.'[12] It was an aspirational vision of social order and harmony 'in which the rich had their special place and the poor knew their place'.[13]

This vision was ingrained in the capital city, Adelaide, which had been laid out weeks before the first immigrants stepped ashore. In order to avoid the industrial slums that were springing up rapidly in British cities, Adelaide's residential districts were divided into large blocks of land surrounded by smaller lots—ensuring that rich and poor would always rub shoulders. The result was often a wealthy family estate surrounded by the homes of its workers. Even today Adelaide strikes the visitor as a vision of the ideal pre-industrial English town, with its gracious parks, churches, schools and tree-lined streets.

The first colonists, we are told, stepped ashore with enthusiasm, certitude and a sense of self-importance bolstered by a shared understanding of their historic significance. After all, as family historian Fayette Gosse reminds us, this was 'the first attempt since the days of ancient Greeks at organised colonisation on scientific principles . . . Hope and zest abounded, along with rigid respectability, to produce a different kind of Australian town from those fabricated over the miseries and cynicism of their penal colony origins, like Sydney and Hobart.'[14]

But idealism soon ran aground on the grim reality of life in a far-flung colonial outpost.[15] Being 'apostles of a new Enlightenment' was no defence against drought, mismanagement, overpopulation and a lack of resources.[16] The South Australian Company soon ran out of money, but the British government was indifferent, believing that the new colony should be self-funding. Despite these hardships, the land proved kind, and good grazing pastures were discovered 300 kilometres south-east of Adelaide. As a result, the colony's earliest pastoral enterprises flourished and with them the city of Adelaide.

By the 1860s the colony's immigrants had created a model society based on English ideals, complete with its own gentry. Fewer than a hundred families, united by prosperity and marriage, would dominate South Australia for nearly a century. Their fortunes would be based on large property holdings, but they would equally play a pre-eminent role in politics, finance and industry—setting the standard for the colony and achieving recognition as leaders within their community. Unlike the penal colonies, which could look to their imperial masters in Britain for support, South Australia relied on its private individuals for political and economic development. The colony's future thus depended on their sense of social obligation. Even today its founding families are household names whose activities are regularly reported on by the local media. People are still identified by their family connections, as are suburbs, electorates and streets. Indeed, the Adelaide gentry, as these families came to be regarded, would leave an enduring mark on the city through their contributions to public architecture and their large and gracious homes.

'They were distinguished not just by wealth, as not every wealthy family became a member of the establishment, but by lifestyle. They lived as they believed aristocrats lived in England, and it was once again a dreamed-about affluence,' observes historian John Hepworth. 'Theirs was a lifestyle of recreation, with lots of parties and tennis, and even croquet, and large houses in which there could be garden parties. There were always a number of residences: a town house, which was often very grand, but also a country estate in the nearby hills where one could escape the heat of summer.'

But for all their aristocratic airs, the South Australian gentry had also inherited the colony's reformist beliefs. These were middle-class families made good, and they held fast to a shining ideal of British justice, tolerance and liberty. 'The South Australian establishment has educational overtones, leadership overtones, political overtones, which simple wealth in the eastern states doesn't necessarily denote. It's a package deal, and you've got to join the whole thing. South Australia has never completely lost its sense of social responsibility and reformist philosophy.'[17]

It is from this potent and contradictory mixture of progressive traditionalism that the Downer dynasty arose. Henry Downer, Alexander's great-grandfather, was one of the colony's earliest arrivals—an English tailor who emigrated to South Australia in 1838. From such solid but (in South Australia at least) unremarkable tradesman origins, his three sons would establish themselves among the upper echelons of Adelaide society. All three would enter the legal profession and join the Bar; two would later become politicians while the other, George, would establish the family's fortunes as a noted pastoralist. (A bachelor, his wealth eventually passed to Alexander Downer's branch of the family, further consolidating its prominent place in the colony.) John Downer, the youngest, began his rise through the ranks while still a schoolboy, winning a scholarship to St Peter's College, the pre-eminent school of the colony, founded by a number of prominent citizens in 1847, four years after his birth.

John 'was probably the most brilliant schoolboy of his time'[18] and on completing his education became one of Adelaide's leading barristers. He soon established himself as a force in South Australian society and politics. In 1878, at the age of thirty-five, he was made a QC, and in that same year was elected to the House of Assembly. Three years later he was appointed attorney-general and in 1885, when he was forty-three, assumed leadership of the government. He held the position of premier twice, and led the colony's conservative forces in parliament for twenty years, before joining the new federal parliament in 1901 as a senator. But, according to historians and family alike, 'perhaps the greatest contribution he made was as one of the founding fathers of the Constitution'. A passionate federalist, Sir John represented South Australia at the 1891, 1893 and 1897–98 federal conventions.

Indeed, much of the Australian Constitution was penned at Sir John's town house, conveniently located a short stroll from the South Australian parliament, where the 1897 convention was held. Today this stately terrace, which still looks out over parklands and the Torrens River towards the city, is home to Adelaide University's leading residential college, St Mark's. Its current principal is former Labor premier and St Peter's old boy John Bannon, a keen student of Federation and, consequently, a leading authority on Sir John's career.

In a somewhat ironic turn of events, John Bannon now presides over formal dinners in what was once Sir John's second-floor ballroom. He considers the room 'a sacred site of Federation' for it was here that the Constitution of Australia was drafted in 1897. Sir John served on the drafting committee with future prime minister Sir Edmund Barton, who stayed with him during this time. A third member of the committee, Richard O'Connor, the solicitor-general of New South Wales, resided just down the road. The three men had been elected by the convention to write a draft for the Constitution that would then be printed and considered by the other delegates. 'At the end of each day there was a lot of work to be done, so the committee would walk back to Sir John's residence, settle down over the port and cigars, and work on into the night. This is the place were the i's were dotted and the t's crossed.'[19]

One of the few, and earliest, remaining photographs of Sir John is from this time. A copy hangs in Alexander Downer's parliamentary office behind his desk, and another in his mother's living room. The photograph shows a man in his prime, a robust, imposing figure with a decidedly determined, if not pugnacious, air. It supports the description bestowed on him by friend and fellow politician Alfred Deakin, as 'bull-headed, and rather thick-necked . . . with the dogged set of the mouth of a prize fighter' and 'smallish eyes'.[20]

Cartoons and sketches of the day, however, tended to emphasise different qualities. They portray Sir John as a jaunty figure, dressed to the nines and sporting a top hat when out of doors. Irrespective of setting, he is invariably smoking a cigar. Although not born to it, Sir John was a man fond of good living, with a reputation for enjoying fine wines and even finer cigars. Despite his professional commitments, he maintained the leisurely lifestyle of the South Australian gentry. In addition to his grand town house, he had (like others of his class) a summer residence, Glenalta, in the Adelaide Hills. Here Sir John's family would escape the heat of the plains from December to April, in a style a little reminiscent of the Indian hill stations of the British Raj. Although it had originally been a cottage, Sir John built Glenalta into a large and comfortable country estate, complete with stables, a well-stocked library and a large and equally well-endowed wine cellar. These trappings did not go unnoticed or uncommented upon.

'The satirical newspapers certainly gave him a fairly hard time, casting him as the ultimate aristocrat, the person of imperial pretensions in a small colonial pond. They had great sport of it,' concedes John Bannon. 'Sir John was a currency lad, but of the South Australian variety. Conservative, Anglican in religion, somebody who believed very much in pulling oneself up by one's bootstraps and establishing oneself, and yet a great imperialist—someone who looked to England for a lot of ideas, styles, stimulation.'

But Sir John combined his imperialism with a sturdy nationalism. In the lead-up to nationhood, he championed the constitutional need for Australia to manage its own judicial affairs, with final authority resting in its own High Court. When others argued that the idea behind Federation was not to 'cut the painter' with Great Britain, he replied: 'We have come to the conclusion that we may cease to be provincial and form the foundation of a nation. We do not propose in any way to separate from the British Crown; in fact we look to it with reverence. We consider ourselves the same people. But the very essence of the difference is that we think we can make laws which will suffice us; in other words, to put it colloquially, we can manage our own affairs.' It was time, he insisted, to 'get out of swaddling clothes'.[21]

It is worth remembering that at the time of Federation, the idea of granting independence to a British colony was a relatively recent one. But Sir John had always exhibited rather progressive tendencies. As attorney-general, he had changed the law to allow those charged with a crime to give evidence in court. He had also furthered women's rights, creating legislation that protected the property rights of married women. He also advocated women's suffrage—a popular issue in a colony that uniquely in Australia had drawn large numbers of women settlers. Most unusually for his day, Sir John did not believe the Immigration Restriction Act deserved a high priority in the affairs of the new nation and as a federal senator he spoke out against 'this general running amok with the name of white Australia'.[22] Sir John's electorate was the Barossa Valley—the winemaking region of South Australia that had benefited so greatly from its German Lutheran immigrants. He was a popular representative among this community and never suffered an electoral defeat at its hands.

For some, a closer look at Sir John's political reforms reveals steadfastly conservative motives. His support for women's rights—particularly to property—has been interpreted by some as a way of bolstering his conservative constituency. (While some believed that women represented a radical new voice in politics, an equal number believed that women, with their concerns for home and hearth, brought a civilising but innately traditional influence to bear on society.) Likewise, Sir John's motivation in supporting Federation has been construed by some as a means of undermining the advances made by the emerging labour movement in individual colonies. John Bannon disagrees with this reading. In his view, Sir John saw Federation as an opportunity to advance the interests of smaller states—an outlook shared by both sides of South Australian politics. Radicals and conservatives alike saw Federation as a great democratic move. And as John Bannon reminds us, Sir John in style and substance was South Australian to his bones.

'South Australia was founded on the basis of ideals as much as expediency. It wasn't just a good place to settle, but a place to work through a number of ideas of progressive democracy in a theoretical sense. And Sir John Downer and most of the nineteenth-century South Australian colonial politicians were aware of that history and were very much caught up in that feeling. Much as they might inveigh against more radical reforms, and what they saw as dangerous left-wing notions, nonetheless they all shared this view that ideas were important in politics.'

Indeed, Sir John clearly believed his birthplace to be ahead of its colonial parent when it came to political discourse. He showed the courage of these convictions at an imperial conference in London in 1887, which he attended as premier despite a looming election. Notes John Bannon rather wryly: 'It's said that Downer went to the imperial conference to make a name for himself, armed with a sheaf of colonial reforms to urge onto the backward British parliament, and this made him cut quite a figure. The cartoonists made great fun of him, swanning around the salons of London, smoking his inevitable cigar, and telling them how advanced the colonies were. The problem was that while he was away an election was taking place in South Australia, and he chose not to return. Some claim this was the passion for his reforms. Others less kindly suggest that his reason for dallying was his hope that he'd be granted a knighthood and that back home, if he could be seen as such an international statesman, his election would be guaranteed. Well, he got his knighthood, but unfortunately not his election.'

Sir John returned to Adelaide to discover that, although he still held his parliamentary seat, his fellow conservatives had been routed at the polls and the choice of premier had fallen to the state's more radical factions. Unlike other politicians more concerned with their domestic standing, Sir John had failed to ensure that his opponents travelled to London with him, nor had he kept his visit brief. Henceforth his role in local politics would be consigned to leadership of the Opposition. Says his grandson more than a century later: 'He was a man of strong convictions but not a man of great ambitions. He wasn't one of those people who foamed at the mouth to succeed. I think he was probably fairly laid back and a bit of a *bon vivant* and, if he lost the premiership as he did, I don't think it would have thrown him into a state of despair. There's probably a bit of continuity there in our family, I think. When things have gone wrong for us in politics—as happens from time to time—it's a pity, but we just shake it off and wait till the wheel turns.'[23]

This apparent nonchalance, however, would result in Sir John's one great disappointment in political life when, contrary to expectation, he was not elected to Australia's High Court, the institution he had worked so hard to establish. Despite his reputation as one of the great constitutional lawyers of the day, and the support of then Prime Minister Sir Edmund Barton, 'his appointment was opposed in cabinet by certain members who disapproved of what they considered were his rather self-indulgent habits'.[24] This rather euphemistic explanation refers apparently to Sir John's continuing fondness for cigars and wine. Most of all, he was perceived again, in the words of Sir Alfred Deakin, to have 'an indolence about him'.[25] This indolence, rather than a lack of talent or skill, would prove Sir John's downfall in the eyes of Deakin and politicians since. 'He wasn't serious enough in that hungry ambitious sense and that probably meant he waited for the call to the High Court rather than actually getting out and furiously lobbying and calling in all the chips from his old friends and associates, and that was probably his undoing.'[26]

But this insouciance may have been little more than skin deep, for Sir John also had the reputation of a canny politician who, in an era of shifting alliances, displayed a pragmatic flexibility and who was prepared to subjugate ideals to the necessity of political success, deal-making and coalition-building. Most notably, Sir John would renege on his long commitment to women's suffrage when, in 1894, he refused to lend his support to legislation devised by his arch-rival, Charles Kingston. To the astonishment of the suffragettes present, Sir John was one of a handful of dissenting politicians in the parliament, ostensibly claiming that while he supported votes for women, he could not support the right of women to stand for parliament. Many believe, however, that he simply could not stomach such a success going to his political nemesis. Although the bill was subsequently passed by a large majority, Sir John, if such eye-witnesses are to be believed, could be pugnacious to the end. He was also a good debater—the best in the South Australian parliament said one colleague of his early days—and the Adelaide *Observer* believed that as premier he had dominated the House in the manner of 'a second Bismarck, with a too yielding Reichstag'. Similarly, a cartoon of the day, depicting the 'political schoolyard', shows him punching his Labor opposition with all the relish of an overgrown schoolboy. None of this suggests a politician lacking in ambition.

Most commentators today suggest that Sir John's indolence may have been something of a smokescreen. Observes John Hepworth: 'There was a leisureliness that the upper classes, particularly in South Australia, cultivated. Even when you were busy, you shouldn't look busy. You should look as if you had time to read and time for tea, and time for talk—as indeed they did. Sir John Downer probably cultivated it to some extreme, but he wasn't the only one. And I tend to resist rather the accusation of indolence.'

John Bannon, speaking from his own experience as a South Australian politician, agrees. 'Perhaps it's a fact that the manner of someone who is an aristocrat—or aspiring to be one—also suggests a certain type of amateurism, in which to seem really to try and be overly ambitious is just very bad form. In politics that can often work to one's advantage, but it can also look as if you're not committed or dedicated enough, with the result that you may be seen as being a bit of a dilettante. But it's more a matter of style, I think. I know a lot of aristocratic amateurs who are as tough and as difficult as those who would see it as their profession.'

Sir John's leisurely aura was a smokescreen in another regard. He had never been among South Australia's wealthiest citizens and had always relied upon work at the Bar to earn a living. (Unlike his brother George who would leave an estate of £400 000—significant wealth at the turn of the century—Sir John's estate at probate was valued at little over £14 000.) Serving in the federal parliament (then in Melbourne) thus put some strain on the purse strings, and Sir John would retire from the Senate in 1903, two years after he had joined. Had he enjoyed greater opportunities to influence events in federal parliament, he may have been tempted to stay, but he retired from the Senate feeling his time there had been something of a waste.

Sir John, however, continued to play a prominent part in local affairs, sitting in South Australia's Legislative Council until his death in 1915. A photograph taken towards the end of his life shows him seated in a cane chair on the lawn, while behind him hovers a young woman with a parasol. It is a characteristically colonial tableau of the elderly statesman at his leisure. The young woman is Una Stella Russell, whom Sir John married when he was fifty-six. She was his second wife and more than twenty years his junior. His first wife, Elizabeth, had died, leaving Sir John with two sons. Frederick, the eldest, would continue his father's interest in law but would become a businessman and community leader, rather than a politician. Una Stella also provided Sir John with a son, and it was she, far more than the patriarch himself, who would pass on the Downer political legacy to the next generation.

As with many of his contemporaries, the Canberra suburb of Downer is so named in recognition of Sir John's contribution to Australia's nationhood. Unlike the suburbs of Barton and Deakin, however, Downer is not among Canberra's inner dress-circle districts. Instead, it is a rather flat, unprepossessing suburb on the outskirts of the city which, to the unholy amusement of those in the know, has been divided into 'upper' and 'lower' Downer.

However, Sir John Downer stands alone in being the only politician to have a fountain dedicated to his memory in the nation's capital. Commissioned by his son, Sir Alexander Downer, while a federal minister, this fountain occupies pride of place in Canberra's main commercial district.[27] A neo-classical sculpture at its centre shows a young boy sitting on his father's lap, his arms outstretched reaching for the chalice held above his head. It expresses the yearning of a man for a parent he never knew, together with an understanding of the goal he is compelled to seek.

The only child of Sir John's marriage to Una Stella Russell, Sir Alexander Downer was five years old when his father died. But in this instance death did not diminish the patriarch's charisma. Left with just 'a fragment of memory', Sir John's son grew up with a strong sense of his father's political achievements, and a determination to follow in his footsteps. This pride, says Sir Alexander's eldest daughter today, 'must have been inculcated by his mother. I think my father put his own father on a pedestal increased by my grandmother's great love and admiration for her husband. She was a great influence and I think she probably wanted my father to go into politics as well.'[28] The daughter of a Queensland pastoral family that also produced conservative politicians, Una Stella was a gifted amateur painter, with strong artistic and social sensibilities. She was an involved and adoring mother, and Sir Alexander in turn would prove a devoted son, living with and caring for his mother until her death. He also named two of his three daughters after her, calling his eldest Stella and his youngest Una as well as building a private chapel to her memory. (Una Stella's ashes were interred, along with her predecessor's and her late husband's, in the Downer family plot in North Adelaide, where a large marble edifice commemorates this and subsequent generations—a monument that has been tended and restored by Sir Alexander's widow, Mary.)

Guided by his mother, Sir Alexander came of age with 'a sense of family tradition that it was a good thing for the Downer family to produce politicians'.[29] (Adds his son a generation later, with all the good humour of a politician in a relatively safe seat, 'I think there would be millions of people who'd disagree with that!') Sir Alexander also grew up immersed in the ideals of the Empire. He was educated with other sons of the Australian establishment at Geelong Grammar, one of the country's most prestigious private schools—as thoroughly imbued with the values of God, king and country as St Peter's and, if anything, regarded by South Australians as a step up the social ladder—followed by university in England where, like his father before him, he read law at Oxford. As with his father, this education and training would instil an unswerving loyalty to his imperial heritage. 'All my life, from my early schooldays, I have believed in what we used to call the Empire, later the British Common-wealth, above all in preserving Australian–British links,' he later noted solemnly in his memoirs.[30]

Sir John's early death appears to have whetted his son's appetite not just for politics but for a connection with the past. And, as seems commonly the case, it would be this second generation that sought to consolidate not just the family's achievements but its reputation among future generations. Sir Alexander would make it his task to write down what he knew of the family history—not for publication but for his own children and grandchildren. 'My father had a strong sense of history and often complained that his father had left so little in the way of personal records,' reflects his son Alexander Downer today; a further indication that it was Una Stella, rather than Sir John himself, who felt the dynastic imperative most strongly.

It was perhaps to ameliorate his sense of lost heritage that Sir Alexander would design a family seat for himself in the Adelaide Hills while still a university undergraduate. (His father's country estate, Glenalta, had gone to his elder half-brother. It would eventually pass, through marriage, to another old Adelaide family, the Rymills, before being sold.) Sir Alexander clearly intended his new home to take its place among older, more established estates in the belief he was 'planting a tradition and a heritage' for subsequent generations.[31] Begun during the Depression and completed in 1936, Arbury Park was built to resemble a large Georgian country house. It was set on more than 40 hectares of garden and farmland, complete with deer park and gatehouse. Perched on its own little hill, its stone porticos looked out over landscaped gardens stepping down to a large stone fountain. Even Sir Alexander's own relatives looked somewhat askance at a young, unmarried man creating such an estate for himself. 'His aunts thought it foolhardy,' says daughter Stella. 'Yet in the end, they grudgingly saw what a beautiful place he'd managed to conceive. My father loved Arbury. He really, really loved it.'

But before Sir Alexander could take up his rightful place in Adelaide society from his new country seat, war intervened. He immediately joined up as a gunner in the Australian artillery, refusing an officer's commission in what was perhaps one of the clearest expressions of his commitment to upholding the democratic ideals of Empire, as he somewhat naively perceived them.[32] He was taken prisoner almost immediately when Singapore fell to the Japanese in one of the greatest military humiliations the British Empire had ever suffered, and spent the next three and a half years as a prisoner in Changi—where, as his son likes to point out, there were no 'cocktails from the Adelaide Club'. Here he earned the sobriquet 'Red Downer' for his opposition to officer privileges. 'Although he had some good friends among the officers, some were very hard on the ordinary ranks even as prisoners, and he didn't believe people should be pushed around by their superiors. He wouldn't do that himself, and he didn't think it should be done to himself, or anybody else for that matter.'[33]

Sir Alexander made it safely home at the end of the war, returning to the bosom of the Adelaide establishment, and drawing even closer to its heart with his subsequent marriage to Mary Gosse. Mary had made her wartime contribution serving in the Land Army, and the couple met at a party at the Australia Hotel, a famous establishment watering hole, shortly after Sir Alexander's return. They were married less than a year later in April 1947. She was twenty-three, he thirty-seven. But they shared similar backgrounds although Mary's heritage, if anything, was even more impressive. Indeed, observers of the Adelaide gentry will tell you that it was this marriage that firmly established the Downers as South Australian bluebloods, for Mary brought with her the influence of power, philanthropy and wealth.

The youngest daughter of Sir James Gosse and Joanna Barr Smith, Mary Gosse was herself the child of one of South Australia's great dynastic alliances. (This was hardly unusual, for South Australia's establishment families were threaded together by an intricate network of marriages. Mary's was simply more illustrious than most.) Her father had been knighted for his services to industry and was the head of a wealthy pastoral empire—established by his grandfather, from the vantage point perhaps of serving as the young colony's surveyor-general.

It was Joanna Barr Smith, Mary's mother, however, who came from the most influential clan of them all—the pinnacle to which all others aspired. The Barr Smiths were the financial backbone of the establishment, the colony's wealthiest family and its first millionaires. Robert Barr Smith, the patriarch of the family and Mary's great-grandfather, had been one of the co-founders of the stock and station firm Elder Smith, the 'gilded prop' of South Australia's economy. In a landscape of mansions, the Barr Smiths' winter seat at Torrens Park was by far the most palatial. Set in the foothills of Adelaide, with its own chapel, out-houses, stables and even private theatre—designed in perfect imitation of the Victorian music hall—it offered a bold and highly visible statement of the family's status, 'a collection of buildings, too big for one family, which crossed the generations and crossed to other families'.[34] The Barr Smiths were far more than merely financial leaders, however. They were also leading philanthropists—responsible for financing the completion of Adelaide's St Peter's Cathedral, among much else. As Stella Downer points out, 'Go to Adelaide and you see the constant references to my mother's family, the Barr Smith Library at Adelaide University, and so on. It shows their sense of civic pride and public leadership, and how they really contributed enormously to South Australia's development.'[35]

The Barr Smiths, perhaps of all the Adelaide families, embodied the colony's ideals of *noblesse oblige*. They were the squires of the district, with a commitment to the welfare of their local community (where they again built churches and schools) as well as to those in their employ. As Alexander Downer's mother makes clear even today: 'I think if you are fortunate in life, you should put something back into it. I'm perfectly certain that it makes things much better if people who have been born, let's say, into a prosperous family, put something back. And I certainly think they *ought* to do something for nothing in this life.'

This outlook found political expression with Mary's marriage to Sir Alexander Downer. 'When he asked me to marry him he said, "Look, before you say anything, I must warn you, I am determined to go into politics, and to get into parliament",' she recalls. 'And I said, well, yes, that was all right, coming from a very non-political family. It was only after the elections, when Alick first became a Member of Parliament in 1949, two years after our marriage, that I suddenly thought, goodness me, what have I done?' Sir Alexander entered parliament as a Liberal backbencher in Sir Robert Menzies's first government, and served with him for the next twelve years, the last six of these as Minister for Immigration. His commitment to national politics, says his daughter Stella, reflected a belief in 'following through what his father had tried so hard to achieve in the Federation of Australia, the pulling together of all the states'. A devout Anglican who would 'kneel down and say his prayers before bed every night',[36] Sir Alexander's career was also marked by his reverence for the noble profession of a father he never knew. He would prove perhaps a more idealistic small 'l' liberal than his father before him, although arguably a less influential politician. 'He always used to say that he thought the two great professions were the Church and politics,' recollects Mary Downer today.

Photographs of Sir Alexander at this time show a tall man with handsome features. Impeccably dressed and with a patrician air, his sense of formality is broken by a broad smile when looking at his young wife. Colleagues remember him as somewhat reserved and aloof—an impression not shared by friends, who knew him as Alick. He was also softly spoken and, as a result, was regarded by some as rather effeminate. Recalls his wife: 'He was a very correct person and liked to do things properly. He always was very meticulous about his dressing, always made sure his tie was straight and his shoes were clean. He used to clean his shoes every morning, which I'm ashamed to say I don't do.' In short, despite his war record, Sir Alexander's bearing was somewhat out of step with the robust stereotype of Australian masculinity.

'He had a royal bearing—well, not exactly royal, but a superior standing without ever intending to be superior,' recalls Clyde Cameron who, in his own words, became the Downers' 'favourite socialist'.[37] A federal Labor MP, he had also joined the parliament in 1949, and although the two men would glare at each other from opposite sides of the House, they would sit next to each other on the plane to and from Canberra. 'I didn't like him on reputation,' Clyde confesses, 'because I knew he was a member of the Adelaide Club, or I thought he was. I knew that he had married a girl who belonged to the Barr Smith family, and that she was very wealthy.' (Sir Alexander was, of course, a dedicated member of the Adelaide Club, in his view 'one of the best men's clubs in the world, but never a reservoir of political wisdom'.)[38]

Despite their ideological differences, the two men became firm friends. In Clyde Cameron's eyes, Sir Alexander was simply 'one of the most honourable men I've ever known. He would never break a confidence and would never break his word.' It was an opinion shared by others, on both sides of the House. Although a loyal and cautious politician who, in the words of one Liberal colleague, 'did not like to rock the boat', Sir Alexander believed that party discipline should not be at the expense of voting one's conscience. (He would exercise this belief conservatively, most notably voting with Labor against Casey's peace treaty with Japan, although he eventually became reconciled to a new post-war relationship.) 'His views were always honestly held. I knew they weren't being stated in order to satisfy some faction, and he knew the same about me. That was the thing that drew us together more than anything,' says Cameron. 'The thing I admired about Alick was that he was always truthful. There were none of the shady tricks that are now played as part of the normal ritual. He had a great respect for another person whose point of view was different from his.'

Mary Downer was at times far more vehemently outspoken than her husband. Clyde Cameron recalls her outrage after a speech in parliament in which he condemned the Liberals for wasting so much taxpayers' money drinking champagne at a function for the Queen. Meeting Alick and Mary at the airport the next day, he found himself squarely in the firing line. 'Lady Downer kept eyeing me off as though I had stolen her purse. Suddenly she exploded: "You are a bloody reprobate to make that speech about the Liberals guzzling grog and eating oysters, when you and all your socialist mates were stuffing themselves with all that was offering as though you had just come through a famine!"' It was, he recalls with admiration, 'a great blast.'[39]

Then, or now, there was nothing reticent about Mary Downer. As a young woman she was striking rather than classically beautiful, with a compelling vivacity even in the most posed and languid of portraits. While her husband, even by his friends, was seen as 'terribly English and proper', she was 'great fun! She likes a joke and is more radical than Alick. One would never guess she is a Gosse–Barr Smith cross. She is one of the few Liberal wives who has a natural attractiveness. There is nothing artificial about Mary, and she doesn't hesitate to call a spade a spade.'[40] These days her wide circle of friends include her companions in exercise at the local pool—the 'aqua aerobic girls'—none of whom share her establishment background, and all of whom admire her for her down-to-earth forthrightness and lack of pretension. (There is almost an implicit expectation and acceptance in South Australia, as elsewhere perhaps, that someone of Mary Downer's background is entitled to certain airs and graces. Mary, secure in who she is, is a great and much loved antidote to this—something that is played on, for example, when, as patron of the Barossa Music Festival, she promoted its accessibility by being photographed with a bikie on the back of his Harley-Davidson.)

Says Lady Mary Downer, who is known as 'Cuddles' among the family, 'I think Alick and I were different. He was more serious than me. He also had an extremely good sense of humour and I think we confused people enormously because with his seriousness, people didn't realise what a sense of humour he had, and it made him laugh very much. He was more introverted and I'm more extroverted, I suppose. Maybe that was a good thing. We got on very well together, and were very happy.' (Agreed one Liberal acquaintance, 'Sir Alexander did have a good sense of humour, but he knew how to keep it private and not to share it with the press.')

Others, faced with Mary's strong personality, have less kindly suggested that it was she, not Sir Alexander, who 'wore the pants in the family'. But theirs would be a devoted partnership and Mary would prove Sir Alexander's greatest ally, both at home and in the political field. 'I think my mother's support was one of the most important things to my father,' recalls their daughter Stella. 'In fact, in the writings he left behind, it's very moving, the tributes he always pays to my mother. They show his deep, deep love for her, and his deep respect for her and everything she did for him.'[41] In comparison, Sir Alexander would urge the wife of his colleague Harold Holt to spend more time in Canberra 'if only to help Harold, and to meet the members . . . I was amazed by how few MPs she knew. Such unawareness, I used to tell her, could detract from Harold's path to the top.'[42]

Mary Downer would prove the consummate politician's wife, often accompanying her husband to Canberra when parliament was sitting, and on excursions through his electorate. 'I was often detailed off to ask embarrassing questions, which I was very happy to do,' she confesses cheerfully. 'I can always make out I'm stupid.' She is, of course, anything but, with a thirst for politics and a fierce party (as well as family) loyalty that reflects a genuine vocation. 'I was very new to politics when I married Alick, and I found it quite difficult to start with, but I've always said it's rather like changing your religion; you become quite passionate about it.' She is often credited as having the best political antennae in the family—and with having been almost as influential in her son's career as she was in her husband's. She has emerged since Sir Alexander's death as the matriarch of the family—although the dynasty's political fortunes now rest on her son's shoulders. (One wonders how far she might have gone if, contrary to tradition, she had been cast in the starring, rather than supporting, role.) Even today, Mary is a tireless campaigner for the Liberal Party, serving alternately as president, secretary and treasurer of her local branch, and handing out 'How to Vote' cards deep in enemy territory. She is always assigned the toughest polling booths, but as she says with a laugh, 'It's important to have a presence in a Labor electorate that we would probably never win, and you can have quite a bit of fun standing there.'

In contrast, Sir Alexander 'could never share' his colleagues' enthusiasm for elections. He found them physically tiring and 'an affront to serious work'. 'He was naturally a shy man,' recalls his daughter Stella, 'so he would have to force himself to get up and speak publicly, and he was always very nervous every time before he did.' Addressing parliament was equally daunting and in his memoirs Sir Alexander admits that 'years passed before I felt at ease in the House, an experience shared by most sensitive members'. One of his most galling memories was of Menzies's response to a parliamentary address Sir Alexander had been asked to give at the start of his second term. 'By words and gestures he ridiculed my apparent nervousness when beginning my speech the night before, an exchange I found anything but endearing.'[43]

Reflects Sir Alexander's politician son today: 'I probably enjoy the rough and tumble of politics more than my father did. In that respect I suspect I'm more like my grandfather. I don't think my father liked debating here [in the parliament] with the Labor Party; being attacked, as is the nature of politics; dealing with the interjections that are going on around you. I can imagine my grandfather would have rather liked that. He enjoyed the theatre of politics as well as the policies of politics. My father enjoyed the policies of politics. I think he was less comfortable with the theatre of politics.'

Sir Alexander's greatest political contribution, according to his family, was in curtailing some of the excesses of the White Australia Policy while Minister for Immigration. 'One of the first things he did was abolish the dictation test, which was a terribly unfair piece of legislation. If a Chinese man wanted to stay in the country, he was given a dictation test, in which maybe he had to speak or write in Arabic. They would do it in a language they knew this poor person had absolutely no chance of knowing, which I think was very unfair.' In Sir Alexander's case, argues his son, a love of Britain and its people formed the basis for a broader philosophy of liberal tolerance. 'As Minister for Immigration he was a prominent advocate of the now fashionable view that migrants and their descendants should not lose touch with their own cultures and traditions, and he rightly predicted that these cultures would enrich Australian life,' wrote Alexander Downer in the 1982 preface to his father's political memoirs.[44]

In this regard, Sir Alexander was far less narrowly an Anglophile than his prime minister, for Stella Una had cultivated a rather dreamy appreciation of Europe and its cultures in her son. In contrast, 'the other side of the Atlantic, apart from Great Britain, held little attraction for Menzies', and Sir Alexander simply could not understand his prime minister's lack of interest in 'the incomparable glories of Italy, Austria, Switzerland, France and parts of Germany . . . these fountains of our civilization.' Their different outlooks were mirrored in their views on immigration, at a time when governments were keen to attract as many new citizens as the economy could absorb. 'On immigration policy he usually gave me his blessing,' wrote Sir Alexander of Menzies, 'but not without growls of disapproval about the stream of Italians and Greeks we were attracting. Settlers from Asia were even less acceptable.'[45]

While the White Australia Policy remained firmly in place, Sir Alexander's appreciation of other cultures clearly influenced his ministerial work. 'For my father, bringing people from different cultures around the world was something that he found very exciting.'[46] In Sir Alexander's opinion, these new immigrants brought 'attributes which our rather stodgy Anglo-Saxon communities are much in need of'.[47] Nor did he advocate an isolationist stance towards Asia, but rather an 'unselfish' embracing of what he believed would inevitably emerge 'as part of our destiny'. Although in many respects very different to his father, Sir Alexander shared Sir John's openness to creative political change.

From the perspective of a new century in which public sentiment has became ambivalent to immigration and turned against refugees—appeased and sustained by what many might regard as a carefully crafted government xenophobia—Sir Alexander's enthusiasm seems particularly poignant. Newsreels of half a century ago show him proudly and personally welcoming the 250 000th refugee to Australia's shores, and assuring journalists that the government would meet its target of an additional 100 000 migrants that year. An older cousin, John

Downer, remembers grateful migrants from Poland and the Netherlands dropping in to Arbury Park for tea with the man who had made it possible.

Another regular guest at the Downer estate was the then prime minister, Sir Robert Menzies, who would generally time his stays to coincide with Test matches at the Adelaide Oval. When not at the cricket, he would walk in the Arbury meadows, 'a mixture of the Australian and English scene'.[48] On Sundays, he would participate in the family's weekly service at the little chapel Sir Alexander had built in memory of his mother. 'It was unforgettable,' writes Sir Alexander, 'hearing that expressionful voice reading the lessons from the lectern.'[49] Stella Downer recollects those visits a little differently, influenced less by her fondness for the great man and more by her memory of always having to be very quiet. 'As we were four rather noisy children, it was actually incredibly difficult.'

Nor was Sir Robert Menzies the only politician to visit Arbury Park. Clyde Cameron has fond memories of being 'treated like royalty' during his many visits, and Gough and Margaret Whitlam also stayed. Even Eddie Ward, Labor's most outspoken left-wing firebrand, who refused to speak to most Liberals, paid a visit. (In his defence, Eddie Ward argued that Mary's grandfather, Sir Robert Barr Smith, had paid off the Trades Hall in Adelaide, so the family's politics had clearly once been sound.) At the same time, Sir Alexander's mansion was a soft target for the Opposition. Labor backbencher Mick Young in particular would regale parliament with his story of timidly knocking on the door of a building several times more palatial than the Prime Minister's Lodge, only to be told that he was at the gatehouse.

For Stella Downer, as would be the case for most children, these political intrusions were often unwelcome. 'I can remember governors-general coming to visit and I can remember having to line up in the hall to meet them and having to be polite . . . I can remember very clearly when my father was made Minister for Immigration and being extremely irritated, having to dress up.

It was so exciting to have my parents home, but then having to dress up in good clothes and having to stand there and be photographed when all I wanted to do was run around. We all were very grumpy, I remember.'

One of Stella's earliest memories is of her brother's christening—another occasion for mixed feelings. 'I must have been three and a half, or maybe four, and my father hung flags from the portico out here, which was very exciting, and I had to sit very quietly outside with my sister Angela because we were dressed up, and read a book. I can remember looking at these words and thinking, why can't I understand what they say, and why should such a fuss be made of this little baby?'

Alexander John Gosse Downer was born in 1951—the third of Sir Alexander and Mary Downer's four children and their only son. For him and his sisters, Arbury Park in all its grandeur was first and foremost a family home; a place with 'marvelous banisters to slide down' and a large nursery in which they would play and squabble. 'It was an idyllic place to grow up,' recalls Stella. 'My father and I would often go for walks together. I can still smell the eucalypts there, and the creek that ran at the bottom of the garden. But the house had a certain sadness for me as well . . . My parents lived very busy lives and would often be in Canberra, and I suppose I felt the responsibility of being left with my younger brother and sisters. I suppose I just wanted my parents there the whole time.'

It was, all the same, a close family and Alexander Downer's response to accusations of privilege is to admit to the privilege of having been raised by supportive and loving parents. Moreover, even federal politics in those days was very much a family affair. During school holidays, the Downer children would accompany their parents to Canberra, making the long drive for a three-week parliamentary sitting. 'It was a bit different when my father was a member of parliament,' reflects Alexander Downer, 'because he and my mother used to own a house in Canberra and would spend long periods of time there. Nowadays, you just realistically can't do that. You have to get away, go back to your electorate, do things in the electorate, and then come back the following week. So I rent a house with a couple of senators. We don't have a lot of space, and it's all a bit more barbaric now than it was back in the fifties and early sixties.' His own children seldom visit the national capital, and have never sat in the House of Representatives to watch their father during Question Time—something Sir Alexander's children were frequently required to do, in what was 'one of the low points' of an otherwise enjoyable holiday.

'We used to be dragged as children into the chamber to sit in the visitors' gallery to watch Question Time. I'd have to admit we found it indescribably boring. But my father wanted to have his wife and children there to watch him perform. It obviously gave him a bit of a buzz, even if it put us to sleep,' laughs Alexander Downer today. 'He quizzed us on everything he took us to. He'd take us to the dining room in the old Parliament House and he'd buy us a chocolate malted milk, and while we were sitting there we'd be asked questions of what we'd seen, and who was who, and we'd be introduced to people as they passed by.' A better time was generally had playing cricket with Sir Robert Menzies's nephews at the Lodge.

Nevertheless, having political parents is an advantage for aspiring politicians, admits Alexander Downer, who points to the high number of second-generation members in parliament today. Nor is this restricted to the conservative side of politics— Kim Beazley and Simon Crean, to name but two in the federal Labor Party, have followed in their fathers' footsteps, although a daughter has yet to take up this role on either side of the House. The exercise of political power in contemporary democracies (as with other forms of government) clearly still lends itself to traditional dynastic arrangements. Only Alexander Downer and Larry Anthony of the National Party, however, can boast of a dynastic lineage going back three generations.

'You probably learn a little bit about the need to be—how can I put it—reasonably cunning to be a successful politician. And you do learn those things on the knees of your parents,' confesses Alexander Downer of having a father in politics. But more than that, he says, politics is an 'all-embracing occupation', and growing up in its vicinity encourages a natural interest and understanding. 'You can imagine at home, just sitting around with my parents, or in the car driving to Canberra for interminable hours, that my parents would in particular talk about politics. You know, the gossip of politics, the policies of politics, are we going to win the next election, or won't we? The problems, the worries, the excitements. The celebrations when my father did well; the disappointments when things didn't go well.'

On election night, the Downer children would gather round the fireplace in Sir Alexander's study to listen to each result as it came in on the radio. Politics was also the main topic of conversation at the family dinner table. But, insists Stella Downer, theirs was 'a liberal household' in the broadest sense of the word, in which 'nothing was censored' and everything was up for debate. 'We would sit down to meals and would have the most enlightened discussions on everything from religion to politics, of course, social conditions, economics, sex, everything,' she recalls. 'We would discuss everything very openly, and Alexander, being a boy and more aggressive, would hold his own very well and make a point of doing so.'[50] At the same time, Sir Robert Menzies was the family hero who, despite his minor differences with Sir Alexander, was 'a great and towering figure, somebody that we were required to admire as a family, and were happy to admire as a family as well'.[51] For the Downer children, Menzies was 'the personification of Australia . . . a symbol of all that was good'. Recollects Alexander Downer, 'We grew up believing that God was in his heaven, and Bob Menzies was in the Lodge, and that Australia was just this fantastic place.'[52]

In this idealised world, politics was seen as a noble calling. 'There was a view in our family there was something very meritorious about playing a significant role in government, which in our family was viewed as a pinnacle of the way society works. In a lot of families it is believed that what you should aspire to is making a lot of money and the definition of success is to be a millionaire or whatever. In our family, the definition of a successful life was making a mark on the way society evolved. In our family that has been regarded for generations as the definition of success.'[53]

But times were a-changing. In 1963, after six years as immigration minister, Sir Alexander was offered the post of Australian High Commissioner to London. Some see his appointment by Menzies as evidence that there was no longer room on the front bench for so well-mannered and benign a conservative. 'I wonder whether he was too decent or he wasn't tough enough?' queries Clyde Cameron—a suggestion staunchly rebuffed by Lady Mary Downer.

The offer coincided with a personal tragedy for Sir Alexander Downer: the loss of his beloved estate, Arbury Park. This injury came, ironically, at the hands of a fellow Liberal, the then South Australian premier Sir Thomas Playford, who was determined to build a six-lane freeway to the city across Sir Alexander's front lawn. The son of a cherry-picker, Playford held strong anti-establishment values, which often placed him at loggerheads with many in his own party. Sir Alexander's entreaties—including an offer to meet the costs of a detour—fell on deaf ears, and he was left with little choice but to sell up and move. So resentful was he of his treatment by Playford that, as he later confided to Clyde Cameron, he would vote for Don Dunstan, the Labor candidate, in the next state election. His wife, however, had never shared her husband's great love of Arbury Park, for it had been in some ways less her house than her mother-in-law's, who had presided there for over a decade before their wedding. (It is also hard to imagine Mary Downer under any circumstances voting Labor.) Although Arbury Park still stands, it is no longer a family home but a corporate office, buffeted by the sounds of traffic.

If Playford's lack of thought for the sensibilities of the Adelaide gentry signalled a new national mood, Sir Alexander Downer, now ensconced in the High Commissioner's residence at Kensington, knew nothing of it. He continued to educate his children in the manner of his class, if anything upping the ante. Sir Alexander had sent his son to his *alma mater*, Geelong Grammar. Now, with his posting to Britain, he enrolled him at Radcliffe, an elite English boarding school. Meanwhile, his two eldest daughters were sent to finishing school in Switzerland. 'I think my father wanted the very best for his children,' reflects Stella Downer today. 'And he was very idealistic, and perhaps I think out of touch with what was really going on.' Sixteen-year-old Stella found the shift from her 'protected and limited' South Australian upbringing bewildering. 'I was with people like Christina Onassis and Saudi Arabian princesses and Kuwaiti princesses. I found it very strange and daunting.'

Her brother found the transition equally problematic. The irony, he says, is that 'I get sneered at by the Canberra press gallery about my English education, but it was not my choice. I was patronised and I put up with that for years [at school].' He was, he recalls, 'pilloried' and 'called a colonial'. Nor was it just by fellow students. 'The staff shared the same attitudes. Even as a child, I found my housemaster's attitude imperious, unfriendly and unsympathetic. I think of those days and I think of the grey and the drizzle and the cold.'[54] The experience, he says, gave him an abiding distaste for Britain's deeply entrenched class system and the forelock-tugging deference of its working class.

Sir Alexander, however, was in his element. On being offered the high commissionership, he had advised his prime minister that he intended to buy a place of his own in the English countryside, both as a family retreat and as an opportunity for 'country house diplomacy'. Unsure of how Menzies would react, he was relieved by his enthusiasm, for 'none of my predecessors in London had interpreted the position in that way'.[55] In October 1965, the Downers duly bought a country estate in Wiltshire. Oare House was 'built mainly in 1740, but more Queen Anne than Georgian in design, set amidst extensive gardens with commanding views over its fields, woods and the Marlborough Downs'.[56] In fact there were over three hectares of garden, including a traditional walled garden with flowers, vegetables, fruit trees and closely cut grasses. Neighbours included the former politician Sir Anthony Eden, then Lord Avon and the noted jurist Lord Devlin.

Once again Menzies was a regular visitor, mixing martini cocktails, talking politics and imparting his wisdom to the young Alexander. 'I must have been sixteen or seventeen, and my father wanted Sir Robert to give me advice about what I should do once I left school,' Alexander Downer recalls. 'Even though we were staying in the same house, an appointment had to be made . . . It was indeed like a child going before the school principal. He was a kindly man, but he was also a great figure, so he was formidable. I walked into the library with trepidation, but there he was sitting with a cigar, and gave me his lifetime advice . . .

'I asked him, if I were to become a politician one day what would be a good early path. He advised me to do law, which I didn't want to do . . . The second thing he said was that you shouldn't become a member of parliament before you were thirty, and you shouldn't become a member of parliament after you were forty. That is good advice. Because after you're forty, you are set in your ways. So I remember that part of it quite clearly.'

Today, Alexander Downer also believes that to study law, as both his father and grandfather had done, 'is the best background' for a politician. He himself would study economics and politics at the University of Newcastle—his early hopes of following his father to Oxford dashed by poor grades. 'In retrospect,' reflects Alexander of his disappointment at not being admitted, 'it was a good thing I didn't [get in]. I think coming out of Geelong Grammar and an English public school, in terms of my development as a human being, it was important I got away from that sort of environment and had a broader experience of society.'[57] But this redbrick university would make no mark on his political loyalties. While other students were bussed to London to take part in anti-Vietnam War demonstrations,

Alexander (as his mother fondly recalls) would seize the opportunity for a free lift home. As an honours student, he wrote his dissertation on the evolution of the Australian Liberal Party. He also became a member of the university's intervarsity debating team as he had made a crucial discovery about himself: he was a good debater, and he liked provoking the Left.

Perhaps most importantly of all, Alexander Downer would meet his future wife, Nicky Robinson, at university. Adelaide gossips will tell you that eyebrows were raised among certain circles on hearing of their relationship, remarking that Alexander Downer had tied himself to a girl whose family was in trade. (No matter that the Robinsons had had their own large and successful manufacturing business, Robinson & Sons, for more than one hundred and fifty years.[58]) In turn, Nicky Downer, as she became, has been known to joke that Alexander married her to bring some common blood into the illustrious Downer line.[59] She still remembers her first visit home to meet his parents. 'He gave me no idea what to expect. I remember I was so shocked when I drove up the drive of their house, I had to stop the car.'[60]

She has since been credited with bringing a keen intelligence and political skills to their partnership. In the tradition of his father before him, Alexander Downer had found in his wife an outstanding ally—someone who would work closely with him behind the scenes, but who was far from relegated to the back seat—and colleagues will often point to the considerable influence of women in the Downer family. Nicky would put aside a promising career in journalism with the BBC to join Alexander in Australia when, in 1975, he joined the Department of Foreign Affairs, becoming one of only thirty-two candidates selected out of hundreds of applicants.

This career move was partly at his father's urging. Sir Alexander had grown increasingly disenchanted with Australian politics and was no longer sure if it was the right profession for his son. Menzies had retired in 1966 after seventeen years at the helm, and the Liberals had undergone a succession of leaders until being swept from power in 1972. Gough Whitlam's new

Labor government, which included Clyde Cameron on the front bench, presided over a political landscape dramatically different to that which Sir Alexander had known. 'He really believed that it had become so much rougher, and the House of Representatives had become a different place to when he knew it,' recalls Stella Downer. 'He would feel very disillusioned about that and I think he would try to protect my brother, and he would say, "What about being a diplomat? That's a more civilised and rewarding life for you."'

In fact Sir Alexander had retired to Adelaide in 1972 somewhat disappointed in diplomacy too. (He had been recalled by Gough Whitlam who, notwithstanding his visits to the Downer home, wanted his own man in the job.) Sir Alexander's final year as high commissioner had been, by his own admission, 'a sad and contentious period in Anglo–Australian relations'. 'At the time,' recalls Mary Downer, 'Britain was going into the Common Market and he became very outspoken and very undiplomatic, and his views ended up as headlines in the London papers. He was very upset about it, and about how Australia was treated.' Sir Alexander knew he was presiding over the final loosening of the ties that bound Australia to Britain, and that subsequent generations would not share his emotional attachment to the Commonwealth. As Clyde Cameron commented in his diary of the time, 'He loves the Queen and is genuinely saddened that the British Empire has gone down the drain.'[61]

In his retirement, Sir Alexander watched this understanding become a reality as attitudes to the Queen as Australia's head of state became sharply divided after her representative dismissed the Whitlam government in 1975. This event also marked a hardening of political divisions, as the then governor-general, Sir John Kerr had acted on the advice of Malcolm Fraser, the new leader of the Liberal Party who had blocked supply in the Senate and who swept into office in the subsequent election. (Interestingly, at the constitutional convention Sir John Downer had been firmly of the opinion that although Australia needed a strong Senate, it should never have the capacity to block supply.) The controversy sounded the final death knell for cordial relations across the House. 'Today they look across and they sneer,' remarks Clyde Cameron. 'You can see hatred in their eyes and faces, and that didn't happen in the days when Alick and I were first elected.'

Despite these changing times, and Sir Alexander's increasing scepticism, the young Alexander could not resist the allure of politics. In 1981 he stood for preselection in the safe seat of Boothby, but narrowly missed out. He went to work as a speechwriter and political adviser to family friend, then prime minister, Malcolm Fraser. By now Sir Alexander was ill with cancer. He would not live to see his son become a federal politician. In 1984, three years after Sir Alexander's death, Alexander Downer entered parliament as the member for Mayo, the Adelaide Hills electorate where both his father and grandfather had lived. At thirty-two years old, he had entered politics before his fortieth birthday, just as Sir Robert Menzies had advised.

'I'm perfectly certain Alick would have been delighted to see Alexander a member of parliament,' says Lady Mary Downer today. 'I remember him saying when Alexander first stood, "I don't know if that boy ought to be doing this." But I'm sure once he got in, he would have been very proud of him, and would have encouraged him too.' Certainly Alexander Downer's heritage surrounds him. Behind the desk in his parliamentary office, portraits of his father and grandfather bear witness to the endeavours of their successor. 'I'm proud of the things my family has done in contributing to the building up of Australia. I'm quite conscious of it,' he says.

Even as a newly elected MP, Alexander Downer clearly had a sense of destiny. Questioned by reporters about his aspirations, he blushingly confessed to an interest in 'rising to the very top'. In turn, among the Canberra press gallery he became 'everybody's favourite target for jolly jibes . . . The rich, pink-cheeked, wet-behind-the-ears establishment boy displaced in time from Menzies's Australia.'[62] It was hard to overlook the fact that on his return to Australia at twenty-four he had become the second-youngest member of the Adelaide Club.

However, Alexander Downer would prove a very different politician to his patrician father. All in the family agree that, in personality, he is closer to his mother, with her extrovert nature and sense of humour. He has his mother's looks too— or perhaps his grandfather's, for the two share a curious likeness. There again are the thickset features and strong jaw. And from the outset, Alexander Downer has enjoyed the political roughhouse, as parliamentary correspondent Dennis Grant observes. 'He relishes the role of headkicker. When you look at the proceedings in the House, and you can hear what people are saying across the dispatch box, they're pretty willing, they're pretty brutal sometimes. And the most enthusiastic observer of that process is Alexander Downer. The Speaker has to shut him up quite often because he won't walk away from a stoush. Sometimes there is a sort of schoolboyish last-day-of-term quality to this debate, but he's never shy. He's almost always in there.'

In his first ten years in the parliament, Alexander Downer also proved adept at aligning himself with the political currents of the day, deftly taking on the colours of the party's right wing or its more moderate elements, depending on prevailing winds. He adapted in other ways too, and his English accent became less noticeable. All who knew him agreed that beneath his laid-back style and self-deprecating humour dwelt a keenly focused political ambition. Noted one adversary sourly, 'He has a personality as tough as old boots, and a skin like rawhide.'

These attributes came to the fore in the last troubled days of John Hewson's leadership. As shadow treasurer, Alexander Downer had been among Hewson's most ardent supporters, tirelessly pushing his dry right-wing agenda for economic change. However, most journalists agree that privately Downer also became one of Hewson's most vocal critics as these policies met growing voter disfavour. In a party increasingly divided between small 'l' liberal traditionalists and a new hard-line right, Alexander Downer with his dynastic pedigree cast himself as the leader behind whom all could unite. 'I am imbued with the culture of the Liberal Party and its values,' he announced. On this note, he ascended the throne with the blessing of his elders and buoyed by the urgings of his good mate, Peter Costello, another emerging star who would take on the role of deputy, believing it too early in his own career to strive higher.

In contrast, Alexander Downer, with his family's backing, declared every confidence in his ascendancy. His assurance that his birthright gave him an innate understanding of the 'broad church' of Liberal politics was popular with voters too. Despite then Labor Prime Minister Paul Keating's best efforts to brand him as someone who 'believes that only those born in big houses have a right to live in big houses', Alexander Downer enjoyed a 70 per cent approval rating in the early months of his leadership—a record high in the polls. Indeed, Keating's efforts to play the politics of class backfired among voters and the press, which pointed to Keating's own considerable wealth and highbrow tastes, noting 'it's a bit rich for a top nouveau toff to scoff'.[63]

But the honeymoon would not last. 'His inexperience and unbounded confidence in his abilities did not allow him to see the minefields,' commented analysts as a series of blunders made Alexander Downer's 'commonsense practical party' look like a 'policy-free zone'.[64] Unable to chart a steady line through the troubled debate around Aboriginal land rights and native title, and unable to find party support for his small 'l' liberal social policies, Alexander Downer committed a final folly by making a joke of his own political agenda. In a keynote speech, he sent up the title of the party's carefully crafted new platform, 'The Things that Matter', in a series of ghastly puns that culminated in the suggestion that the party's policy on domestic violence could be called 'the things that batter'.[65]

This performance effectively achieved what Paul Keating had tried so hard and failed to do. It branded Alexander

Downer an aristocratic amateur who, by virtue of his privileged upbringing, could not be entrusted with the serious business of running the country. As Dennis Grant points out, 'The speech that did him in may have been written by someone else, but it was delivered by him. And that maybe underlines an important point about Alexander Downer, that there is sometimes a capacity to be an intellectual dilettante. Perhaps his breeding suggested that to him, that there was always someone to run around and make the cups of tea, and there was always a nanny in the nursery.' More pertinently, such a public gaffe suggested an astonishing absence of the kind of instinct that most politicians quickly develop for their own survival. Dennis Grant is not alone in seeing this as a consequence of Alexander Downer's carefully nurtured establishment background—his time at a redbrick university notwithstanding. Although Alexander Downer was certainly not alone among politicians in leaving the substance of his speech to a writer, he should have had the foresight to realise that such jokes had no place in a public forum. Was it perhaps the polite deference of South Australia that led Alexander Downer to assume that he was always among friends who would understand and excuse his escapades?

The 'things that batter' debacle was a watershed in Alexander Downer's career, for he was battered in the press and even by members of his own party for it. 'People do learn from searing experiences like that, and Alexander Downer certainly did,' recalls Grant. 'From that point on he required a much higher standard of advice, and a much better standard of staff around him.' But the lesson came at the expense of the Liberal leadership. After only eight months in the job, Alexander Downer stood aside for John Howard, the tenacious flagbearer of the party's hard right. (Once again, the deal was done in a gentlemen's club in Melbourne—this time the Athenaeum, where John Howard and Alexander Downer met for dinner.) Downer's consolation prize was the foreign affairs portfolio, to which he brought his own personal experience and a long-held family interest.

Looking back on those turbulent days, Alexander Downer acknowledges that he in fact did 'very poorly' in the job of Opposition leader, and 'was kind of relieved to move on'. At the time, however, he professed bitter disappointment at losing the leadership, although he remained resilient to the last. 'It's like snakes and ladders,' he shrugged in an interview that same night. 'I'm only forty-three, so if the opportunity ever came again—good.'[66]

'I think there was an assumption that because he was a Downer he was somehow born with the attributes necessary to lead a political party in Australia in this day and age. You're not born with those skills, you develop those skills, and first time round he clearly and spectacularly did not have those skills,' comments Dennis Grant wryly. 'I think he learned from his mistakes, and I don't think you can say it's the same Alex Downer who made a goose of himself back when he was leader. I think he has done what politicians are frequently required to do—he's reinvented himself.'

In 1996 John Howard led the Liberals to a landslide election victory, and Alexander Downer took his place as Minister for Foreign Affairs in a new conservative regime with little time for the old small 'l' liberal values of its predecessors. He would prove himself one of Howard's better ministerial performers, adhering strictly to the policy directions of his prime minister. In doing so, he would demonstrate some of the political pragmatism of his grandfather when he defended his government's refusal to ratify the United Nations' protocol on women's rights, which, in providing a non-binding appeals process for women whose human rights had been violated, sought to improve their global welfare. Ironically, Australia had until then been one of its keenest advocates. Alexander Downer maintained this decision had nothing to do with his support for women's rights—despite the blow it dealt them internationally—but rather reflected his reservations about the United Nations' appeals process.

In fact, the decision to deal the United Nations such a public rebuttal probably had more to do with his prime minister's view that the organisation was an easy target to assuage a right-wing voter backlash against an increasingly multicultural, economically global Australia. Accordingly, Alexander Downer as Minister for Foreign Affairs, warned the organisation that it risked 'getting its nose bloodied if it interfered in domestic politics' when his government was confronted by reports critical of its human rights record on Aborigines and refugees. Criticism would nonetheless continue—most notably of the Howard government's hard-line response to asylum seekers.

The steady diminution of Australia's commitment to take refugees (in the face of an escalating global crisis) and the scapegoating of asylum seekers would mark a new ideological direction in the history of the Liberal Party, for past conservative governments had been keen supporters of the United Nations and upheld the moral imperatives of leadership in meeting the needs of refugees. It would also mark a break between Alexander Downer's pragmatism and that of his forebears—neither of whom had extended their support to such a jingoistic nationalism. Indeed, Sir Alexander Downer had been among the most vocal supporters of Australia's need to show leadership on such issues, warning audiences that the country risked being seen as a 'selfish' and 'insular backwater' if it failed to meet its international commitments and obligations.

While newspaper headlines have proclaimed 'the quiet comeback of Alexander Downer', others have lambasted his lack of leadership on women's rights, refugees and the United Nations. 'I don't mind the criticism,' responds Alexander Downer. 'If you go into public life—my father was able to teach me this—constant criticism comes with the territory. It's not a job for the faint-hearted, and it's not a job for someone who agonises over criticism.' He is, he says, interested only in practical outcomes, whether something will work. This would make him, perhaps, the most professional politician of the dynasty so far—if only by lobbyist Richard Farmer's definition that the mark of a professional politician is that 'they believe in nothing much except outcomes'.[67] Certainly his resilience and determination to do whatever is needed has proven Alexander Downer in the eyes of his colleagues. Many regard him as a better politician than his father. Observes Clyde Cameron, 'The present-day Alexander Downer would find a way of getting around a question without having to tell the truth, without even having to tell a lie. It's very clever. His father couldn't do that. His father wouldn't want to do it. But young Alexander is a tougher politician than his father ever was, more ruthless because his father wasn't ruthless at all, and the young Alexander Downer is a very good politician.'

He has perhaps already gone further than his father and grandfather before him—achieving (albeit briefly) the leadership of a federal party that has traditionally overlooked politicians not from Victoria or New South Wales. Perhaps also, in his handling of foreign policy issues such as independence for East Timor, he has made as much of an impact on Australia's future as his antecedents. It is much more difficult to predict what his political legacy will be—even for those at close quarters. 'His intellectual framework is very much rooted in his small "l" liberalism. He describes himself as a creature of the Liberal Party, and he's certainly that. I mean, the genes are certainly there. But I think that his public school education in Britain, and perhaps his early days in the foreign affairs department, equipped him with pretty strong armour and a level of intellectual arrogance that has served him in fairly good stead. The problem is, when you mesh these things together, a tough exterior, a strong rhetoric, a touch of the political bullyboy (see a Labor target, kick the head) the problem is: will the real Alexander Downer please stand up.'[68] The danger here is that what may be left of the Downer dynasty's political legacy is simply a belief that the family is better qualified than most, by virtue solely of birth and pedigree, to assume political leadership.

What hasn't changed is the Downer family's South Australian roots, despite the fact that many other establishment families have moved east to greener pastures. At the end of the day, Wakefield's reformist vision, hampered by geographical realities, simply could not compete with the economic success of its convict rivals. The Downer family's fortunes too have waned. Despite his silvertail tag, Alexander Downer relies on his parliamentary salary. Although more affluent than the average Australian, he is far from being one of the wealthiest politicians. His old adversary, Paul Keating, is considerably wealthier—as are other Liberal Party establishment politicians such as fellow South Australian Ian McLachlan.

While Alexander still lives in the electorate of Mayo, as did his father and grandfather, his home is a sprawling family bungalow rather than a Georgian mansion. Like his parents before him, he has four children—a boy and three girls—and politics is still very much a family affair. It is often the focus of dinner-table conversation, and the family will converge on election night to watch the results come in. During these suspense-filled and keenly discussed moments, it is easy to see the allure politics still holds. Some commentators believe, however, that with the increasing devaluation of politics by a cynical electorate there will be less inclination for future generations to follow in their parents' footsteps.[69] There is little of this mood in the Downer household where, despite the gruelling schedule kept by today's politicians, the prevailing sense is of the pride and pleasure Alexander Downer and his family share in his job. Certainly there is the hope, if not the expectation or pressure, that a fourth generation will pick up the political mantle.

Alexander Downer himself says he believes in continuity and preserving one's links to the past. If anything, he is perhaps a somewhat more cautious conservative than his forebears, a Burkean who believes not in bringing about change but in adapting to it 'where it evolves with time'. Either way, he eschews comparisons with generations past. And perhaps it is the mark of a successful dynasty that each generation can adapt to changing times. In which case the last word on the subject belongs to Alexander Downer himself:

'There's no point trying to relive the previous generation's experiences as a family. And I don't think, to be fair to our family, other than us being politicians—because we can't really think of anything else to do as a family—that any of us have tried. I mean, my father had a very different lifetime experience from his father—and people say he was very different. I've heard it said that I'm very different from my father. I've been a politician as he was, but am living out a very different life.'

It remains to be seen what the fourth generation will bring.

THE MYER FAMILY

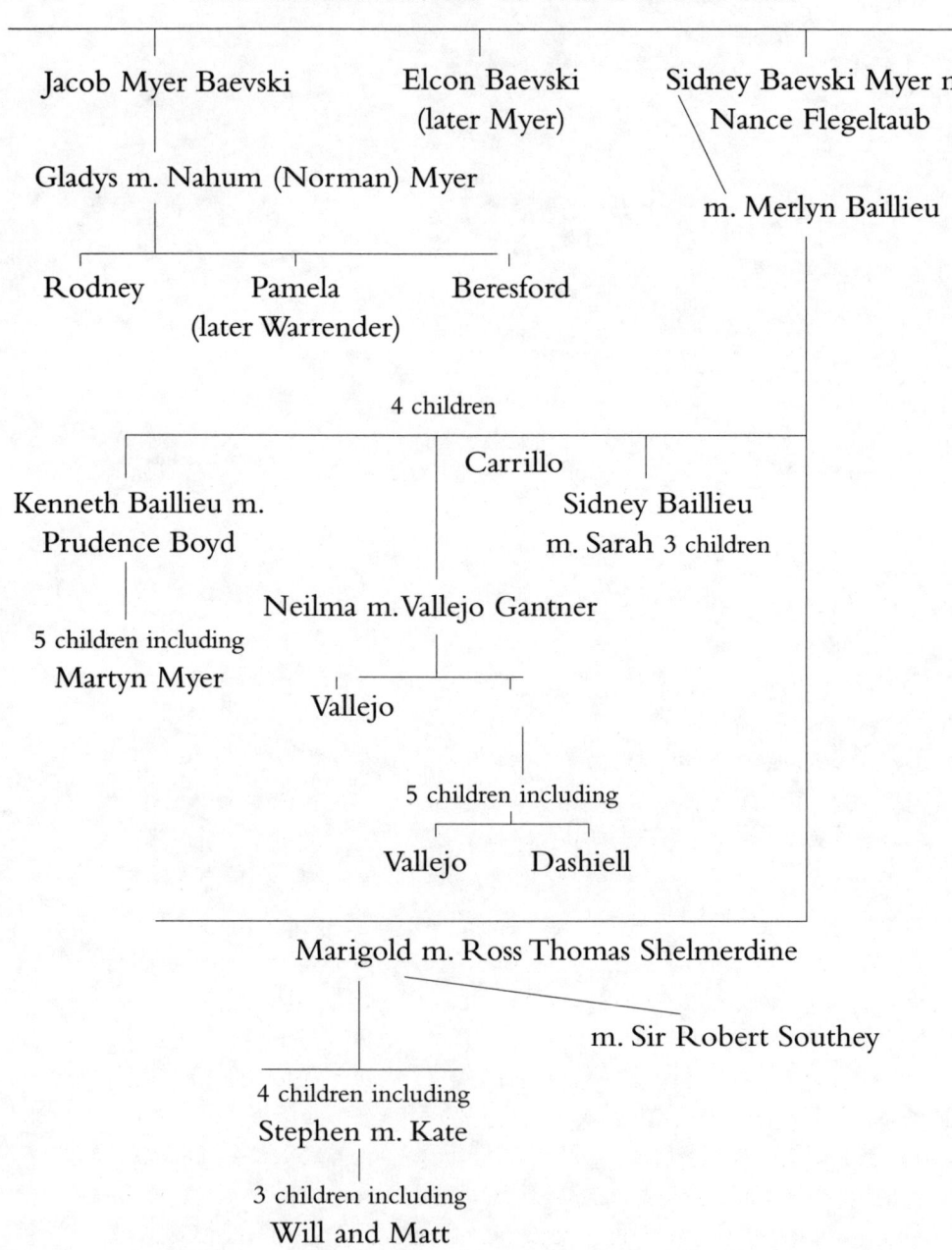

Israel Yeheskial Baevski m. Gina Dabrusha Shur

Jacob Myer Baevski

Elcon Baevski
(later Myer)

Sidney Baevski Myer m.
Nance Flegeltaub

Gladys m. Nahum (Norman) Myer

m. Merlyn Baillieu

Rodney   Pamela   Beresford
(later Warrender)

4 children

Carrillo

Kenneth Baillieu m.
Prudence Boyd

Sidney Baillieu
m. Sarah 3 children

5 children including
Martyn Myer

Neilma m. Vallejo Gantner

Vallejo

5 children including

Vallejo   Dashiell

Marigold m. Ross Thomas Shelmerdine

m. Sir Robert Southey

4 children including
Stephen m. Kate

3 children including
Will and Matt

THE PATRIARCH'S WILL

THE MYERS

LATE in the afternoon on a warm March day, three women sit sipping sugary tea on the front verandah of a rundown cottage in the Melbourne bayside suburb of St Kilda. All in their early twenties, they don't know each other well. What they have in common is heroin—a lethal habit they'd all like to kick.

They chat, but this is no polite, light conversation; it cuts straight to the heart of their lives as heroin addicts. One woman says she's lost her husband, who overdosed two months ago, and she has four children to support. Another speaks of her friend who overdosed two weeks ago, aged eighteen. The third woman nurses her sick eight-month-old baby, and talks over the top of the other two about how she still wants to be using, the pleasure of being 'out of it' and of only having friends who still use. She has visible track marks on her beautiful alabaster skin.

These three women are waiting to see the doctor. All went through heroin detoxification a few days earlier and are finding it hard. This detox centre is not funded by any government—it relies on volunteers and donations. It uses naltrexone, a highly controversial drug which blocks the endorphin receptors in the brain, thereby temporarily stopping both the high offered by heroin and the craving for it. The people coming into this centre view naltrexone as a potential lifeline. Unfortunately for them, many health professionals and the government don't share this view. This centre, First Step, was set up by a wealthy Melbourne couple after they saw their own teenage daughter detox via naltrexone. Their lives now revolve round helping other heroin users.

Inside the house the atmosphere is relaxed and homely. First Step treats addiction as an illness, and addicts as patients in need of both allopathic treatment and human kindness. On any given day the centre is bustling—heroin is cheap and opiate use enormous. But First Step is struggling under the weight of its social conscience. Unlike other more conventional detox centres which charge in the thousands for treatment, First Step asks only $200. This makes the naltrexone course affordable, but puts the centre on a financial knife edge. There's only one doctor, who helps subsidise the centre by donating a substantial portion of his wage and by working excessive hours. There is also one nurse and a varied and dedicated team of volunteers. First Step is desperate for more cash. In particular, it needs to provide better after-care services.

As the women talk on the verandah, several young men wander up the path and stand staring with slight trepidation at the scene before them. People stumble and shamble in and out of the house in an almost constant stream. Some are obviously ill. Inside, all is shabbiness: paint peeling, few furnishings, mattresses sprawling on untidy floors, sheets dishevelled. A window is smashed, shards of glass remaining in the frame—one of today's patients hurled himself at it, unaware of what he was doing.

The young visitors stand out from this crowd: their clothes are clean, their skin looks healthy, their eyes don't have a desperate gaze. These five young men, mainly university students, are all related and are on a unique family outing. They share the same great-grandparents: Sidney and Merlyn Myer. Their ancestry places them in an unusual position. For three generations the

Myer family have been generous philanthropists. Now, as many of the fourth generation reach adulthood, it's hoped they will continue the family tradition. Visiting a detox centre is an odd family excursion, but this is no ordinary family; the Myers are in the business of giving money away and this centre may be a beneficiary of the famous family's so-called 'G4', or Fourth Generation fund.

One of the young men is Dashiell (Dash) Gantner, an olive-skinned, curly-haired, perspicacious medical student with a studiously shabby undergrad lifestyle. Dash is ambivalent about the family wealth and feels the responsibility for using it wisely. He leaves his cousins and strolls into the doctor's surgery to observe the consultation between the centre's frenzied middle-aged doctor, Simon Rose, and some of the patients.

By five o'clock those treated have drifted off. The volunteers and nurse are cleaning up ready for the next day. But the centre won't close for a few more hours—there are still patients to see, although the committed Dr Rose says he can now afford some time to chat with the Myers. Dash is joined by his relatives and a group of former heroin users in the doctor's chaotic surgery. The Myers are about to listen to what the people who have been through the treatment have to say; and Simon is hoping for a donation from the G4 fund.

The Myer family's net worth is estimated to be at least $500 million—based on their shares in the troubled retail giant Coles Myer Limited alone. This is the core of their dynastic riches. The Myer fortune is managed and generated through their private investment company, the Myer Family Company. Wealth enhancement is a, if not *the,* primary family focus. But the Myers justify their collective acquisitiveness by guaranteeing that the greater their resources, the greater the investment they can make in philanthropy. This self-imposed *noblesse oblige* dictates that a small percentage of the family wealth is chan-nelled into good causes. The family's philanthropic organisation is the Myer Foundation—and in 2001 its directors (all Myers) offered the fourth generation $100 000 per annum to assist certain projects. These projects can be social, environmental or cultural—all the directors ask is that the fourth generation show some interest in the projects. The visit to First Step has been arranged by a non-family member, the CEO of the Myer Foundation, Charles Lane.

A few months earlier the Myer Foundation had given several thousand dollars to the detox centre to help provide after-care support for patients. On this warm March evening a young woman with bitten nails and translucent skin describes their after-care as making all the difference for her. She had gone through many heroin detox programs. This one worked because she had people calling to check if she was all right, days after the detox. 'When you're a heroin user,' she explains, 'you think the world hates you. To have someone ring you up, a complete stranger, it puts your faith back in humanity.'[1]

However, the money the Myer Foundation gave to the centre is a drop in the opiate ocean. $5000 is used up in a few weeks. First Step desperately needs more. At the detox clinic, the normally self-assured Charles Lane is anxious. Giving money to the detox centre was a new step for the foundation—a step that might not have pleased some of the conservatives in the family.

The Myer family now consists of more than eighty people and spans an age range from infants to near-octogenarians. There's also a striking diversity of lifestyle. Some are regularly seen sipping champagne at Melbourne's A-list society parties, others are happy to be inconspicuous and build boats in picturesque coastal towns. There are some who, perhaps due to a heightened sense of entitlement, are thought recalcitrant. Luckily the clan also has enough members who wish to seek consensus. Within any family there are disagreements, but wealth and dynastic legacies add further complications. For the Myers, struggling to work together through the often conflicting tasks of business and philanthropy, middle ground can be elusive. In philanthropy, the attempt to find targets on which they can all reach a consensus safely has meant funds frequently travelling a well-trodden charity path to the respectable turf of hospitals, art galleries, museums, theatres and universities. Here in shabby detox-land, the Myer Foundation is on shakier ground. Research is divided as to the efficacy of the treatment, and heroin addicts are often portrayed as thieves and useless people. There's divided community sympathy for addicts—and little kudos for those trying to help them.

The sun sets over suburban St Kilda. The Myer clan listens wide-eyed to the stories of the former addicts. One well-dressed man in his twenties tells them he can go back to work now, thanks to naltrexone. A woman tells of the importance of having support after detox. Paddy Myer meets a worldly teenager who used to attend his old school, the elite Geelong Grammar— heroin is no respecter of class. At various times during the discussion the receptionist hurries in, needing Simon Rose to sign urgent medical documents; he also receives a call from a Perth doctor to discuss complications in a patient. The frenetic physician needs to see other patients; however, before he dashes off, he must quickly make the point to the young philanthropists that because most heroin addicts have underlying emotional problems, the naltrexone treatment has to be followed up with after-care support. This support costs money.

The G4 are impressed by the dynamic doctor and somewhat overwhelmed at the enormity of the problems this centre faces—not merely in staying open, but in giving the addicts the care needed to break their habit. One of the Myer group, Will Shelmerdine, expresses his admiration for Simon Rose and the parents who established the centre. 'I'd always read about it from the paper, from a safe distance, but when you come into an environment like this . . . I couldn't believe how incredible, how amazing it is. There are people out here in society really helping a lot of people.'[2] His teenage cousin, the self-effacing Paddy Myer, chips in: 'I guess we've been born into money—we had no choice in it. I guess it's up to us to help the people who haven't been so fortunate, and I hope we can do some good.'[3] Paddy's comments reflect the general mood of the group.

The Myers are rare among wealthy dynastic families. They've put in place a unique structure to encourage their youngest members to act ethically and benevolently in the wider community. The Myers' *noblesse oblige* is a carefully crafted family enterprise, with few ties to social expectation. The story behind this altrusim lies in the family's past—in the will left by its dynastic founder. Their philanthropy began with a refugee living on the margins and working on the streets over one hundred years ago: Simcha Baevski—otherwise known as Sidney Myer.

In August 1899 a tall dark-haired young Russian Jew stepped off the European mail steamer *Karlsruhe* and breathed the cold salty air of the Melbourne docks. Simcha Baevski had been travelling for three months after being smuggled out of Czarist Russia (like his brother before him).

In the dying days of the Russian imperial regime, the unpredictable and murderous anti-Jewish pogroms were on the increase. Russia's five million Jews were confined to an area known as the Pale of Settlement which stretched from the Baltic to the Black Sea. For Russian Jews life was generally harsh and deprived. During Simcha's childhood anti-Semitic violence was a rarity in his isolated home town, Krichev. But by the late 1890s it was on the rise. In the months before his forced departure, arsonists destroyed several Jewish houses and businesses in Krichev. The Baevski family worried about their future security. Adding to their concerns, Simcha was in hiding from the Russian army. The Czarist regime, seasonally at war either with other nations or with its own civilians, always needed new recruits. Jewish men faced a forcible conscription of twenty-five years in the notoriously ill-equipped and undisciplined army. Young Simcha and his resourceful parents carefully plotted escape from this fearful bleakness.

In early 1899, Simcha's mother Gina Dabrusha Baevski decided now was the time to close her successful drapery business and make good the plans for the family's escape. It was clear her beloved Simcha should join his brother Elcon in

Australia. Elcon had spent the last three years in Melbourne working for a brother-in-law, Lasar Slutzkin. Lasar had offered to pay for Simcha's fare to Australia. With relatives and a manufacturing business already established in Australia, it made sense that Simcha should accept the offer. Gina then determined that she and her Talmud scholar husband, Israel Yeheskial Baevski, should flee to Palestine. Gina and Israel were never to see Simcha again.

It took Simcha three months to reach his adopted homeland. He wore his one and only suit and clutched a carpetbag 'stuffed with personal linen and oriental curios and a threepenny bit'.[4] He knew no English and had little money. But he was young, ambitious and flamboyant—attributes that in his adopted homeland would stand him in good stead.

Simcha stepped off that boat and into this country on the very cusp of a new century—one that would give birth to the consumer economy. The gold-rush years had forged a community that was boisterous and open to fresh ideas. Simcha turned out to be the entrepreneurial showman Victorians wanted. According to family legend, his first transaction on stepping from the boat was to spend his threepence on a beer. He was to assert later that this was the best money he ever spent, because he knew it belonged to him.[5] Perhaps Simcha drank the refreshing beer as he waited for his brother to meet him. Elcon, having the wrong information for the steamer, never arrived to pick up his brother. But finally the Baevski brothers were reunited at Lasar's home.

Simcha was quick to find his feet, energetically seeking out ways of making money and fitting into his new surroundings. His name was Anglicised to 'Sidney'. In the same vein his brother now called himself EB (short for Elcon Baevski), and they both adopted the readily pronounceable surname Myer as a tribute to their dead eldest brother, Jacob Myer Baevski.

Sidney knew that to succeed in his adopted homeland he would have to master the language and try to assimilate into its culture. Victoria was emerging from an economic depression and there was little sympathy for the plight of penniless refugees. It was commonly felt that Jews were among the least desirable migrants as they were reluctant to adopt Australia's dominant mores and religion.[6] He spent his evenings conscientiously studying English and reading classic English texts, including Shakespeare. By nature extroverted and theatrical, Sidney would later join an amateur dramatic society. His performance as King Lear was remembered for years—never had the audience heard the king played with such a heavy Russian accent.

But the theatre was to be an occasional diversion; employment was the main game. Once established in the relative stability of Australia, far from the conflicts of Russia, the Myer brothers put their minds to the matter of starting their own drapery business. Lasar Slutzkin, despite not wanting his Myer relatives to leave his business, supplied them with £300 worth of stock and introduced them to two importing firms.[7] The Myer brothers were ready to branch out on their own. But they knew that family would always be the place from which one could build.

With expectation and their new hawking licences, they travelled around Victoria's thriving commercial centres—Melbourne and then Bendigo and Ballarat. Simcha and EB knew that hawking was the lowest rung on the business and social ladder. It was left to men with foreign accents, usually Afghans and Chinese. In the regional press, hawkers were constantly portrayed as confidence men and all faced discrimination and harassment in a country just about to introduce its White Australia legislation. However, setting up as hawkers was a necessary first step. The brothers at least knew the rag trade. In the Krichev Pale settlement, employment for Jews was severely restricted. Consequently, their mother had meticulously taught her sons the drapery business. Under her tuition and adding his own retail flair, Sidney had quadrupled the turnover in the family shop in the year before he left Russia. From this background sprang the brothers' confidence.

Whether the day was hot and dusty or wet and windy, Sidney

traipsed around the bustling towns, carrying a heavy wooden box filled with an array of buttons, ribbons, cotton and needles. His days were long and frequently exhausting.

The family enjoys a favourite, although apocryphal, story of Sidney's hawking times. One hot day, they say, a fatigued Sidney staggered into the town of Maldon. The town publican saw him and invited him to have a drink and rest. The publican poured him a drink and gave Sidney a basin of water for his blistered feet. The hardworking hawker, too tired to wash his own feet, had to be helped by this good Samaritan. The shoes were worn and the socks torn. As his aching feet lay soaking, Sidney fell asleep. The solicitous proprietor gave him a bed for the night and the next day a grateful young man went on his way.

As his business grew, Sidney rarely went into Maldon—but didn't forget the publican's kindness. By the time of the Great Depression, years later, Sidney Myer had become one of the most successful retailers in the country. In those hard times a stream of down-at-heel jobless men from all over Victoria came knocking for work at the door of the Myer Emporium. As Sidney walked into his store one day, he came face to face with one of the job-hunters. Sidney recognised this penniless character as the Maldon publican, now down and out after the Depression had left his business—and indeed the entire town of Maldon—ruined. Sidney took the fallen publican to his managers and told them that this man was a friend and that he was to have a job with the Myer Emporium for as long as he wanted.[8]

However, in the early years of the twentieth century, the glory days of the Myer Emporium were barely imaginable. The brothers dared only climb the rickety retail ladder one rung at a time. In 1900 they opened their first store in Pall Mall, the centre of Bendigo. For these aspiring migrants this thriving regional town was an ideal location. The gold rush was over but the 40 000 residents still enjoyed the wealth generated by the gold mines. For the Myer brothers this meant ample income and people to support their nascent retail business. It was more a cramped depot than a shop, with Sidney delivering purchases to their out-of-town customers on his travels. This little business was delightfully and officially called 'Myer Bros., Drapers and Importers; Ladies Underclothing a Speciality. Skirts, Blouses, etc., Made to Order'.[9]

It appeared no match for their established competitors Craig & Williamson and Beehive. Myer Bros was minute and the clientele sparse, but the brothers had two advantages: their goods were generally cheap and they sold ready-made clothes as well as those made to order. Women who had always sewn the family outfits were being offered a time-saving alternative. The Myer brothers' ready-made clothes began to make an impression on all but the well-to-do.

The good-looking Sidney was a natural salesman, outgoing and charming. His brother EB preferred to be behind the scenes and was a meticulous administrator. The brothers differed in personality and attitude, but this only became a problem when it came to their faith. Judaism had been the spiritual bedrock of their upbringing. But once in Australia, Sidney enjoyed a life with few religious restrictions. While others sought security within Victoria's tightly knit Russian-Jewish community, Sidney was determined to transcend this enclave. He believed that to succeed in Australia meant keeping his ties to the Jewish faith and community at a minimum. His brother was perturbed by Sidney's transformation. One of the busiest trading days was Saturday, the Jewish Sabbath. For EB the shop had to be shut, at least until the evening; Sidney, always a religious pragmatist, wanted it open. The differences between the firm believer and the firmly businesslike created a temporary schism.

In 1903 EB returned to work with Lasar in Melbourne. Sidney bought out his brother and stayed with the Bendigo shop. The decision almost proved disastrous. Sidney still spoke English haltingly and his style was foreign and too flashy for many straitlaced Victorians. Customers stayed away and Sidney, now bound to the store, was unable to travel around the towns to sell his goods. After a year going solo his shop was almost lost.

THE MACARTHUR FAMILY

John Macarthur, the founder of one of
Australia's oldest dynasties. Seemingly the
epitome of the assured English gentleman,
he was a tailor's son and a self-made man.
(State Library of NSW)

The first matriarch, Elizabeth Macarthur, in her
widowhood. Although instrumental in creating
the family's pastoral empire alongside her
husband, Elizabeth would inherit none of the
business, though she continued to take a keen
interest in its affairs. (Macarthur-Stanham family)

The dutiful sons of the second generation, James (left) and William Macarthur. With none of their
father's flamboyance, these two men did much to consolidate and increase the family empire.
(State Library of NSW)

Helen Macarthur Stanham, matriarch of the fifth generation of Macarthurs. This photograph was taken as she prepared to attend the first Buckingham Palace tea party held after World War II and just before she returned to Australia to take up her inheritance at Camden Park. (Marion Millwood)

Quentin Macarthur Stanham with his first wife Andalusia and their two eldest children, Mark and Anne, at Camden Park. The marriage was soon to end, and Miss Andy (as she was known) returned to England, leaving the two children behind. (Marion Millwood)

From left to right: John, Helen, Mark and Jane
Macarthur Stanham. (Marion Millwood)

Left to right: Victoria, John, William, George and
Edwina Macarthur Stanham. (High Life magazine)

THE DURACK FAMILY

Patrick 'Patsy' Durack (back left): The dynastic patriarch and founder. From impoverished beginnings in Ireland the ambitious Patsy and family acquired vast landholdings in New South Wales, Queensland and the Kimberley. Patsy stands here with members of his family, including his brother 'Stumpy Michael' (back right). (Enid Durack)

Patsy's son MP Durack. MP tried to uphold his father's pastoral dreams, but he never felt at home in the wilds of the Kimberley. Two weeks before his death MP sold the bulk of the family's Kimberley leasehold, leaving the dynastic hopes in tatters. (Enid Durack)

Among Enid Durack's many achievements was setting up the first primary school in the district for many of the station workers' children. (Enid Durack)

Patsy's indomitable grandson Reg Durack, who was determined to stay in the Kimberley despite the loss of most of the family's land. With his wife Enid he established an isolated property deep in the Northern Territory. In this remote region they raised five children including (from left) Anne, Ruth, John and David. (Enid Durack)

Mary Durack saved and collated the family records, which she used as the basis for her two bestselling books Kings in Grass Castles *and* Sons in the Saddle. *Mary's pioneering tales gave her family a visible place in Australian history, though by the time* Sons in the Saddle *was published all the Duracks' Kimberley stations had gone. (Patsy Millett)*

THE DOWNER FAMILY

Sir John Downer, a politician in his prime and a product of South Australia's colonial society, on his appointment to the Third Federal Convention in Adelaide.
(Mortlock Library, State Library of SA)

The wedding of Sir Alexander and Lady Downer. Not unusually for South Australia, their marriage marked the joining together of two well known establishment families, although her heritage was more illustrious than his.
(Lady Mary Downer)

Sir Alexander, Lady Mary Downer and family on the steps of Arbury Park, the estate Sir Alexander built in the Adelaide Hills. This family photograph marks Sir Alexander's appointment as Minister for Immigration in the Menzies cabinet. From left to right: Alexander junior, Una, Angela and Stella. (Lady Mary Downer)

Alexander Downer and his wife Nicky with their children. Like his parents, Alexander has three daughters and a son – but will any of this fourth generation go into politics? (Nicky Downer)

Not just the matriarch of a political dynasty, Lady Mary Downer promotes the Barossa Music Festival, of which she is patron, from the back of a Harley-Davidson. (Lady Mary Downer)

According to the *Bendigo Advertiser*, shoppers preferred to buy from the established and more staid emporiums. Sidney despaired as he tried in vain to keep his small shop open. As he watched his losses mount up he felt forced to sell up and went to the manager of one of the bigger firms who agreed to buy Sidney's stock at less than cost. Just before the sale contract was signed Sidney mused: 'If I am to receive only these low values then why should I not sell my wares at these prices to the people who have supported me in the past?' Accordingly he spent all one night in marking his stock at the lower values. Always recognising a bargain, people flocked to his shop and soon the stock became exhausted. Young Myer found he had enough money to purchase more stock, and to his delight the patronage continued. It was the turning point of his life.[10]

Serendipity had played its part in Sidney's mercantile drama. From misfortune there emerged a technique that became his signature: the sale. This, and other versions of the cut-price deal, became the trademark for all future Myer stores and the foundation of the family's immense fortune.

Spurred by his immediate success, Sidney now conjured up gimmick after gimmick. He soon became known for bargains and blitzkrieg advertising. On one occasion he bought 5000 hats and announced he would sell them for a few shillings each as soon as the Town Hall clock struck 8 pm. Bendigo's main street was bedlam; women fainted as the throng pushed towards the bargains. The chaos abated only when all the hats were sold.

His youngest daughter, now Lady Marigold Southey, claims that when her father set up his business in Melbourne in 1911 he changed the prevailing washing routine. Traditionally Monday was washing day for Melbourne households. However, when the Myer Emporium opened, Monday became its weekly sales day. People would flock to the city to get the bargains.[11] The washing could wait when a sale at Myers was on. Unlike his staid competitors, Sidney's business thrived on high turnover; the bottom line was selling as much as possible.

It was Sidney's ostentatious daring that gave Myers a distinctive quality. His sales and mail-order catalogues were new, brash and eye-catching. He also found his customers enjoyed being able to touch the cloth and inspect the quality for themselves rather than wait for a salesperson. They enjoyed the informality of shopping at Myers and now came again and again.

Sidney had a few opponents. A handful of the fashionable wealthy ladies of Bendigo remained unconvinced and stuck to the conventional shops and up and down the tree-lined Pall Mall; rival Bendigo retailers waged bets as to when this upstart with his cutthroat discounts and ubiquitous advertising would fall into bankruptcy. But Sidney Myer wasn't going to give them any such pleasure. In a few short years he became Bendigo's most successful retailer. His ambitions were far from satisfied, however; he set his expansionist sights on marvellous Melbourne. In the early post-Federation years, Victoria was ebullient. Indeed, Melbourne was home to the new federal parliament and had overtaken Sydney as the nation's financial and industrial heartland.

In 1911, Sidney made the move from Bendigo to Melbourne. He was thirty-three and in just over ten years he had risen from penniless refugee to wealthy entrepreneur. He opened the Myer Emporium in Bourke Street—the commercial heart of Melbourne. The store was an immediate success. Despite this, Sidney couldn't yet bring himself to break all ties with Bendigo and the Pall Mall business would remain open until 1914.

To his new home in Melbourne he brought his cantankerous wife. In 1905 Sidney had married Nance Flegeltaub, the daughter of a wealthy Jewish retailer. The marriage would never be happy. At the time of their 1904 engagement Sidney probably thought it useful to marry the daughter of a successful Ballarat businessman. Nance was eight years her husband's senior. When the couple first met she was thirty-four and her parents were keen to arrange a good marriage for their eldest daughter. She was smart, quick-witted and apparently possessed of some charm, but she lost her sense of humour with Sidney. To her, he had the manners and the education of a peasant; but despite these perceived flaws, she preferred to marry him than be a spinster, forever beholden to her parents.

In this loveless union no children were conceived. Sidney later described their marriage as 'wretched and turbulent'. He was to spend most of their eleven years together buried in business-building, preferring the demanding workplace to the chilly atmosphere of home. It was, perhaps, a marriage born of Sidney's apprehension that, despite his growing wealth, he would always be considered the Jewish outsider. His friend and biographer, Ambrose Pratt, believed the marriage was the result of pressure from Sidney's relatives who felt his bachelorhood was in defiance of Jewish custom.[12]

In matters of religion he was pragmatic; his abiding passion remained his Baevski family. He had wanted to bring his parents to Australia but they died in 1904, the year his business nearly collapsed. Now, with a successful store in Melbourne, Sidney wanted to be surrounded by family. Relations with EB and Lasar remained strong and Sidney turned his attention to making the Myer Emporium a family concern.

In 1913, perhaps because he had no heirs, Sidney sponsored and 'adopted' two nephews, Samuel and Nahum. Nahum was the son of Sidney's dead brother Jacob Myer. Jacob had died when Nahum was a baby and the child had been raised by his mother and a stepfather who apparently terrorised his stepson. When the news arrived that his uncle offered a chance of escape, fifteen-year-old Nahum was delighted.

Sidney, holding dear the Jewish saying, 'He who brings up, not he who begets, is the father', doted on his heirs apparent and gave them all the education and encouragement they needed. Nahum was renamed Norman and began to be groomed for a life in the family business. The boys' uncle promised them a grand future, urging them to make Australia, whatever its drawbacks, their home. Sidney led his nephews by example. His growing prosperity had opened many doors and Sidney was a novel feature of Melbourne's business circles. He diligently entertained business and political leaders. Would-be prime minister Robert Menzies was an occasional visitor. Some years later he would liken Sidney to a warm-hearted fifteen-year-old, noting patronisingly that Sidney's outstanding characteristic was 'simplicity'.[13]

At home with Nance, Sidney had little scope for warm-heartedness. To those who had known him in Bendigo he was gregarious and extroverted; in Melbourne he established only a small circle of loyal friends. For the few guests that came to the home of Mr and Mrs Myer, it was difficult to ignore the frequent barbed comments made by Nance to her husband across the dinner table.[14]

The worse the marriage became, the more successful the store. Here Sidney could give rein to an exacting despotism and with energy, brilliance and mercurial temper he dictated every detail of the business.[15] In 1914, a mere three years after his move to Melbourne, a new and more grandiose Myer Emporium opened. It was based on noted emporiums in San Francisco. The chic epitome of the modern department store, it included a luncheon hall, bargain basement, rooftop garden and the most expensive and the cheapest of a variety of goods from clothes to carpets. The new Myer store was a commercial centrepiece for a city revelling in its new-found modernity and sophistication. Even World War I did little to halt the growth of the business—the trademark Myer cut-price bargains guaranteed the store customers through the wartime austerity.

In his first twenty years in Australia Sidney had made a fortune. The doubters of Bendigo never predicted Simcha Baevski would one day employ a driver to chauffeur him to and from the office—now he need never walk the streets again. He enjoyed the luxuries his money could buy, and could satisfy a weakness for flashy cars and exotic art.

He also had some family to share his good fortune. His brother EB was working with him again, and his rather erratic nephew Norman was itching to become a fully fledged member of the business. But Sidney was still shunned by many conventional retailers, who continued to disparage his sales tactics and predicted his undercutting would lead to eventual ruin. By 1918 life was at a low ebb for this 'godless blow-in'; he had few close friends, his marriage had come to a grinding halt and tragically his promising and much loved nephew Samuel was killed in a motorcycle accident. Sidney's dynastic hopes now rested with his other nephew, the twenty-one-year-old Norman. But by the end of the year he engineered another seismic shift in his life.

Extravagant risk-taking was a mark of Sidney Myer's business and also of his personal life: he was falling in love with a woman who should have been beyond reach. Sidney was living alone after separating from Nance when he became smitten with a teenager from a well-connected family: Marjorie Merlyn Baillieu. The Baillieus were a prominent force in Melbourne. Leading light William (Big Bill) Baillieu was a giant in mining, stockbroking and banking. To the older-established Port Phillip pastoral families, the Baillieus were *nouveau riche* upstarts, but among the more relaxed business class, they were commercial and social leaders. Big Bill Baillieu, the family patriarch, had numerous siblings, fifteen in all, and eighteen-year-old Merlyn was his favourite niece.

Sidney had known Merlyn since she was a child. Her mother was one of his wealthy customers and would frequently invite the delightful Sidney and his nephews to spend the afternoon at her spacious St Kilda home. Some suspect Agnes, a widow, initially hoped Sidney might become her second husband. Certainly it was Agnes, not her teenage daughter, who first found Sidney appealing. But his eye was on Merlyn and ultimately she became captivated by her blue-eyed suitor.

Sidney was twenty-two years Merlyn's senior and many of her Baillieu relatives disapproved of the budding relationship for that reason alone. For some, any association between their lovely niece and a Russian Jew who dealt in handkerchiefs and undergarments was unthinkable.

However, Agnes Baillieu was a no-nonsense sort of woman. She was Sidney's greatest supporter, having warmed to his solicitous nature. The Baillieu family were well connected, but the widow Agnes only possessed a small portion of the family's wealth and did not hold with the elitist values of Melbourne's social set. She knew her daughter had certain charms: she was statuesque, but certainly no beauty. With their prosperity coming from Victoria's land and mineral booms, the Baillieus had emerged as an Anglo-Australian dynasty, which several generations later would continue to rank amongst the country's wealthiest and most influential families. When Agnes weighed up her daughter's options, the handsome Sidney was a good catch. He was considerate and loving—not to mention very wealthy. The fact that he was not only a Jew but also married were, to Agnes, mere obstacles to be overcome. For Sidney, the chance of personal happiness was now at last within reach. He was like a teenager in the first throes of love.

The newspaper gossip and innuendo surrounding this union barely concerned Sidney after his intolerable first marriage. But extricating himself from the vengeful Nance would be a trial, almost literally. In stuffy postwar Australia it was all but impossible to divorce. Under Victorian law, divorce was permitted only in cases where the applicant could prove 'matrimonial wrong-doing' such as cruelty, adultery or desertion.[16] The situation was further complicated for Sidney, for even if he obtained a divorce it would not be sanctioned under Jewish law.

Sidney looked to ways of bypassing the divorce laws. He was aware that the state of Nevada in the United States had some of the most relaxed divorce laws in the world. In Reno, Nevada, you could get a divorce after six months of residency; but the settlement would only be recognised in America. Ignoring protests from family and colleagues, Sidney risked everything by leaving Australia and heading to the United States.

His right-hand man at the Myer Emporium, Lee Neil, tried hard to dissuade him from this course. Neil wrote to Sidney urging him to forgo the partnership with Miss Baillieu. A devoted Christian and astute businessman, Lee Neil not only feared the wrath of God but also that of conservative customers outraged by such a liaison. The prospect of having to manage the retail empire with his visionary boss—who was now an American citizen—exiled must have been daunting for the strait-laced lieutenant.

Sidney had created a hornets' nest—which he attempted to calm by converting to Christianity. At the very least, this conversion pleased Merlyn and the couple hoped his baptism would pave the way for his eventual acceptance by the Baillieus, a family with strong ties to the Anglican Church. Sidney was baptised into the Christian faith by the charismatic minister, the Reverend Brewster Adams. Sidney's eldest son, Kenneth (Ken) Myer, would later remark that Sidney's baptism 'was a matter of convenience . . . rather than conviction'.[17] Like so many of Sidney's moves, this conversion was rooted in his assimilationist dreams. He wrote to his loyal nephew Norman, exhorting him to convert as well. Expediency dictated that the Myers should be Christians; from here on, their Jewish heritage was to play no more than a token historical role.

It was not an easy time for either Sidney or his young beloved. The estranged Nance refused to cooperate, even moving to New Zealand to avoid having to contest the divorce in court. Despite her recalcitrance, the matter was finalised under Nevada state law. The gossip columnists in *Punch, Table Talk* and *Truth* enjoyed the juicy spectacle and waded with gusto into 'the matrimonial affairs of a leading Melbourne commercial man', regaling their readership with as much detail as they could muster about the shocking liaison between a 'prominent businessman and a young debutante'. The papers were adamant that if the couple married they would be shunned by polite society. Other slanderous scuttlebutt claimed Sidney was only marrying Merlyn for her name and position. Sidney tried to ignore all the gossip and the dire warnings, although at times he worried that Merlyn's reputation would be permanently sullied if the union went ahead. Despite these misgivings, on 8 January 1920, Merlyn's twentieth birthday, they were married. The ceremony was conducted by Brewster Adams in The Palace, a discreet hotel in San Francisco. The wedding party was tiny; the couple's joy immense. On their wedding day the couple ignored Nance's threat to sue for bigamy if Sidney returned home.

Melbourne lapped up the tantalising details of the Myer marriage. The February edition of *Punch* reported:

> . . . *the much-talked of marriage of a well-known businessman was celebrated last Monday. Rumour runs that the first partner of his joys and sorrows refused to divorce him. At any rate he went off to America to obtain the necessary divorce at the divorce-making town, Reno. About the same time, a Melbourne woman bearing a well-known name and her daughter, also went over to America. After his Reno-made divorce had been granted, he married during the first week in January, the said daughter on her twentieth birthday. She is a pretty girl with a poetic name, is clever and charming. The many Melbourne friends and acquaintances are wondering and arguing about it all. The divorce is not legal outside the USA, therefore when they return here—as they must do for all his business interests are here—can he be prosecuted for bigamy? First wife is reported to be waiting for their return anxiously. Will they be received, if the second marriage is no marriage outside the USA!!!*[18]

In March 1920, two months after the wedding, Lee Neil, having reconciled himself to Sidney's foolhardiness, wrote advising the newlyweds to remain in America until the furore had dissipated. Neil warned his boss that if he returned he would be 'courting unenviable notoriety' which would be 'seriously injurious to our business'.[19] It was a sacrifice the couple made happily. Merlyn never complained about the price paid for marrying her Russian divorcee. But as one relative put it, Merlyn was now at the 'bottom of the social table, and no longer at the head'.[20]

The couple was to live in the United States for the next nine years. Only when Nance had remarried and Melbourne had new scandals to feast over could Sidney and his bride return to live permanently in Australia. However, life for Sidney and Merlyn was lavish. They enjoyed their second home in San

Francisco and their access to the best that money could buy. For Sidney, this racy metropolis was a welcome relief from the snobbish stuffiness of parochial Melbourne, with its old-world reverence for gentility and class hierarchy. Sidney's Russian-Jewish background didn't concern the business entrepreneurs in the United States; indeed, his ethnicity was positively embraced.

Sidney took advantage of the situation. He had long admired the emporiums in the United States and his Melbourne store was already modelled on emporiums in San Francisco. If Myers was to keep its commercial edge, it had to be one step ahead. Sidney was perfectly placed to follow the local trends and relay them back to Australia. The United States was not only modern in its divorce laws, it was also sophisticated in its fashions. From a distance Sidney could still give Melburnians what they wanted—the most comprehensive range of merchandise from around the world in one store.

Sidney's deputy Lee Neil ably managed the day-to-day operations of the business and precisely oversaw the translation of his boss's vision into practice. Like all good entrepreneurs and budding dynasts, Sidney Myer was an 'ideas man' and relied on a safe pair of administrative hands to make his vision a reality. Every few months a trepidatious Neil would await Sidney's visit to Melbourne. Like the King on a royal tour, Sidney would arrive brimming with boundless energy and enthusiasm, injecting new life into the store and expecting all his new ideas and strategies to be adopted immediately. During his tour the autocrat was to be found pacing the shop floor, rearranging stock, talking to customers, training staff. However, when this tornado of energy left once more, his loyal Chancellor most likely released a sigh of relief, happy to return to the details of his meticulous management. Between king and chancellor the Myer empire continued to flourish.

But, as with all ambitious patriarchs, Sidney was always restless for more. And expanding the business demanded a full-scale return to Australia. The trick would be to find a way to go home without any more details of his second marriage being publicly pored over. This was so successfully achieved that until the 1980s public accounts of Sidney's life rarely mentioned his first wife Nance and his subsequent United States divorce. According to Ken Myer, his father never mentioned his first wife and he only learnt of the marriage after Sidney's death. The years in America were casually explained away as Sidney having business interests and furthering his 'retailing education'.[21] Even today, some older members of the family appear uncomfortable with this history.

It was philanthropy that helped smooth the path back to Melbourne—it would spirit him home as surely as Dorothy's ruby slippers returned her from Oz to Kansas. In 1926 Sidney had been several months in Melbourne and during this time a long-running headline story was the financial crisis at the University of Melbourne. Sidney had just taken the step of making Myers a publicly listed company. Motivated by the example of American philanthropists such as Rockefeller and by the ideals of meritocracy, he now decided to give 25 000 fully paid Myer shares to the university, valued at the time at £50 000. No conditions were placed on how the university could use the money.

Over the years Sidney had spent liberally on newspaper advertising and now the papers, careful to maintain good relations with their wealthy client, reported his gift in detail. In the Melbourne papers Sidney was profiled as a great, civic-minded business leader, even though he was still living outside the country.

Lee Neil further encouraged his employer's philanthropy. Both men agreed it would set an example to other businesses, and as Myers made money from the community, the company should endeavour to give some back. These acts of social largesse were once again given prominence by the local newspapers. The much noted gifts lent Sidney a new respectability and to him it made good business sense. He felt the more successful his business could be, the more he could return the benefit to the community; and the more closely he bound himself to the community, the more his business would prosper.

By 1929 many other businesses were looking shaky. The Great Depression was looming in the United States, and what had been a golden way of life was losing its sheen. The couple decided that now was the time that they and their four children—Kenneth, Neilma, Sidney Baillieu (Bails) and Marigold—could and should return to Melbourne. The Myer family made their home, predictably enough, in establishment Toorak, where they were attended to by a staff of nannies, maids, butlers and a governess. Ken Myer would later joke that it was the family chauffeur, Harry, rather than his parents, who raised the Myer children.[22]

Given the ongoing success of the emporium and a relaxing of social attitudes, few snubbed the homecomers. They were welcomed at Melbourne society parties; Sidney lavished gifts on his adored wife, and indulged himself by buying flashy Cadillacs and adding to his Asian jade collection. Occasionally the family were reminded they weren't of the Melbourne establishment. Both Ken and Bails were refused membership of that bastion of conservatism, the Melbourne Club. On another occasion a young Marigold was quietly told by a member of the Baillieu family not to apply for membership to one of Melbourne's exclusive golf clubs, because as the daughter of a Jew she wouldn't be accepted.

Sidney, perhaps still worried that his family's status in polite society hung by a thread, was keen to establish his position as a leading and caring Melburnian. His first well-publicised benefaction on arriving in Melbourne was an £8000 gift to the children's hospital. But his most celebrated charitable endeavours were precipitated by the Great Depression.

The world's stockmarkets crashed in October 1929. Many businesses were shattered, but Myers was large enough and popular enough to weather the storm. By 1930 the unemployment rate had reached 20 per cent. Neither federal nor state governments provided any answers and largely relied on charities to look after the burgeoning ranks of the 'deserving poor'. More than every before, Melbourne was marvellous for some, desperate for others. The capitalist free-market bubble had burst and throughout the once bustling city, businesses were laying off workers. The slums were overflowing. Here people lived cheek by jowl in the neglected tenements; epidemics were frequent, food basic and work practically non-existent.

At the Myers store in Bourke Street, not a single person was laid off. Sidney took the unprecedented step of taking a cut in his own salary and persuaded all the staff to follow suit. He was disappointed by the general attitude in the business community that little could be done to stem the tide of recession. He remained a staunch free-market capitalist, believing the Depression could be defeated through private spending. According to grandson Stephen Shelmerdine a favourite saying of his was that 'It is the responsibility of capital to provide work; if it fails to do this it fails to justify itself'. He encouraged business and political leaders to spend. The same energy he had given to creating the Myer Emporium he now directed towards addressing the recession. He instituted a number of employment schemes (the building of the Yarra Boulevard round Como Park was one), and he also brought forward a rebuilding program for the store.

As Christmas 1930 drew desperately near, newspapers implored the wealthy to give generously to a Christmas appeal so that all children would have at least one toy. In Melbourne, charitable Christmas lunches for the poor and their families were an established tradition. As unemployment rose ever higher, it became a more earnest public gesture. In keeping with his flamboyant character, Sidney Myer decided to provide a lunch on a grand scale. While other charitable meals were held around the city, nothing could compare with the Christmas feast Sidney Myer laid on at the Exhibition Building. Unlike other charitable dinners or lunches, there was no committee behind this one—it was shaped and organised down to the last detail by the fastidious Sidney.

He 'invited' ten thousand unemployed men and their families for lunch. The actual number fed was closer to twelve thousand—at five enormous sittings stretching through the afternoon. Sidney was host and head waiter as well as diner. According to the *Argus* newspaper: Tables stretched in all directions within the building, and before each guest were laid plates of corned beef and ham, tomatoes, pickled onions, a slice of Christmas cake, two rolls, sliced peaches for dessert, apples, dixie cups to be filled with beer or soft drinks, and a packet of toffee.[23]

Throughout the day a Santa Claus sweltered in his red suit and beard as he entertained the crowds of children and each was given a gift. At the final sitting three thousand people came to the tables. Staff and family helped serve the tonnes of food, including Norman's young daughter Pamela. Rather wistfully, she still remembers it as a wonderful day, one that made her feel that she was part of something 'very special'.[24]

Sidney told news reporters these people were his guests, not the targets of his charity, and that it provided a boost to people experiencing extremely difficult times. There were photos and a cartoon of Sidney wearing a Santa Claus hat, carrying a Christmas pudding. Some of Melbourne's prim establishment must have smouldered to see the Jewish draper casting himself as a symbol of Christian goodwill.

Irate competitors declared him mad; others dismissed the lunch as a rather superficial self-aggrandising stunt. His daughter Marigold waves off any suggestion that her father's Christmas lunch was anything but a compassionate gesture as 'he genuinely wanted to help mankind'. Sidney's grandson Stephen Shelmerdine is devoted to his grandfather's memory and understands Sidney's philanthropy as 'a genuine expression of someone who had come from a deeply disadvantaged and a repressed background, realising that he had an opportunity and the privilege of being able to help others who were disadvantaged—and he was in one sense a soft touch for that sort of thing. He received thousands of letters from people wanting clothes and shoes in the Depression. He had people come to his house; they came to his door seeking simple acts of charity.'

Sidney Myer's acts of charity during the Depression years built his personal legend to new dimensions. To many Melburnians, he had become something of a hero. But he would have only four years left to enjoy his iconic status.

On 5 September 1934, Sidney told his driver Harry to meet him on Toorak Road as he needed a short walk. He'd had a bad night's sleep and felt weary. As he set off down the gravel drive of the family mansion, he felt a tightness across his chest. Moments later he collapsed, felled by a massive heart attack a few metres from his home. He was fifty-six.

Sidney Myer's position in the community was illustrated at his funeral the following day. Thousands of people quietly lined the 11-kilometre stretch as the funeral cortege wound its way through the streets of Melbourne from his home in Toorak to the Box Hill cemetery. Floral tributes filled eight cars—many from people Sidney had met while hawking goods back in those tough early years. Seven hundred people travelled by rail to the cemetery—three special trains had to be added for the day. They all wanted to pay their respects to this larger-than-life benevolent entrepreneur.

Sidney died a millionaire who held the controlling interest in Melbourne's largest department store and a civic hero. He now left it to his family to continue the business and the philanthropy. His wife and children were to be guided by the patriarch's will, signed on 3 June 1930. Typically patriarchs favour the eldest son, encouraging a smooth transition from father to heir. Sidney Myer, innovative to the end, favoured a more long-term collective approach, inviting his family to hold together for at least one generation. Sidney's will exerted his personality and influence well beyond the grave. Indeed, his four children's lives would be forever linked to their father's dreams and ambitions.

The patriarch gave twelve pages of detailed instructions to the executors of his estate. His widow and children only had rights to the income earned by the estate's assets during their lifetimes. The actual assets would be passed on to the grandchildren. This secured the family holdings for at least a generation. After payment of various monies to Merlyn and several contemporaries, Sidney Myer directed that a tenth of the residue should be used to fund a philanthropic trust, the Sidney Myer Charitable Trust; the remainder would then be divided into ten parts. Income from two parts went to Merlyn; their four children, Ken (thirteen), Neilma (twelve), Bails (eight) and Marigold (six) were to receive the income from one part each; and a half part each went to his brother EB and nephew Norman.

The remaining three parts were earmarked for Ken and Bails on condition that they were a part of Myer management before they turned thirty. Lured by this substantial legacy, both sons would later move into the family business.

The Myers are one of the few Australian families possessing both the wealth and the inclination to operate a family office, and it is from here that various Myer businesses and philanthropic organisations are based. Almost seventy years after Sidney Myer's death, his moral authority is manifest from the moment you enter the Myer Family Group office. His portrait, painted posthumously, hangs centre stage, between two windows that open panoramically to the towering business centre of modern-day Melbourne. He is the family icon, lending a virtuous command to his descendants. This dynastic office sits above bustling Collins Street, well removed from street level, at the choice end of two floors of a concrete and glass tower in the heart of the city's business district.

Much has been gained and lost in the years since Sidney's death. The family has undergone its own evolution—from strong patriarchal founder, through the sibling relations and rivalries of his offspring, and into third and fourth generations featuring an alliance of cousins and a more collective governance. Although the 'Store' still dominates a block on Bourke Stree, the great Myer Emporium is no longer the jewel in the family crown. The family has pulled back from the hands-on grit of the retail business, preferring the more dispassionate enterprise of investment. The family are now significant minority shareholders in what has become the biggest retail corporation in the country—Coles Myer Limited. Only one Myer, Sidney's grandson Martyn, has a place on that board. The loss of direct control of the Myer Emporium was a protracted and painful operation surrounded by bitterness and a sense of decline.

After Sidney's death, his nephew Norman became head of the business. Since leaving school both Sidney and Norman had assumed Norman would eventually succeed his uncle. The young Norman was a mix of joviality and devil-may-care insolence, often exasperating Lee Neil who had to supervise the young man's training while Sidney lived in the United States. On one occasion the headstrong Norman had every window of the Bourke Street store displaying a model with 'Nude' silk stockings. Lee Neil declared Norman's marketing stunts too crude and vulgar for Melbourne.[25] If the young Norman perhaps struck Neil as crass, his uncle was committed to having his de facto heir well placed in the company. In 1928 he ordered the thirty-year-old Norman to manage the newly acquired Myer store in Rundle Street, Adelaide.

The prince regent always did as directed by the retail king, looking to Sidney for guidance on the most important aspects of his life. He followed Sidney's direction and was baptised an Anglican, despite having no spiritual connection with the Christian Church. Sidney had drummed into his young nephew that their Russian Jewish background was of the past. They had to look to the future, and that future was Christian and Australian. Consequently, it was only after Norman's death that his daughter Pamela discovered her father was Russian and Jewish and that his mother—her grandmother—was still alive.

Around the time of Norman's Anglican baptism, Sidney encouraged his heir to woo a beautiful seventeen-year-old, barely out of school, even though Norman already had a fiancée. Five months later the twenty-three-year-old Norman married his new teenage sweetheart, the golden-haired Gladys. She became a regular feature in the glossy social pages; a wonderful 'clothes horse' and advertisement for Myer fashions.[26]

A short, rather pudgy man, Norman never had Sidney's charisma, but he did have the ambition and acumen to make his mark as a retail giant. His daughter Pamela calls him an egotistical genius; to others he was dictatorial. He copied Sidney's autocratic style but never had the endearing charm of the founder. Norman's approach was abrasive and at times ruthless. But during his reign the Myer Emporium was carried to new heights. Norman ran the Myer Emporium with obsessive energy and pragmatism and under his tenure the business underwent a tenfold increase in turnover. He decentralised the company and opened new stores in Adelaide, Brisbane, Geelong and Ballarat. By the time of his death in 1956 Myers was the fifth-largest store in the world.

Norman's family enjoyed living in fabulous opulence in exquisite homes, with a sizable domestic staff to pick up after them. But it came at a price. Norman was a distant husband and father to his three children Rodney, Pamela and Beresford—the Store was his passion. Gladys was left to amuse herself by spending money, which apparently she did.

Unlike Sidney, Norman didn't guarantee that all his offspring would continue to enjoy their accustomed privileges. A few years before he died, Norman Myer divorced Gladys and married a woman younger than his own daughter. This marriage produced two children and on his death Norman's second family became his main beneficiaries. For Norman's older children, in particular his daughter Pamela, the days of plenty were gone forever. Even Pamela's husband, the Honourable Simon Warrender, found his insurance services for Myer business interests terminated immediately after his father-in-law's death. The Warrenders are now the poor relations to Sidney's children and grandchildren. In a bitterly fought and very public 1970s court case, Pamela tried but failed to get a larger slice of her father's estate. One of the executors of Norman's estate was the man who replaced him at the Myer Emporium, Ken Myer.

With Norman's death it was time for Ken, Sidney's eldest son, to take his dynastic place as the head of the Myer business. The generational shift brought many changes. Under Norman's direction there were some sixteen Myers working in the company. This number immediately declined as an autocratic and nepotistic style was replaced by a corporate one. The Myer retail empire was beginning to discard the family connections.

Not that a complete separation between the family and the business could happen too rapidly. Sidney's sons, Ken and younger brother Bails, had little choice but to join the company. Their father's will had set this course, but neither Ken nor Bails had the bombastic style of his predecessor. Ken had many non-business interests in the arts and philanthropy. From the mid-1960s to mid-1970s he chaired the Myer board while leaving the day-to-day operations with the uncharismatic Kenneth Steele, a man dubbed 'Stainless' by his staff. The unconventional and beguiling Ken Myer usually caused ructions outside, rather than inside, the Myer business. He upset Melbourne's establishment when he signed a public letter supporting the Labor Party during the 1972 election campaign. His disapproving and conservative mother Dame Merlyn and brother Bails immediately fired off their own missiles by contacting the Liberal Party to declare their support.

Bails was always the more conventional of the two brothers and Sidney's second son moves naturally in Melbourne's establishment milieu. He has been known to play host to visiting British royalty and, on the surface at least, epitomises the society that once snubbed his Jewish father. For many years Bails was on the Myer board of directors, but found himself occasionally without executive function and free to run a variety of other corporate interests from a separate office. He was the Myer chair when the company accepted the takeover bid by Coles in 1985.

Ken and Bails entered the family business in their early twenties, both claiming they had retail 'in their blood'. But unlike their father and Uncle Norman, they were never passionate hands-on retailers. They had grown up knowing only the best life could offer; slogging away at the Store was neither necessary nor, perhaps, inviting. Like so many dynasts, Sidney's legacy cast a long and at times stifling shadow over his sons. They revered the memory of their father and knew they could never relive his unique greatness.

From the time of Norman's death in 1956 to the 1985 merger, Myers changed from a groundbreaking emporium to a labyrinthine corporate entity juggling reduced profits. In those thirty years Myer department stores had spread throughout Australian cities and their outer suburbs, along the way buying the down-market Target chain. As the tentacles of the retail octopus grew, the family's daily connection became more tenuous. By the 1980s there were only four members of the family working for Myers.

Typically the patriarch never considered his daughters to be fully fledged dynastic heirs like his sons. Neilma and her younger sister Marigold were not encouraged by Sidney's will to get involved in the business; the sisters watched from the sidelines as the Store left family hands. It's probably no coincidence that the 1985 Coles merger occurred a few years after Dame Merlyn Myer's death. Despite Myers being a publicly listed company since 1925, the family had always held approximately 20 per cent of the company's shares. With such a substantial minority holding, any merger would more or less depend on the family's blessing. Perhaps only with the death of the patriarch's wife—a woman who never remarried and revered the memory of her dead husband—could the family really opt out of the nitty-gritty of retail. Neilma is still convinced that it wouldn't have happened if her mother had been alive.[27] Merlyn would never have agreed to her children washing their hands of the retail empire her husband had created from nothing. Some in the family still cleave to the potent memory of a uniquely dynamic family enterprise. For others the loss of the Store was something of a relief—gone was the oppressive expectation that they should spend their lives immersed in the retail business.

However, the remaining members of this successful dynasty do not intend to walk away from the ideals of the founder.

After the patriarch has left the throne, a dynastic family can only hold together if they are able to claim a shared identity. Sidney's will secured family cooperation. With one of the founder's legacies, the Store, now gone, his ancestors want to ensure that the other legacy, philanthropy, goes from strength to strength. Myer blood is now apparently built on the DNA not of retail but of benevolence.

Three of Sidney's children, Bails, Neilma and Marigold, remain the income beneficiaries of his estate. The eldest brother, Ken, died in a plane crash in 1992. In the next twenty years the rest of the third generation, Sidney and Merlyn's grandchildren, are set to inherit the assets. When this happens, the Myer family will no longer be compelled to work together in either investment or philanthropy. Few want this to happen—many regard the advantages of sticking together as outweighing any drawbacks. They feel that for their dynasty to be enlivened they need philanthropy both as a link back to the founder and as a basis for future possibilities.

However, for the ever-expanding tribe to continue the patriarch's charitable legacy into the fourth generation, much work is needed. There are now more than eighty members of the family, covering the second, third and fourth generations—all of them, once they become adults, free to participate in the range of family business and philanthropic endeavours. It is a divergent group. Aside from the investment company, the Myers have created family structures to voice ideas and provide extra strength to the adhesive. There's the Family Council, a forum to discuss ideas and values, which can provide an ethical voice in discussions on investment.

And there's the Family Muster. Every two years the eighty or so family members hire a lodge and skilled advisers, and—in the words of Sidney's daughter Marigold—'go to the mountains or somewhere . . . and for three days we'll meet together to discuss all the issues that we as a family care about'. These Musters keep the family in touch and introduce the teenagers to the variety of things the family does. For the junior members, the Muster acts as something of a careers advisory service. The youngsters know they can turn to this kinship gathering for advice on setting up their own business or moving into the family enterprise. Through a variety of discussion groups and formal game-playing the older generations can also observe the talents and ambitions of the fourth generation.

What motivates the family to keep working together is quite simply money; the money that is tied up in Sidney's estate. As the most outspoken member of the family, Vallejo Gantner (Sidney's great-grandson), puts it: 'If money left tomorrow, I think a lot of the reasons for the idea of a Myer family wouldn't be there any more—and that's because philanthropy wouldn't be an option and the kind of way that the business structure is set up as a single business wouldn't be there. We've . . . constructed these frameworks around the idea that it is the family which is the Foundation, the business structure and the Family Council . . . and they buttress your sense of what it means to be in a family— and if the dollars that supported that weren't there, everyone would get on with their lives. I mean, I don't think anyone would be shattered.'[28] Whether they'd be shattered or not, the family works hard to keep these structures together—and to enhance the family wealth.

Unlike Vallejo, two members of the family, Lady Marigold Southey and her son Stephen Shelmerdine, can always be relied on to give smoother accounts of the family's history. Justifiably proud of their heritage, they never seem to tire of telling the well-known high points in Sidney's life: the 1930 Christmas lunch, the building of the Yarra Boulevard at Como Park, Sidney's revolutionary sales techniques. Like all powerful dynasties, the golden moments in the family's history are what's generally told and retold to both the family and to the public. The more unsettling or disruptive episodes, such as Sidney's first marriage or losing control of the family business, are usually glossed over. The 'official' family history is told as a selection of iconic vignettes, that also serve to reflect well on the dynasty and its current preoccupations.

Stephen and Marigold are well-chosen spokespeople for the Myers. Both are amicable and hold a genuine belief in the importance of philanthropy and therefore the family's significance. Sitting in the Myer meeting room, high above Collins Street, Stephen Shelmerdine comments that the family acts '. . . through this philanthropic foundation because we believe we should. Clearly there may be some who feel that it is purely self-serving or it's not addressing all the right issues at the right time . . . but we essentially believe that we've made most of the right decisions.' Stephen also expresses concern about the growing disparity between the haves and have-nots in Australia. He likens Australia's current polarisation with his grandfather's days; like Sidney, he believes business must be mindful of its civic and employment responsibilities.

Moments of cynicism about the Myer munificence tend to intrude when the lifestyles enjoyed by many of the family are observed. The Myers have grand houses, domestic staff, expensive cars, designer clothes and frequent overseas travel. It's not unknown for Myers to flit overseas merely to enjoy a birthday party in an unusual and exotic location. Those on the fringes of the family watch the lives led by some and mutter about the deadening hand of affluence. The commitment the second and third generation have to their working lives is variable. There are plenty of stories of Myers enjoying overseas sojourns (so-called 'sabbaticals') that last for months at a time.

On the other hand, Lady Marigold Southey stands as a good example of Myer altruism—although her good work often doesn't involve money, but time. Lady Southey, Sidney's youngest child, is now in her early seventies. A Collins Street farmer of Hereford bulls and vines, she is also chair of Philanthropy Australia and Victoria's lieutenant-governor. Her office is based in the mansion the family has owned since they returned from the United States in 1929, Cranlana. In these spacious surroundings, tended by a contingent of domestic and gardening staff, Marigold gets on with the business at hand. The position of lieutenant-governor suits her: she has a certain regal bearing and keeps a distance, preferring to be called Lady Southey rather than Marigold by all but her family and closest friends. Once in a while her voice can be heard snapping orders at her assistant, but the impatience is momentary.

Lady Southey's strength of character shines when she leaves the pleasant surrounding of Cranlana and climbs into a garish orange ambulance. Once a fortnight she swaps her immaculate clothes for a pale blue cotton dress and an ordinary red cardigan. This is her Red Cross uniform. For twenty-five years she has taken paralysed polio patient June Middleton out from her hospital bed for a day trip.

June can move only one finger. From the age of twenty she has lived in hospital. These outings are one of the most pleasurable aspects of her difficult life. Driving the cumbersome ambulance, Marigold takes June wherever she wants to go: to the sea, the shops, the park, or even to Cranlana—June loves the tranquil garden. On these days Marigold is at June's beck and call. She feeds her, keeps her comfortable, swats away flies, and chats. They usually go out and buy a Scratch Lotto ticket, hoping to win a few dollars. For a woman in her seventies it's a long and tiring day, but Lady Southey is June's friend and she believes she has a moral duty to give back to the less fortunate. The old-fashioned notion that 'from those to whom much is given, much is expected' still influences Lady Southey.

On a cold Friday morning in May 2001, the Myer Foundation is having one of its regular directors' meetings. Lady Marigold Southey is the chair, ever the responsible matriarch (the other matriarch, her elder sister Neilma, dislikes the formal and rather stuffy nature of Myer business, and frequently runs late for such meetings). The foundation was begun by Ken and Bails in 1958. Based on the Rockefeller Foundation in the United States, it has a loose brief to benefit humankind. Ken bequeathed a significant proportion of his estate to the foundation. Other foundation funds come from the member contributions (including dividend income) derived from the family investment company.

Lady Southey fastidiously checks the details and protocol of each document presented to her by CEO Charles Lane. Despite all the directors being related, these meetings are highly professional and corporate. A key difference between this and other business boards, of course, is that here no one can be sacked, a situation that at times must cause problems. Certainly there is no sense that this is a cosy informal family get-together.

These meetings approve or reject funding requests from a variety of nonprofit organisations. The approach is more structured than in Sidney's days—no whimsical gifts to pet projects—but there is a more informed sense of what can make a difference. There are several philanthropic trusts in family hands, all coming under the umbrella of the Myer Foundation, and each year the foundation donates between four and five million dollars to a vast assortment of social, cultural and environmental projects. Among many other causes, Myer money helps promote the environmental health of the Snowy River, funds a plethora of performance groups and youth employment schemes, gives assistance to the homeless and fosters an Aboriginal health service. A glance at the Myer Foundation Annual Report provides evidence of how seriously the family takes this work—and the usefulness of their donations. In a country where private and public social service is on the wane, the Myer family are justifiably proud of what they do.

Traditionally the Myers avoid projects that may be seen as too political or controversial. The family occupy a central place in Melbourne's social as well as business establishment. The days of sneering at one's Jewishness or retail origins have largely passed and have been replaced by a commercial pragmatism of which Sidney would have approved.

Three generations of Myers are seated at the table, aged from mid-twenties to late seventies. The one board director from the fourth generation, the G4, is Vallejo Gantner. Vallejo, a T-shirted, ebullient former law student, now an arts festival organiser, has been coming to meetings since he was at university, but his appointment as a director is relatively recent. He wants the G4 to 'shake up' the foundation; to inject it with a new commitment.

The Myers all want the foundation, unlike the Myer Emporium, to stay in family hands and they know this can only be achieved with the youngsters' energetic involvement.

The G4 have a certain street savviness. None has lived such well-tended lives as their grandparents. They were not raised in the care of countless butlers, nannies and maids as were Neilma, Marigold, Bails and Ken. Their youthful smartness could prevent the foundation from becoming too staid. For Vallejo, the eldest of the G4, it's philanthropy that will bind the family together well into the future. Business is a cutthroat game, and philanthropy allows the family to come together to share more noble concerns.

So Vallejo, working with Charles Lane, came up with the idea of the fourth generation having their own good works com-mittee looking after its own pot of money. The G4 committee operates within the foundation and introduces the generation to the foundation's activities. The committee is granted $100 000 a year to pump into projects they deem worthy and pressing. Both Charles and Vallejo want the G4 committee to draw its members into deep involvement in projects: '. . . not just signing a cheque and washing your hands of it . . . I guess hopefully we're setting the G4 up in a way that the members will actually love being part of a philanthropic thing for the rest of their lives.'

Vallejo talks effusively of his hope that the fourth generation will liven things up, will provide new approaches to shake up the long-established way the family has gone about its philanthropy. He is the perennial joker, the party boy. He doesn't fit the stereotype of the do-gooder. Avoiding both the businessman's suit or the plain clothes of most charity workers, he's more often bedecked in baggy pants and loud shirts that promote the boutique beer he's helped set up. Venture capitalist meets venture philanthropist. Like his great-grandfather, Vallejo has an energy, a rakish charm and a determination that add up to a formidable presence. Luckily for the Myers he is currently hustling for the family's future philanthropic endeavours.

Sitting at Vallejo's crowded kitchen table, far removed from the swish Myer offices, Vallejo and his younger brother Dash tend hangovers and discuss what it's like these days to be born into privilege. Unlike others born to wealth, they appreciate some of its benefits without adopting the full-tilt materialism their money could buy. Instead they choose relatively unassuming lifestyles. 'No one wants to be Donald Trump,' says Vallejo with a characteristic sweep of his hand. 'No one wants to be in *BRW* or any of that garbage. It's not what we're seeking to do.' However, Vallejo admits he has a financial security that provides him with a certain freedom. 'We're not given trust funds with millions of dollars. That doesn't happen in my family anyway, and so I don't have things that are against my name worth a lot of money . . . The money you might inherit you might not get until you're sixty, but it gives me the freedom to go out and do what I would like to do as an artist, and not have to worry as much as other people about my financial foundation.'

Dash is quieter than Vallejo and keen to distance himself from the rich kid tag. He doesn't exactly cry poor, but quibbles at the suggestion that he and his brother have lived privileged lives. By most criteria he has and he does, but along with the wealth Dash shares great-grandfather Sidney's sense of social responsibility. However, unlike the patriarch he has little interest in hoarding wealth; rather he believes the fourth generation have a responsibility to 'redirect that money . . . in a way that would be beneficial to the community or the environment or the social good . . . I don't see the money as being directly connected to me.' And Vallejo chips in with agreement: 'I don't have a personal connection to whatever the Myer family wealth is. It's not something I've earned and it's not something I've done anything for.'

The brothers share an education and a confidence typical of the wealthy, but it doesn't carry through into arrogance. They don't subscribe to the consumer trappings that others in their position have chosen. Instead, Vallejo and Dash articulate the ideals the family wants to instil in the upcoming Myers. They're born to wealth but not spoiled by it. The visit to the detox centre was part of their education into philanthropy and of the handing down of the family values.

By 7 pm the young Myers troop out of Simon Rose's consulting room. The five boys have seen and heard enough. The doctor still has to see a handful of people patiently sitting in the waiting room; he won't be out of the office until around nine. His total dedication to the centre and the addicts who seek his help has impressed the Myers. They leave feeling more informed, excited by the possibility that Myer money can help. They, with the other members of the G4, decide to give their first grant to the centre, providing a much-needed boost of £10 000.

The visit has been a success for First Step, and for the G4 as well. They've seen at first hand something of what their money can achieve, this family fortune established by a great-grandfather who arrived in Australia with threepence in his pocket. While most of the wealthy have a reluctance to part with any portion of their money, the Myers are conscious of their good fortune and the implications of a certain responsibility to those less fortunate.

Vallejo puffs animatedly on another cigarette before dashing off for a night out. 'I guess what I hope that we get out of the G4 committee in the foundation,' he says, 'in terms of how we end up as a family in twenty or thirty or forty years . . . is actually not really as a family at all, but a collection of individuals who are really committed to the same set of goals in terms of working and helping the community.'

High above the street, Simcha Baevski smiles from his gilt-edged frame. His store may be gone, but his dynasty is still bonded together by his altruism and an ironclad will. It is now up to the fourth generation to ensure the Myer legacy continues well into the twenty-first century.

THE MURDOCH FAMILY

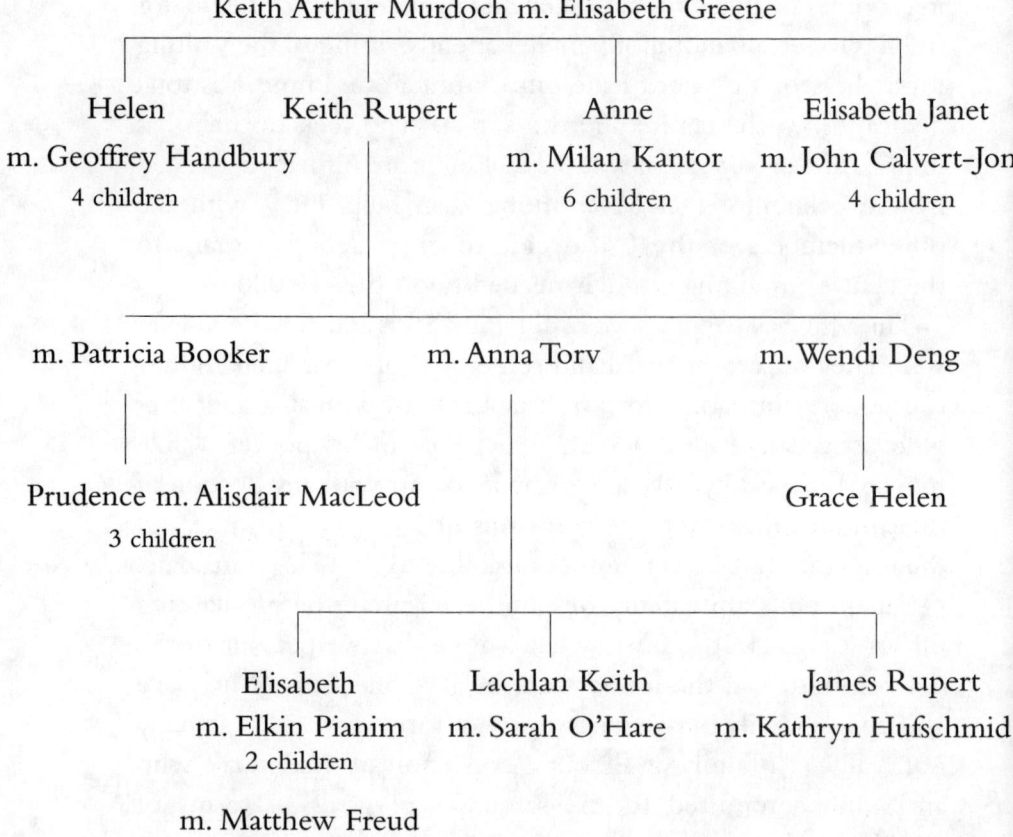

Keith Arthur Murdoch m. Elisabeth Greene

Helen   Keith Rupert   Anne   Elisabeth Janet

m. Geoffrey Handbury   m. Milan Kantor   m. John Calvert-Jon

4 children   6 children   4 children

m. Patricia Booker   m. Anna Torv   m. Wendi Deng

Prudence m. Alisdair MacLeod   Grace Helen

3 children

Elisabeth   Lachlan Keith   James Rupert

m. Elkin Pianim   m. Sarah O'Hare   m. Kathryn Hufschmid

2 children

m. Matthew Freud

1 child

A WINNING STREAK

THE MURDOCHS

THE year 2001 brought mixed blessings for seventy-year-old media tycoon Rupert Murdoch. On the one hand, he was back to his usual rude health with his prostate cancer in remission and his beloved new wife Wendi gave birth to his fifth child, and her first—a dark-haired baby girl, Grace Helen. On the other hand, he had ultimately failed in his biggest business deal that aimed to combine his satellite television operations with the largest United States satellite broadcaster, DirecTV. If it had succeeded, Murdoch would have created the world's first satellite service covering Asia, the Americas and Europe. It was a bitter loss.

This business setback came hot on the heels of a more personal problem. In August Rupert's ex-wife Anna went to the press to declare him, in effect, a liar and an adulterer. Her public allegations about her ex-husband's infidelity revealed cracks in a family that has always been proud of its unity and discretion.

For more than thirty years the coolly blonde Anna Murdoch and her craggy, powerful husband appeared perfectly suited, both immersed in the sober corporate existence of Rupert's making. She supported his every move as he skilfully built his business empire, News Corporation. Although this corporation is a public company, the family has a controlling interest of 30 per cent, and Rupert has made it a dynastic organisation with the strategic placement of his sons, a daughter and a son-in-law.

While her husband was building his kingdom Anna had enjoyed a sumptuous lifestyle, the price for which was loneliness. Former Murdoch butler Philip Townsend recalls Anna spending many evenings sitting alone in the study at their London home, eating dinner off a tray while Rupert held a business meeting-cum-dinner upstairs. When she tried to launch a separate life for herself as a novelist, her husband offered no support and would roundly criticise her admittedly rather florid prose. But she continued her career and always defended her husband in public. In early 1998 Anna opened a new movie lot at Twentieth Century-Fox headquarters in Los Angeles. The entrance to this lot was dominated by a wood-and-metal sculpture featuring Rupert's thumbprint.

Anna had grown used to Rupert's fingerprints over her life. Loyal but not subservient, she implored her husband to spend more time with her. But Rupert wouldn't oblige. The couple's domestic and dynastic uncertainties emerged in April 1998 when Rupert and Anna Murdoch officially separated. Friends and family were stunned by the split, which was considered a bolt from the blue. The official News Corporation line was that they had merely grown apart. The word was that Anna had tired of her peripatetic husband refusing to countenance retirement. Investors were also perturbed and News Corporation's share price fell; apparently the markets had approved of the media king's stable marriage. In the eyes of the traders, domestic uncertainty morphed into corporate weakness.

Their 'amicable' split turned more acrimonious when Anna was removed from the News Corporation board by Rupert six months later. Divorce proceedings dragged on as their lawyers wrangled over the detail of the settlement, including the inheritance for their children, Elisabeth, Lachlan and James, and Prudence, Rupert's daughter by his first marriage.

In June 1999, seventeen days after his second marriage came

to a sorry end, Rupert Murdoch married Wendi Deng, a woman less than half his age, aboard his luxurious yacht *Morning Glory* in New York harbour. Anna quickly married another bil- lionare, William Mann and moved to a $5 million mansion in the Hamptons, America's aristocratic heartland on Long Island.

For three years afterwards she said nothing, but Anna finally broke her silence via a Kerry Packer publication. She claimed that the marriage had failed because of Rupert's infidelity with Wendi. She told the *Australian Women's Weekly*: 'I think that Rupert's affair with Wendi Deng—it's not an original plot—was the end of the marriage. His determination to continue with that. I thought we had a wonderfully happy marriage. Obviously we didn't.'

Anna, a devout Catholic who secured a papal knighthood for Rupert just months before their separation, wanted to hold onto the marriage, but said her husband was 'determined that he was going through with this no matter what I wanted or what I was trying to do to save the marriage . . . I believe you take a vow to be loyal to someone and look after someone all your life and you try hard to stick to that.'[1]

When Anna dropped her bombshell, her ex-husband did what he always does when faced with bad publicity—ignored it. Rupert Murdoch has spent fifty years glossing over unpleasant- ness of any kind, preferring to attribute criticism to people's 'jealousy'. Rupert Murdoch would never get into a public slanging match with his ex-wife. He might have made millions from his sensationalist tabloids, but has no desire to appear in salacious headlines himself. When asked about Anna going public with these allegations, Rupert replied, 'Yeah, right, well, these things happen,' and denied he was seeing Wendi before the end of his marriage to Anna, claiming, 'that really developed later'.[2]

Rupert revealed no animosity towards his ex-wife. In 2001 he and his third wife Wendi looked forward to the birth of their child. The couple already knew it would be a girl and were determined that she would grow up bilingual, speaking both her mother's tongue, Mandarin, and English.

When news of Wendi's pregnancy was first revealed, Murdoch observers were astonished. Aside from the fact that Rupert was in his seventies and just recovering from radiation treatment for prostate cancer, the birth of this fifth child increased dynastic speculation even further. After all, the patriarch had spent years grooming his children to succeed him. Adding another child from a new relationship to this dynastic mix transformed Murdoch's once stable personal life into something of a B-grade soap opera.

Anna claims the divorce agreement with her ex-husband stipulates that the future successor to the company cannot be Wendi or her children. She remains bleak about the inevitable succession problems. 'I'd like none of them to [succeed Rupert]. I think they're all so good that they could do whatever they wanted, really. But I think there's going to be a lot of heartbreak and hardship with this [succession]. There's been such a lot of pressure that they needn't have had at their age.'

Rupert's business acumen has guaranteed that each of his five children will be extraordinarily wealthy. According to Anna, her children have financial trusts that cannot be broken. But the ultimate prize is not the money; it's the corporation. Who will be the chosen one, the successor to a family enterprise begun by grandfather Sir Keith Murdoch and built by father Rupert? Two of Rupert's grown children, sons James and Lachlan, are already competing for pride of place in the family firm. Rupert has said, 'They are running against each other and I'm too weak to say it's you and not you. In fact they are enormously close.' For several years eldest son Lachlan was regarded by his father as 'first among equals', but to date Lachlan has failed to impress the markets as the rightful prince regent to his father's throne. When Lachlan was appointed deputy chief operating officer, placing him in the inner circle of Rupert's executive team, News Corporation's share price fell.

But the uncertainty surrounding this succession rests with Rupert. For fifty years he has been at the corporation's apex, making all the crucial business decisions. News Corporation is a global media giant because in business Rupert is both an astute gambler and a visionary. He can take full credit for the remarkable expansion of News Corporation, but this growth has weakened the Murdochs' shareholding in the company. Rupert has also had to forge business alliances outside the family. As he enters his eighth decade he won't put down the chips and leave the roulette table. He has become both the best and worst of patriarchs.

Rupert may be betting that, as in the past, difficulties will eventually disappear. Throughout his life, his determined gambles have paid off, and generally the Murdochs have been blessed with a long-term winning streak. For three generations Lady Luck has smiled on the dynasty, placing them in the position they enjoy today. From the family's provincial roots in the Melbourne gentility, the Murdoch dynasty is now amongst the world's most powerful families. No other Australian dynasty has come so far. Why should that change?

On any given day you will find Rupert's indomitable mother, Dame Elisabeth Murdoch, sitting by an enormous fireplace checking her busy schedule. Dame Elisabeth is the grande dame of Melbourne society, well known for her generous financial gifts to art galleries, medical research and hospitals. Much of this charitable money is from her News Corporation dividends. Dame Elisabeth is in her nineties, a tiny, delicate woman with a warm smile and a bright conversational tone. She is almost universally admired and loved. But underneath the chirpy demeanour Rupert Murdoch's mother is of firm character.

For a woman of more than ninety, she is certainly physically tough. The flickering blaze in her fireplace produces the only heat in her coolly formal 1930s residence at Cruden Farm, her commodious home and 36-hectare farm that gives refuge from the bland red-brick suburbia of Langwarrin—southeast of Melbourne. Dame Elisabeth continues to be endearingly frugal despite her extraordinary wealth. She has refused to put heating in her chilly home and the windows are still framed by seventy-year-old fraying curtains. She eschews taxis and is known for hopping onto London double-decker buses when she visits the United Kingdom. She continues to drive an old Peugeot. Frugality is a trait shared by her son Rupert. He doesn't spend money on fleets of luxurious cars and is reported to have expensive items of clothing replicated by the dozen, using cheaper fabrics and sewn by Hong Kong tailors.

Dame Elisabeth knows she has lived a fortunate life, thanks to a combination of her determined optimism and luck. She says in recent years two events have cast a shadow over her life. One was the untimely and terrible death of a grandson; the other, Rupert and Anna's divorce.[4] She, like everyone else, was taken completely by surprise when her son and his second wife separated. But regardless of her personal opinions she has long given up offering any advice to her strong-willed son—like him, she doesn't dwell on the unfortunate, but moves on.

Seated in a comfortable armchair by the fire, Dame Elisabeth speaks with gratitude of her good fortune. Born in 1909, the daughter of an improvident gambler, she has taken few chances herself, but has nevertheless been dealt a hand of aces. She recalls two events that laid the foundations for her long and lucky life: her meeting with newspaper baron Keith Murdoch and her father's escape from a pecuniary disaster in 1914.

As Australia stood on the brink of World War I, Elisabeth's suburban Melbourne family found itself under a more immediate siege. Her father, Rupert Greene, a compulsive gambler and chronic drinker, had once again lost the family's money betting on the horses and at the card table. It was far from the first time this had happened. The Greene family's wealth had always been precariously placed, but this time the debts were more serious and the creditors less inclined to be patient.

For years Rupert Greene, an all-round sportsman, had been regarded by Edwardian Melbourne society as debonair and charming. He held a senior position as a wool expert for the New Zealand Loan and Mercantile Agency, which supported his wife Bairnie, three young children and domestic staff in a modest Toorak villa. In the Collins Street gentlemen's clubs—the sedate Melbourne and the more raucous Boomerang—the pipe-smoking Rupert was regularly seen drinking, playing cards and having a wager on the horses. At the Boomerang enormous wagers of £100 on the result of a horse race were not uncommon. Rupert's port-filled gambling evenings often stretched into the wee small hours. Occasionally his youngest and favourite daughter Elisabeth would call the head porter to see if her father was still there. Once he received the message, Rupert would go home.[5]

His belated homecomings were occasionally difficult. A drinker and gambler at the clubs, Rupert was a disciplinarian at home and in the office. At his workplace he was known as 'the martinet'. At home with the port wearing off, his affability could disappear rapidly. Behind closed doors the head of the house could be heard raging at his dignified and stoic wife Bairnie. These rages could erupt even when he was sober. Rupert once told Elisabeth that he would chop up her mother and place her in a black box in the garden.[6] Despite these vicious verbal attacks, his wife had little choice but to stay with him—divorce was almost impossible. So Bairnie did her best to maintain at least the semblance of gentility and decorum.

In 1914, when his world was ready to crumble beneath the weight of his debt, Rupert Greene's friends came to his rescue. They didn't give him money but used their influence to secure him a position as official starter for the Victorian Racing Club. The starter was forbidden to bet on the horses he flagged away—imposing on Rupert a degree of restraint. The squandering of the family earnings was thus significantly reduced and Greene could pay his irate creditors. Remarkably, he continued to display responsibility and diligence in the job, which he held for thirty years, saving the family from disaster. Elisabeth bears no grudges towards her father; rather she is his greatest apologist. She likes to chuckle over his erratic behaviour and remember the good times—such as his demanding that she perform gymnastic tricks for admiring visitors—rather than speak of his shortcomings.

In the same year that Elisabeth Greene's father was brought back from the brink, another Melbourne man was putting his own plans into action. Keith Murdoch was twenty-eight years old and suffering from a stutter. In 1914 his life was being shaped by two opposing traits—shyness and ambition. Despite his debilitating reserve, Keith Murdoch had set out relentlessly in pursuit of his media aspirations, once writing to his parents that he hoped '. . . with health [to become] a power in Australia'. At first disappointed when their son informed them that journalism and not the Church was his calling, his Scottish Presbyterian parents watched with some amazement as their son's ambition bore fruit. His aspirations were realised thanks to World War I.

When the war broke out, Keith Murdoch applied for the position of Australia's official war correspondent. He was pipped at the post by the respected journalist CEW Bean. Nonetheless the tenacious Murdoch found his way into the war. After losing out to Bean, he was appointed London editor to a minor news agency. Using this appointment, Keith then approached the prime minister, family friend Andrew Fisher, for permission to stop in Cairo en route to London. He told Fisher he wanted to investigate complaints made by Australian troops in Eygpt about delays in receiving their mail. Keith Murdoch arrived in Egypt in August 1915, four months after two divisions of Australian and New Zealand soldiers had landed on the treacherous shores of Gallipoli.

When Keith arrived in Cairo he wrote to the British commander-in-chief of the Dardanelles campaign, General Sir Ian Hamilton, asking permission to visit what Keith referred to as 'the sacred shores of Gallipoli'.[7] Hamilton agreed on the proviso that Murdoch observe the usual censorship regulations. During his week-long stay on the peninsula Keith spent most of his waking hours in the press camp. In between penning his dispatches he befriended an alcoholic war correspondent from the British *Telegraph*, Ellis Ashmead-Bartlett. His stories, highly critical of the conduct of the Dardanelles campaign, influenced Keith who agreed to take an uncensored letter from Ashmead-Bartlett and deliver it to the British prime minister, Herbert Asquith.

On his journey to London, Keith was caught with Ashmead-Bartlett's letter by a British intelligence officer who confiscated it. In his anger Keith then wrote an 8000-word tirade to the Australian prime minister. In it he described in highly coloured language the daily dangers befalling the gallant Anzac troops. 'It is stirring to see them, magnificent manhood, swinging their fine limbs as they walk about. They have the noble faces of men who have endured.' In contrast he depicted the British troops as '. . . without strength to endure or brains to improve their condition'. His most vicious phrases were reserved for the British command, including Hamilton whom he accused of 'murder through incapacity'.[8] The letter dramatically overstated casualties by around 40 per cent and stated without proof that the upper-class British officers shot injured men who were lagging behind.

The dispatch was seized by censors but eventually reached Prime Minister Fisher. Under pressure from the British Cabinet, Murdoch then sent a copy of the letter to Prime Minister Asquith. Despite, or because of, the misleading hyperbole, his correspondence had an extraordinary impact and General Hamilton was recalled from the Dardanelles. Three months later, when the Allies realised invasion was impossible, the Australian troops were withdrawn altogether.

The controversy proved to be the most significant piece of luck for the progenitor of the Murdoch fortunes, Keith Murdoch had witnessed the power of sensational prose and bold assertions. It was a lesson he would later teach his son Rupert. Many years later his son financed the highly romanticised and successful film *Gallipoli*.

In Britain, Keith's correspondence gained a notoriety that he used adroitly to promote his career. He spent the remainder of the war in London, establishing himself at the centre of imperial power. He became the de facto representative of the new Australian prime minister, Billy Hughes, and a close friend of Fleet Street media baron Lord Northcliffe. The latter, who had long opposed the Dardanelles campaign, took Keith under his wing and set about promoting the enterprising young colonial.

With the end of the war Keith reluctantly returned to parochial Melbourne. The board of the media group the Melbourne *Herald and Weekly Times* (HWT) couldn't fail to notice the return of Lord Northcliffe's protégé. They offered him the position of editor of their evening paper, the *Herald*. Northcliffe urged him to take the position.

In his first few months at the helm, Murdoch turned the tired paper around. His 'bible' was the written advice of Lord Northcliffe. He would send copies of the papers to the UK publisher, seeking counsel about ways to grab readers and boost circulation. Northcliffe's directives were to improve layout, increase pictures (especially those showing action), to 'exploit' sport and run a women's page every day.[9] Keith was lampooned for being so closely tied to Lord Northcliffe's vision of a paper and was dubbed 'Lord Southcliffe'. But Northcliffe's advice was sound, and the fusty *Herald* was transformed into a populist and popular publication with its circulation skyrocketing.

While he took a tabloid approach to newspapers, Keith was a stickler for staff keeping up appearances. He insisted on journalists wearing business dress, and was apparently suspicious of men sporting beards. To some colleagues Murdoch's mission was no more than the 'acquisition of money, possessions, position and power'.[10] To others he was generous and genial.

By 1926 Keith was on the board of directors and worked as editor and empire builder. The management of the HWT were impressed by Keith's radical vision for the company. He advocated the fiscal benefits of a national chain of newspapers and magazines and steadily sought out publications for the HWT to purchase in all Australian states. In 1928 he was appointed the company's managing director and the following year became the first newspaper publisher to enter broadcasting. Under his management the HWT could claim to be the most important media organisation in the country and Keith Murdoch its most influential newspaperman. He was a king-maker and confidant to leaders in both Australia and Britain.[11] He also made many enemies, with the Labor paper *Smith's Weekly* referring to him as the 'would-be press and radio dictator'.

In his twenties, Keith had enjoyed friendships on both sides of politics; however, in his middle age he had solidified into a trenchant conservative. Many in the Labor Party despised his politics and roundly accused him of using his papers to proselytise for dry conservatism. Years later the same charge would be routinely levelled at his son. Both father and son would dismiss such criticisms.

The forty-two-year-old Murdoch was still shy, sombre and thickset—his demeanour more avuncular than dashing. In his staid South Yarra mansion he was surrounded by antique furniture, fine art and silver and tended to by his household staff. Nevertheless, this successful *arriviste* wanted a family and an heir for his successes. He had been engaged once, but this relationship had recently ended. It was then he saw a photograph of debutante Elisabeth Greene.

By now Elisabeth was a petite eighteen-year-old. While Keith Murdoch was establishing himself as a 'power in Australia' young Elisabeth had been growing up. Despite her father's 1914 rescue, the family lived on a limited budget and were regularly forced to let their Toorak villa and rent in down-market accommodation. However, Elisabeth's mother Bairnie refused to slide down Melbourne's social ladder. Elisabeth's father grumbled, but her mother was adamant her youngest daughter should at least go to an elite secondary school. Once again Lady Luck played her part when Elisabeth's godfather secured this education by offering to pay her fees. So at the age of twelve the tomboyish Elisabeth attended one of Victoria's best and most unconventional boarding schools, Clyde.

Set in the foothills of Mt Macedon, this spartan school—there was little heating and often no warm water—gave its girls some education and the prerequisite amount of social skills. Elisabeth never matriculated. By her own admission she had no academic ambitions but had a great many friends and 'went to parties, played hockey . . .' She adds with insouciant glee, 'It sounds terribly useless.' The Clyde education provided all that the aspiring Bairnie had wanted for her daughter: Elisabeth was equipped with the necessary social requirements for a 'good' marriage.

In 1927, eighteen-year-old Elisabeth Greene 'came out' at a Melbourne society party attended by the Duchess of York (later to become Queen Mother and a friend of Dame Elisabeth's). A rather severe photograph of the young Elisabeth was published in *Table Talk*, a gossipy paper managed by newspaper baron Keith Murdoch. It was this rather chaste image that the middle-aged bachelor noticed. Keith was struck by Miss Greene's looks and sought an opportunity to meet the young woman. He called one of Melbourne's society matrons to inform her that he could, after all, attend a Red Cross charity ball—and could she then please introduce him to Miss Elisabeth Greene.

At the ball, Elisabeth Greene was enchanted by her new admirer. To this teenager fresh out of school, Keith was urbane and charming, although too shy to ask her to dance. The following day he telephoned, and Elisabeth risked her parents' wrath when she sped off with Keith in his expensive Sunbeam sports car to the Victorian coastal town of Portsea. Elisabeth's mother Bairnie was horrified—no respectable girl should be out with a man unchaperoned. But despite Bairnie's initial reservations, the relationship blossomed.

In the straitlaced upper reaches of Melbourne society, their engagement made tongues wag. The couple were snubbed by some long-time acquaintances, including the overbearing Dame Nellie Melba, who didn't approve of Keith's youthful choice. Elisabeth's friends worried that she was seeing a man old enough to be her father. Her godfather even threatened to cut her out of his will if she continued with the relationship.

Her father's reaction was perhaps the most sanguine: when Keith asked Rupert Greene for the hand of his favourite daughter, Greene's reply was: 'Well, Murdoch, I suppose you can keep her.'

With the match provoking obvious disapproval from some quarters, Elisabeth insisted on a simple and small wedding; she wore her sister's dress. On the appointed day in June 1928 the couple's happiness was toasted over afternoon tea at her parents' Toorak home. The most extravagant gift for the newlyweds was from Keith himself. He presented Elisabeth with Cruden Farm—named after Cruden Bay in Scotland near where Keith's father had been the Presbyterian minister.

Elisabeth never regretted her marriage; in her words it was 'quite wonderful'. Keith enjoyed living on the grandest scale and introduced his adaptable young wife to his sumptuous lifestyle. She enjoyed the position this wealth accorded but never adopted Keith's more lavish extravagances. Nevertheless their country seat was quickly transformed from a simple villa to an Alabama-style mansion, and the South Yarra town house was later replaced by Heathfield, a palatial home in Toorak.

With what she calls 'the arrogance of youth', Elisabeth took immediate charge of the houses, sacking one male staff member as early as her honeymoon. To her ten or so house staff 'Milady' was firm, even stern. Today Elisabeth muses on the feudal quality to these arrangements, but believes the staff were content, pointing out that many stayed for years. In Toorak and at Cruden Farm the Murdochs formally entertained a vast array of business and political leaders. Keith and Elisabeth, in their grand homes and with their well-disciplined staff, sat comfortably within the high walls of Victoria's moneyed class.

In 1929 Elisabeth gave birth to their first daughter, Helen. Two years later on 11 March 1931 the son and heir, Keith Rupert, entered the world. Two more daughters, Anne and Janet, completed the family. Janet now jokes that she was meant to be the second boy in the family, but 'there wasn't room for two' because Rupert would always 'have won'.[12]

Their mother was a commanding figure in her children's lives and when both parents were with them, an air of formality prevailed. As friend and neighbour Joan Lindsay once observed: 'The Murdochs out riding on Sunday mornings made an unforgettable spectacle—a sort of medieval cavalcade of children, servants, outriders, horses and dogs . . . At the head rides Keith, mounted on a massive charger, an upright rather heavily built figure immaculate in English tweed and riding boots.'[13]

Elisabeth says she was the loving disciplinarian to her four children. 'I think children must know what your thoughts are and what the rules are and they must obey them.' The children were expected to carry out household chores and earn pocket money. She had inherited her father's martinet approach to child rearing. She once threw her five-year-old son into the pool on board a luxury liner. No one was allowed to rescue him and the screaming Rupert was forced to dogpaddle to the other side. All the while the pool water moved up and down as the liner pitched. At least the lad had learned to swim.

Rupert was a gregarious little boy, all smiles and blond curls. From a young age he cheerfully displayed an irreverent disregard for authority. His nanny, governess and sisters were regular targets for pranks—dead snakes in the bed being one favourite. Sir Keith worried that his young heir had inherited a little too much from his maternal grandfather. The regular visits by the ageing Rupert Greene were a reminder of the family's apprehensions. 'Pop' Greene was adored by his grandchildren, and perhaps sensing Keith's disapproval, he would encourage their disobedience. He would let them puff on his pipe or drive his car despite their feet not reaching the pedals. Helen once drove through a neighbour's fence as she tried to steer Pop's car.

Elisabeth still feels that her son was rather an ordinary little boy. To her, little Rupert's most outstanding characteristic was a lack of imagination. 'He only liked things that worked and I think that is something that is perhaps quite significant: he is motivated by this desire to make things work.' A house guest once remarked to Elisabeth that her then four-year-old son had something tremendous in him and would go on to be more successful than his father. Elisabeth was not amused at such impertinence, but nonetheless both parents hoped he would be a worthy heir. As she says now, 'We only had one possibility'— Rupert.

The four children lived a sheltered existence, enjoying the freedom to play in their lavish Toorak gardens or to roam the fields at Cruden Farm or their grazing property near Gundagai in New South Wales. They would ride thoroughbred horses, play tennis and cricket and hunt the rabbits that burrowed under the Gundagai farm. Janet remembers a childhood of pure happiness surrounded by indulgent grandparents, ponies, beach holidays, picnics and games.

From childhood Rupert Murdoch was eager to grab entrepreneurial opportunities. The oft-told family stories involve Rupert railroading his sisters into either collecting manure to sell, or catching rabbits. Older sister Helen was given the unpleasant task of skinning them. Rupert would pay her one penny a skin, then sell them for sixpence each. The profit thus gained would then be spent gambling when he got back to boarding school. According to Janet, her brother always knew the value of money. 'I can remember he could not resist telling people how much their Christmas presents had cost him and would tease us and put it in such a way as to not quite tell us but let us know that he had been very generous and spent two-and-sixpence.'

Although sometimes slow to show affection Sir Keith drew great support from his young family.[14] Despite his position Sir Keith still felt some insecurities. Early in his career, before World War I, he believed he was snubbed by the British media establishment. In Melbourne Keith was only too aware that the snobbish Victorian squattocracy regarded him as a tedious *arriviste*. He also distrusted the motives of some of his HWT colleagues. In his own mind he would turn this disadvantage into an advantage. Sir Keith argued to his son that social networks compromised your newspaper business, and impressed upon Rupert the importance of a media scion to stand apart from any elite. Rupert took his father's words to heart.

The young Rupert wanted to please his father, but it was difficult. Sir Keith could be indulgent but was quick to criticise and slow to praise his son. Some of Sir Keith's associates thought the boy feared his father.

By nature Rupert was a loner who favoured rebelliousness over conformity. He spent eight years at Geelong Grammar. His mother insisted he attend this establishment boarding school perched on Corio Bay with the Antarctic wind whistling along its corridors. Geelong spelt the end of Rupert's golden childhood. He made few friends and was a target for bullying. Some pupils from pastoral dynasties made it known that their families considered Sir Keith a *parvenu* whose business of media was rather less than savoury. The angelic-looking boy with the wide smile was lampooned as being both a bullshit artist (Bullo Murdoch) and a communist (Commo Murdoch).

At Geelong not even sport could save him. Never a team player, Rupert delighted in winning but had no wish to share the glory. His mother recalls him doing acrobatics while supposedly fielding for the school cricket team. On a Saturday, he would frequently disappear for a flutter at the Geelong races. Rupert was not an academic and he bided his time, waiting for the day when he could enter the world his father was carving out for him.

Rupert had inherited his maternal grandfather's gambling streak, but also his father's media ambitions. Sir Keith would sometimes take his heir apparent around the *Herald* offices. The boy enjoyed the buzz in the office, the noise of the printing presses, the smell of the ink, the power it accorded his father. At home Sir Keith would take any opportunity to talk earnestly to his son about the business, newspapers and Rupert's future.

Elisabeth herself sometimes wondered if her husband expected too much too soon from Rupert. To his wife, Keith explained his anxious belief that he was living on borrowed time and had only a short while left to mentor his son. Unfortunately Sir Keith's bleakness was well founded. He had suffered from ill-health for many years. In 1934 his position at the HWT group was jeopardised first by a heart attack and then by an attempt by its board to move him aside. He survived both events—the boardroom coup by a single vote—but more than a decade later and now in his sixties, he suffered from a litany of ailments, most seriously heart complaints and bowel cancer.

Sir Keith's other concern was the family inheritance. By the late 1940s he was still the most influential newspaperman in Australia—but he had spent his life as a manager, not a working proprietor. He was chair of the HWT group but was not a major shareholder. Over the years Keith had become dissatisfied and faintly bitter at the remuneration from the group. He knew he needed to increase his shareholdings in newspaper companies. In a series of swift and slick moves Sir Keith bought a 48 per cent share in News Limited (an Adelaide company) for what some regard as a fraction of its real worth and placed this in the family firm, Cruden Investments.[15]

Along with building up the family media shares, Sir Keith put his energies into getting his 'wild' son to shape up. In 1950 as spring beckoned, he travelled with Rupert to help him settle in at Worcester College, Oxford. In the United Kingdom, Sir Keith introduced the nineteen-year-old to the *Herald*'s London correspondent, Rohan Rivett. The Rivetts looked after Rupert, trying to hide his fondness for racing and gambling from his parents. Rohan was impressed by the Murdoch heir, writing to Sir Keith in praise of his son's abilities. Sir Keith wasn't impressed, responding by telling Rohan not to 'inflate' Rupert.

Thousands of kilometres from his powerful and demanding parents Rupert was free to be a wealthy dilettante. At Oxford he became the Worcester College secretary of the Labour Party (he was later expelled) and displayed a bust of Lenin in his room. The fact that the young media scion also occupied one of the best rooms (De Quincey) and was one of the very few students to have a car (a beige Austin A-40) somewhat undermined his anti-elitist gestures.

At Oxford Rupert's interests were politics, horseracing and drinking beer. Some of his peers regarded him as spoilt and shrewd. He'd always had a rebellious sense of humour: his one claim to fame at university was as co-founder of the bogus Voltaire Society. This 'society' claimed a general opposition to organised religion; it claimed eleven elected officials, including the office of gardener (as Voltaire was a keen horticulturist); and its patron was listed as Bertrand Russell. This larrikin association was basically a dining club.

During his three years at Oxford, one of Rupert's closest friends was Robin Farquharson, a flamboyantly gay South African regarded as one of the most brilliant students at the university. Farquharson was an ingenious conversationalist and a mathematician who expounded to all who would listen a revolutionary idea called 'game theory'. It was an abstruse mathematical thesis, but when simplified and applied to business or political life suggested that when individuals break unwritten rules and ignore conventions they are more likely to succeed than those who 'play by the book'. It was an idea that the iconoclastic Rupert Murdoch later applied to his media business with remarkable success. After he left Oxford, Rupert lost touch with the eccentric and showy Farquharson, who later died a pauper.

In 1951 Sir Keith, worried that his son was having too good a time and that his leftist politics had become too extreme, wanted to drag him back to Australia to work on his newspapers. Elisabeth intervened but warned her son that this was his last chance. A year later, as Rupert's whimsical idyll at Oxford was coming to an end, he showed signs of becoming his father's son. In the European autumn he attended the British Labour Party's annual congress in the dowdy seaside town of Blackpool. He wrote a long letter to his father about the weekend. Dame Elisabeth remembers the day the letter arrived. 'We hadn't heard from him for a little while . . . I remember it was a Thursday morning and . . . I remember Keith saying, "Well thank God, I think the boy's got it".' The letter no longer exists, but at last the prodigal son had impressed his father. Two days later Sir Keith Murdoch died in his sleep. He was sixty-seven. Dame Elisabeth was comforted in the knowledge that her husband's last days had been spent in a renewed hope for his son's dynastic future.

The family was in deep mourning. For the forty-three-year-old widow it was a 'terrible, terrible loss'. Rupert didn't attend his father's funeral; the journey from Britain to Australia took three days, and Elisabeth insisted her husband be buried two days after his death. Throughout the ordeal the young widow drew on her inner steeliness. Elisabeth would never marry again, devoted to the memory of her husband.

But the tragedy bore rich dynastic fruit. Rupert, says his mother, once forced to assume the Murdoch mantle at the age of twenty-one, was able to develop in a way never possible under the shadow of his father. 'It was a terrible thing for Rupert . . . I think the challenge that Rupert was under at that early age was terrific and . . . in overcoming that, he grew tremendously.' In other words her cheeky son buckled down and now followed the path his father had set.

In his will Sir Keith expressed his ambitions for his heir: 'I desire that my said son Rupert Murdoch should have a great opportunity of spending a useful, altruistic and full life in news-papers and broadcasting activities and of ultimately occupying a position of high responsibility in that field . . .' Still not entirely confident his son would be prudent, Sir Keith added '. . . with the support of my trustees if they consider him worthy of that support'.

At the time of his death, Sir Keith Murdoch owned a country and a city residence, two cattle properties and substantial shares in two newspaper groups, Queensland Newspapers in Brisbane and, in Adelaide, News Limited. All his assets were held in the family company, Cruden Investments. Dame Elisabeth took charge of the Murdoch finances. Her son was dismayed as his mother settled Sir Keith's debts cautiously and conservatively.

Elisabeth had grown up with financial insecurity and refused to be swayed by her son's protestations that the family business could carry debt. With advice from Harry Giddy, the chairman of the trustees, who was also chairman of the HWT group, she sold a large share in Brisbane's *Courier-Mail* to the HWT group to cover outstanding debts and probate costs. Rupert tried to retain the *Courier-Mail* by attempting to broker his first deal with the *Argus* in Melbourne and the *News*. But his business associates weren't prepared to trust the vision of an impulsive twenty-one-year-old undergraduate, no matter who he was. Sir Keith's children were then left with roughly a 50 per cent stake in News Limited between them. It was now the responsibility of the son to build the family company with the family inheritance. He took to the task with relish.

A year later, after leaving Oxford with third class honours in politics and economics, Rupert became a director of the struggling Adelaide *News*. Unlike his academic studies, Rupert approached business with rigour. He moved to Adelaide to oversee operations. His father's friend Rohan Rivett was editor-in-chief at the *News* and they worked together to transform the paper. Naturally enough Rupert adopted the tabloid techniques taught to him by his father.

The *News* was the number two paper in this small city—a position Murdoch was determined to improve. It was out-circulated by the Adelaide *Advertiser*, backed by the HWT group. Only months after Sir Keith's death, the *Advertiser* moved to take over the flagging *News*. In a letter to Elisabeth they offered to buy the paper for £150 000. Rupert took up the challenge. He published the letter on the front page of the *News* with the headline 'Bid for Press Monopoly'. For Rupert, this set the tone for how he would always portray himself: the outsider taking on the powerful establishment.

The *News* headline was snappy and eye-catching—standard fare for the paper that became a recipe of sex, scandal, human interest and sport. It disconcerted conservative Adelaide and circulation of the *News* soared. The softly spoken Rupert was in the thick of it. All boundless energy, sleeves rolled up, wreathed in cigarette smoke, he would oversee every stage of the paper's daily production, regularly subbing major stories and writing the sledgehammer headlines himself. He cut costs, whittling staff to a minimum; senior reporters were asked to write up to twenty stories a day. The money poured in.

Setting his sights on becoming a national player, Rupert determined to make the big jump from Adelaide to Sydney. And there would have to be other changes—among them dumping family friend Rohan Rivett. He, Murdoch believed, was 'too crusading a journalist' and his fiscal skills could no longer be relied on. For the ruthless boy publisher with something to prove, there was little room for sentiment.

More than half a century has passed since Rupert Murdoch inherited the Adelaide *News*. He is now CEO of arguably the most powerful media corporation in the world—a man Bill Gates has referred to as the world's most powerful media player, and who CNN creator Ted Turner has likened to Hitler. He is the William Randolph Hearst of the twenty-first century.

Over the years Rupert Murdoch has stamped his populist template on his ventures worldwide. To his critics, the King of News Corporation desecrates all he touches; to his supporters, including his family—and to himself—Rupert is a risk-taking innovator and a welcome agent for change. He is proud of all he has achieved and regards News Corporation as a reflection of himself, created in his image: a powerful, entrepreneurial and iconoclastic empire.

From his small Adelaide launch pad, Rupert has rocketed around the globe—first by seeking out papers in Australia's major centres, Sydney, Melbourne, Brisbane and Perth. From Canberra he launched Australia's first national newspaper, the *Australian*, in 1964. He said at the time he wanted to create a paper his father would be proud of. By the mid-1960s Australia was too small for Rupert's ambitions and he turned to his father's old stomping ground, Fleet Street. In 1969 he snapped up the *News of the World* and a year later a floundering union paper, the *Sun*. He transformed both into salacious rags with an emphasis on crime, sex, sport and bold conservative editorials. The *Sun*'s topless page three girls provided an extra boon to its circulation. It was a revolution led by bare breasts, and the British establishment reviled him as 'the Dirty Digger'.

Dame Elisabeth Murdoch laughingly remembers that when Rupert bought the *News of the World*, it nearly 'killed me'. She raised her concerns at the time, in her direct way. Her son justified the content to his mother along the lines that 'There are tens of thousands of people living in London and around England who have nothing in their lives practically, and they want this sort of thing.' He was right: the punters loved it and the *Sun* was a cash cow for Rupert's next ventures.

He entered the American market in 1973 with the purchase of two Texas dailies, and in 1976 he snapped up his favourite newspaper prize, the *New York Post*. It was a bastion of liberalism when Murdoch bought it. He transformed it into the Big Apple's most conservative (and often most humorous) sex and scandal daily. Rupert now had a voice and a home in the heart of the capitalist world.

By the 1980s he was on a roll, his deal-making in full flight. His ideological heroes in government were Margaret Thatcher in the United Kingdom and Ronald Reagan in the United States. Rupert, a professed meritocrat and a radical free-marketeer, found much in common with Thatcher and Reagan. He embraced the social agenda of America's Christian Right, together with hard-line views on a variety of issues from drugs to defence.

In this entrepreneurial climate Rupert made extraordinary advances. He also moved into the British broadsheet market with the acquistions of *The Times* and *The Sunday Times* in 1981. In 1985 he ventured into film when he bought a 50 per cent share in Twentieth Century-Fox. Hot on the heels of that deal he bought six metropolitan television stations and started up America's fourth television network, Fox Broadcasting. In the

United Kingdom he transformed the British television industry with the creation of Sky, later to become BSkyB. Back in Australia he had a sentimental win when he managed to secure the Herald and Weekly Times Group in 1987, a takeover that would have greatly pleased his father.

Rupert's biggest fight of the decade came in 1986 when, determined to increase productivity and profit, he set out to destroy the Fleet Street print unions. Under strict secrecy he organised for new high-tech newspaper headquarters to be created. Over several months a bleak building at Wapping was covertly filled with the latest in computer technology, rendering the notoriously obstreporous Fleet Street printers redundant. It was a year before Murdoch could claim absolute victory against the print unions—a year in which thousands would angrily protest outside Wapping. Many in the United Kingdom still can't forgive the 'The Beast of Wapping' for his ruthlessly sneaky actions. Murdoch shrugs off any criticism as inevitable: 'You can't be an outsider and cut through and be successful without leaving a fair amount of scar tissue around the place . . . I think that is the price one pays.'[17]

Wapping was a triumph for Murdoch. The 'game theory' learnt at Oxford had yet again proved a dramatic success. By the 1990s his sights turned to Asia. He bought the Hong Kong-based television station Star in 1993. This expensive and risky purchase was even a surprise to News Corporation directors. One, Gus Fischer, was flabbergasted when his boss rang to say he had just spent $600 million to purchase a 64 per cent holding of Star. Rupert asked Fischer to inform the other News Corporation directors of the Star deal.

Rupert Murdoch also entered the United States' cable industry by creating the FX entertainment network. He then made moves into the world of sport, building up his Fox Sports network with a vast selection of local football, baseball, basketball and hockey. He saw the lucrative potential of owning sporting teams and so made a winning bid for the Los Angeles Dodgers. By now News Corporation was one of the major generators of television product in the world. It, and hence Murdoch, has a controlling interest in television stations in Europe, North and South America, Asia and Australia.

Despite Rupert believing his father taught him that media ownership carried with it 'moral obligation'[18], it can be argued that this obligation has never been much in evidence. During the 1980s, while the size of the corporation dramatically increased, its content remained steady. Rupert Murdoch kept with the tried and trusty formula of sport, sex and gossip to drive his expansion. Many were unimpressed, including his former Geelong headmaster Sir James Darling. Commenting on Rupert's career he quoted from the Australian novel, *Lucinda Brayford* by Martin Boyd: 'Sir, your newspapers for two decades have engaged in the degradation of the proper feelings of our people. What is vile they offer to gloating eyes, what is vindictive they applaud. You have done more harm to this country than any of its external enemies . . . I beg you to leave before my butler throws you down the steps.'[19]

For Murdoch, business expedience always comes before political ideals. The rabidly conservative *Sun* in the United Kingdom has twice championed Labour Prime Minister Tony Blair during election campaigns—in both cases when a landslide for Labour was on the cards. During the 1980s, Murdoch papers were passionate Cold War warriors against the Soviet Union, which they referred to as the 'evil empire'. Yet in the 1990s, as business interests put China in his sights, Rupert softened his official line towards the communist regime in Beijing. If he wanted to do business in China he had to tread carefully. After a 1993 speech in which Rupert proclaimed that technology had become an 'unambigous threat to totalitarian regimes everywhere', the Chinese government placed a ban on satellite dishes—a move that stymied Star's potential reach. Since then Murdoch has gone to various lengths to please Chinese authorities. An early move was to drop the BBC from the satellite broadcast—the Chinese government had been hostile to the BBC since it criticised the Tiananmen Square massacre.

Murdoch prevented his publishing company HarperCollins from publishing the memoirs of the last Governor of Hong Kong, Chris Patten.[20] He has condoned the Chinese occupation of Tibet and dismissed the exiled Tibetan spiritual leader, the Dalai Lama, as a 'political old monk shuffling in Gucci shoes'.[21] Of all the Murdoch companies, the Hong Kong–based Star has been the most difficult to grow and has yet to reap substantial profits. However, in the main his astute gambles have paid huge dividends.

There has been an overarching and voracious logic to his frequent buying sprees involving television stations, film companies, newspapers, cable technology and professional sports teams. Murdoch wants News Corporation not only to transmit the news and entertainment but also to control its production (sport, films and television shows) and the forms of transmission (cable and satellite technology).

Murdoch controls the flow of information and entertainment on a scale unprecedented in history. News Corporation is a public company; however, with the Murdochs owning 30 per cent of the shares, Rupert can run it as a family enterprise with himself securely at the apex. His children refer to News Corporation affectionately as 'a family business'; its shareholders are content with this as long as Rupert remains at the helm.

While politicians, business leaders and royals the world over try to curry favour with Murdoch, he continues to portray himself as an anti-establishment maverick. Sir Keith impressed on his son the need to be above obligation, beholden to no one. In 1999 Rupert commented that 'I try to maintain a position as an outsider to the establishment . . . I try to influence events and take part in events, but I think you must try and keep a distance from people with special interests, whether they be in business or government.'[22]

Like his grandfather Rupert Greene, Murdoch has had a yearning for a punt, a risk, a flutter. He has built the world's most powerful media empire through a series of radical gambles; his adult life a race from one adventurous deal to the next. However, despite the risk-taking, he has only once faced ruin. In 1990, seventy-six years after Rupert Greene's passion for gambling nearly brought him down, his grandson faced a similar fate. Such a fall would have had widespread consequences, and not just for his own family. Moneylenders feared the downfall of News Corporation could send the international share market into a tumble.

For nearly four decades News Corporation had expanded relentlessly. But its massive build-up also made the company vulnerable: Rupert's global vision had brought over $10 billion worth of debt to the corporation. As 1990 drew to a close, he and his bankers faced the task of rescheduling more than $7 billion of this debt. To complicate matters, this debt was spread across no fewer than 146 banks.

Until this point, Rupert Murdoch had looked invincible. News Corporation was his creation, forged in his image. But Rupert had to juggle objectives that were often in conflict: on the one hand, his passion to expand through the making of deals, and on the other his determination to retain the company as his fiefdom—a company that would stay in family hands. Public companies worth billions of dollars don't often operate like the nepotistic courts of absolute monarchs; however, with his significant dominance of the company's shares, Rupert Murdoch had managed just this.

To finance his deals, Rupert had borrowed heavily rather than sell family shares. Then in 1990 the international lending market dried up. He found fewer and fewer banks would lend on the short-term money market. To add fuel to the fire, none of his cash cows—not even his British *Sun* tabloid—could come close to covering a fraction of the costs of his latest expensive entrepreneurial move—his venture into the emerging United Kingdom pay television industry. News Corporation's share price plummeted. For the first time in his career Rupert was in peril of defaulting on scheduled loans.

As Christmas 1990 approached, News Corporation was scheduled to repay a billion-dollar loan. The company couldn't meet the 7 December payment deadline. Unless all the creditors agreed to reschedule their loans, News Corporation faced liquidation.

However, like his grandfather, Rupert had friends with influence who were ready to come to his rescue. He employed a network of Citibank executives to work night and day to sort out the financial tangle. They had marshalled the banks to reschedule News Corporation's debt. There was just one bank, the Pittsburgh National, refusing to be brought into line. This small lender was owed $10 million—just one per cent of the total loan. The Pittsburgh loan officer refused to reschedule the debt, saying he was prepared to see News Corporation go under. Rupert Murdoch made a personal call to the loan officer, but Pittsburgh wouldn't take the call.

Hours before the loan deadline was reached, Citibank's chairman made a call to the chairman of Pittsburgh National, warning him that if the latter bank refused to reschedule the debt, the company would go under. And if News Corporation went under, he predicted the stock markets would go into freefall and the world would face a grim recession. When this nightmarish flow-on effect was outlined to the Pittsburgh chairman he predictably relented. Rupert Murdoch was in the clear.

A slight variation of this story comes via Philip Townsend who was the Murdochs' butler in London for five years. According to his version of events, on 6 December 1990 Rupert made a call from his London triplex to the White House. Within moments he was speaking to President George Bush (snr), telling the President the story of his tussle with the Pittsburgh National Bank. He emphasised to President Bush that without Pittsburgh National coming on board, everything would fall over. According to Townsend, Rupert finally asked, 'Can you help?' Within the hour of his phone call to the President, the Pittsburgh Bank called Rupert Murdoch, agreeing to reschedule the loan. A relieved Rupert got off the phone and uttered, 'Phew, that was a close one.'[23]

While Rupert was pursuing risky business deals, his wife Anna was raising their three children and her stepdaughter

Prudence—Rupert's daughter by his first marriage of ten years to Patricia Booker. Anna and Rupert met when she was a junior reporter at the *Daily Mirror* and went to interview her boss, Rupert. The thirty-six-year-old media entrepreneur and the enterprising twenty-two-year-old married in a quiet suburban Sydney church in 1967. Elisabeth, Lachlan and James are the children of this marriage. For three decades Anna was the dutiful wife and charming hostess, taking care of the children and managing the seven family mansions, including the home in Aspen Colorado which has a swimming pool in the living room. She was his staunchest defender, unceasingly supporting him in his global ambitions. Their family was a tight and loving unit. Rupert once commented to journalists, 'We're a close family, and I think that reflects in our papers . . . We really value the idea of family ties.'

The devoted Anna would sometimes rouse her sleepy children so they could have a pre-dawn breakfast with their father before he jetted off. She was even known to raise her slumbering offspring so that they could greet their father as he walked through the door at 5.30 am. At home and at work, Rupert was king. He was also often absent, his global interests and relentless business deals keeping him away for long periods. Even when he was at home, his children would complain that he wasn't listening to them. If his children wanted their father's attention they needed to enter his orbit and talk media and politics.

The eldest son, Lachlan, was born in London in 1971. His parents, despising the stuffiness of London, fled to the United States in 1974. For Lachlan, his childhood in the United States evokes strong and fond memories. He remembers the grand dining room at their New York home. Dinners were often formal and oddly old-fashioned, given their father's pride in his nonconformity. 'We always had staff serving us. My father would come home; we'd have to get dressed up to see him. We would have half an hour with him alone before the guests came over.'[24]

The dinner guests were a mixture of politicians, newspaper editors, authors and business leaders. The children revelled in the atmosphere of those dinners, the lively conversations over good food and expensive wines. They would listen attentively. When the governor of New York came over, the sleepy children would stare agog as they trotted up to bed past security guards stationed on the stairs.

The unobtrusive and rather quiet young Lachlan enjoyed the debates and discussions round the family dining table. He says that even now, if the family goes out for dinner and conversation is waning, one member of the clan will look to take a position against another Murdoch. 'We don't really believe in it, we just want to cause excitement.'

Prue remembers her father as being an ordinary sort of father, '. . . he never tried too hard, you know, he was always behind a newspaper'. When he was playing 'normal' dad, Rupert loved competitive games. According to Elisabeth, family games of Monopoly were highly animated—and everybody was prepared to cheat. Winning was deemed essential. The family would also seek riskier leisure pursuits, skiing and scuba diving together. Even when his children were small Rupert sometimes took them on a daredevil ride. Elisabeth recalls as a seven-year-old hanging onto a plastic sleigh while her father pulled her and her younger brothers along behind his snowmobile. 'I remember him going like a bat out of hell basically, across the ice and lake and up the bank with me on the back having the time of my life but being absolutely terrified out of my wits.'[25]

Rupert involved his children in the workings of the media from a tender age. Over the years they have absorbed the family's *raison d'être*. If their father was in town, breakfast would be spent talking of the family business. Recalls Lachlan: 'Lis, James and I would come up for breakfast before we had to get the bus to school and all the papers would come out and we'd have the *New York Post*, the *New York Times*, the *Daily News* and the *Wall Street Journal*, and as we read the papers my dad would be handing out the stories and saying, "Read that" or he'd say,

"Look at the headline—that's a shocking headline" . . . that often led [to] what he was doing that day and things that he was involved with that might have been in the papers. So from a very early age—I'm talking now seven or eight years old—we began to understand that we were part of the media business.'

When it came to his children's education, Rupert flung his anti-elite rhetoric out the door after he tried sending eldest daughter Prudence to a London comprehensive. The child, used to a certain level of cosseting, was withdrawn after one term and sent to an establishment private girls' school headed by a baroness. Lachlan and James went to exclusive boys' schools in Manhattan; Elisabeth to an elite girls' school. James and his sister Elisabeth were the most rebellious, although they couldn't quite match their father's schoolboy insouciance. James, sporting dyed blond hair and earrings, argued with his teachers; Elisabeth was expelled from her girls' day school in Manhattan for smuggling rum into the grounds. Lachlan, on the other hand, formed a club for young conservatives.

Rupert's eldest son is wary of being seen as privileged. Perhaps because he mixed with children from other enormously wealthy and powerful families, although rarely as rich as his own, Lachlan portrays the Murdochs as an ordinary family though 'perhaps in extraordinary circumstances'. He talks of the grimy hustle and bustle of New York as a grounding experience: everything happened on street level, people caught buses and cabs, no one drove fancy cars. Childhood friends remember the Murdoch children travelling by bus to school, and Elisabeth in particular running out of money and having to borrow a few dimes. In describing family life as 'ordinary', Rupert's children continue a family propensity—public denial of their exceptional power and status.

The Murdoch children are smart; they understood that their father had an unusually prominent place in the world. As a six-year-old, Lachlan Murdoch saw a front cover of *Time* magazine '. . . that had my father as King Kong on top of the World Trade Center with little planes trying to shoot him down'. No one else's dad, he realised, was publicly portrayed as a 'monster'.

To get attention from 'dear old Pop' Rupert's kids had to engage with the business. During school holidays they were encouraged to take summer jobs in News Corporation. With the exception of the laid-back and jovial Prue, they grabbed the opportunity. Rupert made it clear that they were expected to work hard and be persistent. The children grew up with their father's Presbyterian work ethic, and to gain his approval have had to show utter dedication. According to Lachlan, 'There's no sense of turning business on and off, so News Corporation business is my life as it is my father's and brother's and the whole family—you'll wake up in the middle of the night and you'll be working . . . every lunch, dinner and even your friends that you make are somehow connected to your work . . . I hope it's healthy because it's the only thing I've ever known.'

The children hope that their dedication will pay off and eventually one child will succeed their father. Hard work is a prerequisite to gaining Rupert's praise, but to him the bloodline is paramount. His children's involvement brings 'experience and tradition' to News, says their proud father. 'I think it would lose a lot if it was just another public company, run by a board with the approval of fund managers.' Being part of this family means being part of the enterprise that gives the family its identity. Rupert offers his children heaven on earth, so it's not surprising that they venerate their godlike father. James Murdoch says of being his father's son: 'I hope there are more similarities than differences.' Rupert holds their future in his hands and they worship him.

Rupert Murdoch's own dynastic leanings only became clearly evident in the 1990s. It was in this decade, as his sons reached adulthood, that Rupert bought out his sisters' News Corporation shares for a total price of around $A650 million and thus concentrated ownership within his immediate family. His sisters and their children have benefited greatly from Rupert's business prowess. Today only Rupert's branch of the family retains ownership of the family company his father started in 1947, Cruden Investments—News Corporation's primary shareholder.

As he shored up the dynastic fortune Rupert fast-tracked his children, particularly his sons Lachlan and James, through the company hierarchy. Both prince regents now anticipate that their bloodline, coupled with hard work and perseverance, will take them to the top. Many non-Murdoch managers have left the company, frustrated because they will never be able to have a crack at the top job. For a man who has spent years railing against the establishment, Rupert Murdoch has contrived a fresh nepotistic elite. As ex-employee Andrew Neil puts it, Rupert has produced 'a new media aristocracy'.

Lachlan's first job was back in Australia, working as a jackaroo on one of News Corporation's properties. His next summer job was cleaning the printing presses, helping to print the now defunct Sydney tabloid the *Daily Mirror*. By the time he was seventeen, the boss's son found himself back in the United Kingdom, subediting the *Sun*. Lachlan says these summer jobs 'helped me in understanding the business from an early age. I understand that I'm not the best subeditor in the world, but I can certainly appreciate good subediting . . . so those are very important jobs in the business.'

His younger brother enjoyed a similar entree into the Murdoch empire. James's first work experience was as a photographer's assistant at the HWT group. The heir had an inauspicious start when he fell asleep during the press conference announcing Kerry Stokes's purchase of Channel Seven. Unlike his more relaxed brother, the mercurial and spiky James found these summer jobs difficult. 'I can't complain, but when you're working in the company and you're fifteen and you have a job whether they have a job for you or not, it's very difficult. People are touchy about yelling at you if you fuck up.'[26]

In 1994 the tough-talking scion even dropped out of Harvard to form his own music company, Rawkus. But the lure of working in the family company soon brought him back. By 1995 twenty-two-year-old James was made head of News Corporation's music and new media ventures. He was dispatched to Sydney to improve the performance of music label

Festival. In true Murdoch style he restructured the company, sacking staff all the way through from management to tea ladies. Festival employees went on strike, calling him 'Son of the Beast of Wapping'.

Since then James has enjoyed a meteoric rise, becoming executive chairman of Star TV in Hong Kong in 2000. He's touted to be the smartest of the children, described by his mother Anna as more of a Renaissance person than his brother or sister: 'He finds space in his life for quite a lot of interests and is very knowledgeable about them . . . He has his father's powers of memory and intellect.'[27] Like his great-grandfather Rupert Greene, James likes to gamble—sometimes betting thousands of dollars at the gaming tables. But unlike Pop Greene, James knows when to stop. It is a lesson he has probably learned from Rupert who has said: 'When it is going well, we'll push it. And when it is going bad, let's go home. So you shouldn't limit what you think you could win, but you must limit what you lose.'[28]

Lachlan has been the most predictable, steadily following the path laid out for him. At university the tanned and disarmingly polite Lachlan was an average student, spending a great deal of time rock-climbing. He says that at the time he was considering pursuing rock-climbing more seriously, but after reading a biography of his grandfather, Lachlan was impressed by Sir Keith's achievements and wanted to be part of the next generation, upholding his grandfather's legacy. In 1994 after graduating from Princeton, Lachlan made the most of being a member of this elite family. Rupert sent him to work in News Corporation's Australian division, News Limited. After just a year subediting on the *Courier-Mail*, the twenty-five-year-old was promoted to second-in-command of News Limited—whose papers reach 70 per cent of the Australian market.

Displaying the great confidence that comes from growing up a business heir, Lachlan immediately initiated an editorial overhaul. One of the first papers to be remodelled by the young dynast was the *Australian*, the national daily his father created in 1964. Lachlan sought a younger readership, giving short shrift to lengthy or obscure articles. Senior staff left—some pushed, others jumping. Management were in no doubt that behind Lachlan's gallant demeanour was a man with sharply honed business instincts. Dame Elisabeth describes her grandson as 'caring and unspoilt'. Business associates characterise him as like his father, politically conservative and at times ruthless. In 1996 he was placed in charge of News Limited after Rupert's loyal lieutenant Ken Cowley retired early. News Limited insiders claim Cowley was frustrated at increasingly finding himself out of the loop, with Rupert speaking more to his son than to him.

That same year Lachlan was named heir apparent of the parent company, News Corporation, but more recently the anointing oil has been wiped from his brow. Rupert has claimed Peter Chernin, currently chief operating officer, as his likely successor. Lachlan was appointed Deputy Chief Operating Officer of News Corporation in November 2000, making him the third-most powerful executive in this multibillion-dollar empire.

But his performance has had several shaky moments. In 2001 News Corporation lost $532 million as telephone company OneTel failed. With the collapse of OneTel, the Australian press, at least the non-News Corporation outlets, looked to place some of the blame squarely with Lachlan. After all, he had spear-headed News Corporation's multimillion-dollar investment and was a director on OneTel's board. But Rupert doesn't blame his son, saying, 'It was a corporate decision. We were all involved in the decision, it was not Lachlan's decision or his deal. And it was a great embarrassment to all of us, and certainly to us as the two biggest investors, the Packers [James and Kerry Packer] and ourselves.'

Unlike other executives who can expect a 'bollocking' when they mess up, Rupert Murdoch is positively sanguine when speaking about his children's errors. In an interview in his commodious Los Angeles office in August 2001 he said, 'Mistakes have been made by them and there have been very, very few, but they've been the first to come in and discuss them.

There are many more mistakes made by me every day than by them collectively.' His flexible attitude has given his children a particular confidence. Elisabeth says her father has fostered in them a sense of bravery and acceptance that it is 'okay to make mistakes' as long as 'you work hard and think laterally'.

In the fifty years since he inherited his father's dream, Rupert has been served by many loyal retainers, but most senior lieutenants eventually leave. In News Corporation, only Rupert holds the company's corporate memory and has sworn in as many words that he won't be leaving the company until he's taken out in a wooden box. Rupert is regarded as an exacting boss with a unpredictable temper, his charming demeanour suddenly giving way to a vicious tongue-lashing. Former employee Andrew Neil sees his ex-boss as a hopeless manager who can strike fear into the hearts of his vast team: 'He rules over great distances, through authority, loyalty, example and fear. He can be benign or ruthless, depending on his mood or the requirements of his empire. You never know which; the element of surprise is part of the means by which he makes his presence felt in every corner of his domain.'[29] The only people who can't be sacked and don't experience the vitriol are his children.

To date, Rupert has ensured Lachlan and James a smooth run through the company, but Elisabeth's path has been bumpier. Despite being (like her father) resolute and energetic, the well groomed and beautiful Elisabeth hasn't been promoted by her patriarchal father in the same vigorous manner as his sons. Rupert is known for his unease with female executives and his old-style chauvinism has slowed her pace through the company. He has ruefully admitted that this daughter is, like him, 'a bull at a gate' but he's been uneasy about giving her the same succession rights as her brothers. Elisabeth's husband, public relations supremo Matthew Freud, has said of his father-in-law, 'misogyny is too strong, but Rupert has an old-fashioned attitude [towards women]'.[30]

Still, he has given her advantages that most women could only dream of. In 1995 Rupert lent his twenty-six-year-old daughter several million dollars to buy two Californian television stations. He recalls saying: 'Get out of the [family] company and you'll come back with better credentials. I thought she'd be gone for four or five years. She was back after twelve months with a $10 million profit. You can't argue with that.' In her bid to please her father, Elisabeth restructured the Californian television companies. Through massive job cuts, she earned a reputation as a slash-and-burn entrepreneur. After one year she sold the companies and rejoined News Corporation.

Like her brother Lachlan, Elisabeth is renowned for working long hours and displaying a ferocious edge. She wants to be judged on her merits, irrespective of the advantage that underpins them. However, Elisabeth knows it's her bloodline more than her skills that placed her in the position of senior executive at the British satellite station BSkyB when only in her twenties.

Despite her aspirations, Rupert has told his daughter that Lachlan, as the eldest of his sons, should be considered 'first among equals'. In 2000, apparently frustrated with her father's chauvinism, she left the company and set up her own British-based production house, Shine. Rupert says she is welcome to return to the family business 'whenever she chooses'. Perhaps Elisabeth feels there is no point unless she's treated on a parallel with her brothers. Elisabeth's mother Anna has supported her daughter's move out of News Corporation. 'My mother would exercise her anger towards my father and say, "Good for her. At last!"[31] Perhaps Anna feels her daughter will have more freedom to prove herself as the CEO of a small company, shaped in her own image, rather than have limited power in a major corporation shaped by her father. Rupert says of Elisabeth's new venture, 'If it is a bit of a success she'll be the one who will hit the jackpot first, because she'll probably sell up for hundreds of millions of dollars and maybe come back into the company. She has not given up her ambitions by any means to play a part in the company.'

As an unashamed nepotist, Rupert has engineered his children's, and in particular his sons' rise through the company.

THE MYER FAMILY

Russia, 1897: Dynastic founder Sidney Myer, born Simcha Baevski (second from right) seated between his parents Gina and Israel. He would soon escape Russia and arrive in Melbourne with threepence in his pocket. (Gael Hammer)

Sidney Myer's marriage to Merlyn Baillieu in Nevada, January 1920, was grist to Melbourne's gossip columns. For 20-year-old Merlyn, her sensational marriage was made possible because her mother Agnes (far left) was Sidney's great supporter. (Myer family)

By the mid 1920s Sidney Myer had converted to Christianity and was welcomed into Victoria's business circles. However, within Melbourne's establishment many continued to regard him as an upstart. *(Myer family)*

Father Christmas: On Christmas Day 1930 Sidney Myer hosted a Christmas lunch for 10,000 unemployed men and their families. The lunch helped secure Sidney's image as a caring civic leader. *(Myer family)*

Merlyn Baillieu with her four children: in 1929, after spending almost 10 years in the United States, Sidney and Merlyn returned permanently to Australia. Their four children Ken (seated, right), Neilma, Baillieu and baby Marigold would enjoy the many luxuries the family could afford. *(Myer family)*

THE MURDOCH FAMILY

The demure 17-year-old, Elisabeth Greene, not long before she met the media publisher, Keith Murdoch. Their marriage proved strong. Elisabeth's charm and inner strength have ably assisted the matriarch of Australia's most discussed dynasty. (Dame Elisabeth Murdoch)

The patriarch and his heir: Sir Keith Murdoch and his irrepressible son. Rupert was sent to the elite Geelong Grammar, where he was a loner and frequently teased and called 'Commo' or 'Bullo' Murdoch. (Dame Elisabeth Murdoch)

Elisabeth and her children. The Murdochs had a sumptuous life, with staff, luxurious cars and overseas travel. They had several homes, including their Melbourne mansion Heathfield. In this photo Rupert is on his tricycle and elder sister Helen sits next to her mother, who holds baby Anne. (Dame Elisabeth Murdoch)

The contented patriarch: By the 1990s Rupert Murdoch was among the world's most powerful media magnates. Here he is with his four adult children Prudence (front left), Elisabeth, James and Lachlan. By his side is Anna, who supported her husband for thirty years in his drive to build News Corporation. She worked hard to keep the marriage together, but in the end did not succeed. The couple divorced in 1998. (Austral International)

Shortly after his divorce from Anna Murdoch, Rupert married his third wife, Wendi Deng. A former News Corporatrion junior executive, Wendi is generally considered very smart and ambitious. The birth of their first child, Grace Helen, increased speculation about the inheritance of the 'family business'. (Rupert Murdoch)

THE DE BORTOLI FAMILY

Childhood sweethearts who founded a dynasty: Giuseppina and Vittorio celebrate their wedding in Griffith in 1928. *(De Bortoli family)*

This portrait of a carefree Vittorio taking a punt holds pride of place above the winery's cellar door. In fact, Vittorio anxiously tended the family fortunes alongside Giuseppina, leaving little to chance. *(De Bortoli family)*

With his marriage, Deen also assumed stewardship of the family winery – here celebrating a successful vintage with fellow workers and his mother, Giuseppina, on far left. Deen is leaning on the cellar door at far right. (De Bortoli family)

The third generation of De Bortolis would move closer to the Anglo-Australian mainstream, while proving as adventurous as their predecessors. From left to right: Darren, Leanne, Kevin and Victor. (De Bortoli family)

Vittorio and Giuseppina celebrate 50 years of marriage and winemaking with their children Flo, Deen and Eola, shortly before Vittorio's death. Although he often disagreed with Deen's management of the business, Vittorio was a traditionalist, leaving everything to his son and not his daughters.
(De Bortoli family)

However, Rupert's dynastic dreams sit awkwardly with his own self-interest in further elevating the company with himself still king. All Rupert's life his energies have been directed to the next business gamble; now he can't give it up. Unlike his father, Rupert hasn't been able to tackle the issue of his own mortality and smooth the way for the media crown and sceptre to be handed to one of the prince regents. By Rupert's own optimistic reckoning, he'll still be working at the age of a hundred. Rupert is a gambler, not a natural manager, and he hasn't been able to settle down and consolidate his creation.

During the 1990s Murdoch's global ambitions expanded, but the family shareholding in News Corporation declined. Rupert has come to rely on alliances to help fund his expansionist dreams. Most importantly he has formed a powerful business alliance with American entrepreneur John Malone who holds an 18 per cent (non-voting) share in the company. Thanks to this partnership and other strategic coalitions, Murdoch's information empire now reaches more than two in every three people on earth. But it has come at a price for his dynasty. Rupert Murdoch has a weakening hold on News Corporation shares while John Malone's shareholding has strengthened. As it currently stands any decision on who succeeds Rupert will have to be approved by John Malone. Neither Lachlan nor James is guaranteed an easy ride to the top of the 'family business'.

Rupert's children are very loyal to their father and he in turn shows them great affection. Both sons speak to their father on a daily basis. But they talk deals and developments; according to Lachlan they don't discuss their personal lives. As a family they are not reflective, always looking to the next business deal.

Rivalries are par for the course among large dynastic families, but to date Rupert's children have behaved remarkably well towards one another. With a certain American-pie sweetness, Lachlan says he feels lucky to be a member of such a close family. 'We all live in so many different places and [it] keeps us in constant communication. But my father . . . is a great father, a very loving father, so it's not an unusual father–son relationship in any way. If it's unusual in any way, it's unusual that it's such a strong relationship.'

Lachlan argues that News Corporation has been shaped primarily by the two sides of what the family likes to see as the pre-eminent Murdoch characteristics. On the one hand, they're risk-takers and thrill-seekers à la great-grandfather Rupert Greene. On the other hand they're descendants of a strict Presbyterian minister. Lachlan understands this genetic mix as 'playing itself out in all our lives every day. Everything from the fact we all tend to work too-long hours and sacrifice a lot for it, but at the same time we all enjoy . . . taking risks and making quick decisions.'

The Murdochs believe in the power of genetics, in the passing of 'family traits' down the generations. This set of supposedly shared Murdoch characteristics is, in Lachlan's view, the key to the family's continued success as free-market entrepreneurs. The overriding imperative for the Murdochs and their business is to do what's necessary to expand the company. The worst nightmare would be to see the corporation standing still, stagnating.

The family's self-image is suitably enhanced by a solid collection of favourite family tales, regularly brought out for interviews or speeches. Rupert's children are well versed in the tale of Sir Keith's Gallipoli letters, the generational disdain for social clubs, and the anti-elite rhetoric. Dame Elisabeth—denying the ambition of both her husband and her son—regards Rupert as a modern version of Sir Keith. 'His father was interested in finance too; I can see him with his little red notebook and pens working out negotiations. And I can see it with Rupert. It's not the money, or the power, no; it's the challenge, like his father.'

Rupert Murdoch has no plans to retire. He describes the company in artistic terms as 'a work in progress', with himself as the artist ahead of his time, always impatient to start something new. His plans are endless. For the time being his two sons appear content for 'Pop' to control the business—and to a great extent, their lives.

Although now in his seventies, and after placing his sons in strategic positions, Rupert hasn't been able to set any apparent timetable for devolving corporate control to any of his children. His father Sir Keith sought to secure a firm business path for his heir, but his obsessive son can't bring himself to give the game away. The business is his life. However much he may want the global empire to continue in family hands, however much he might dream of his dynasty continuing, the monarch is unable to allow his children to emerge strongly from under his shadow. News Corporation was created in his image, not theirs; it is what it is because of Rupert's unceasing drive. Few, if any, could match his unrelenting pace. To hold on to News Corporation in its entirety would require the same ingenious authoritarian mindset—but Rupert is unique.

It's not only in his business life that Murdoch has stopped short of securing the dynastic future. His decision to create another family, with a third wife whose careerist drive probably equals his own, has weakened family cohesion. Wendi Deng, an MBA graduate from Yale, is originally from Guangzhou in mainland China.[32] When she met Rupert, she was a junior executive at Star TV in Hong Kong. Fluent in English and Mandarin, Wendi acted as Rupert's interpreter on several trips to China. Expanding the business in mainland China is one of his 'works in progress'. Wendi is the perfect partner for fostering good relations with the Chinese government. His 1999 marriage looks to be a perfect synthesis of his personal life with his Asian media interests.

Although Wendi has no official role in the company, News Corporation insiders say she has identified potential investments for the company and acts as her husband's liaison. In China she is seen not just to represent the company but also its owner. In a country where families and business deals are inexorably linked, this is a distinct advantage.

Their union has been accompanied by a change of lifestyle. Rupert was encouraged by son James to move to downtown New York; he now lives in the trendy and wealthy Tribeca neighbourhood. He and Wendi maintain a loft apartment near Lachlan and his wife, model Sarah O'Hare. Rupert has adopted chic Armani clothes, replacing his former trademark blazer and tie. His four children were 'amazed' when they first heard about their father's new relationship. His eldest daughter Prue, who is ten years older than Wendi, jokingly called her father a 'dirty old man'. But Prue, Elisabeth, Lachlan and James say they are happy for Rupert and find Wendi 'delightful'.

After his marriage to Wendi the Murdoch family rearranged the family company Cruden Investments—Cruden owns 30 per cent of News Corporation. Under the new arrangements, Grace, Rupert's daughter with Wendi Deng, is likely to inherit 10 per cent of Cruden shares from Rupert's individual entitlements. Rupert has placed his other four children in the position of controlling Cruden Investments and the related family company, Kayarem. Between them these four children will inherit at least 40 per cent of Cruden Investments.

Rupert Murdoch's former wife Anna is adamant that a successor to Rupert cannot come from his new and third family. It is believed that the divorce settlement ensured Anna some say in succession planning, making it difficult for Wendi Deng and her daughter to have any effect on Rupert's other children. In addition it's understood that Rupert and his children have signed prenuptial agreements with their respective spouses, which aim to secure the Cruden shares.

Rupert Murdoch is tired of the endless speculation about who will succeed him. He has said there is '. . . plenty of room for twice as many children to have satisfying, worthwhile lives in this company'. He is confident that his four eldest children 'will get together and they will work it out'. Perhaps Rupert is blind to the fierce jealousy that frequently emerges when siblings are left to sort out a rich dynastic heritage. He was lucky to be born the only son in an era when it was assumed that only boys would inherit a business—and to a father who did all he could to ensure his heir would inherit.

Then there is the 70 per cent of the company owned by

non-Murdoch shareholders. The major investment institutions will have their say in ensuring the company's success well beyond Rupert's demise. Shareholders have been happy with Rupert's reign, but this confidence has yet to extend to any of his children. Indeed, as the empire has grown there has been endless speculation about his children's talents and abilities. Many observers believe it's impossible to run a massive public corporation along nepotistic lines and Murdoch genes can't be enough to secure the top position. However, James, Lachlan and to a lesser extent Elisabeth are in the running because they have what it takes to run a corporation, they're competitive and dedicated, sometimes ruthless and aren't afraid to take risks.

But they have a father who remains infatuated with deal-making. It is said that Rupert is at his best when cornered and facing adversity. Even when he loses he looks to the next deal. He is a gambler not a manager. But what his children need now is for Rupert to consolidate the family's shareholding. They need Rupert to manage, not gamble, but for a man who is driven by the thrill of the deal it's unlikely he will change the habits of a lifetime, even for his much loved children.

For close to ninety years, gambling of one form or another has been part of the Murdoch tradition. It has usually paid off. His old headmaster James Darling once remarked that Rupert's only god was himself; now his autocratic style, coupled with boundless ambition and the hunger for risk-taking, has created a business of too great a complexity and too weak a share-holding to be smoothly handed to either of the prince regents, Lachlan or James. When Rupert leaves it will be the investors, including Malone and the Murdoch children, who will do battle over control of the second-largest media company in the world.

Rupert is tied to an image of himself as iconoclastic gambler and he continues to thumb his nose at the world. As a result, this greatest of all Australian media empires waits in uncertainty while its ageing ruler, in both his business and personal decisions, juggles with its future.

THE DE BORTOLI FAMILY

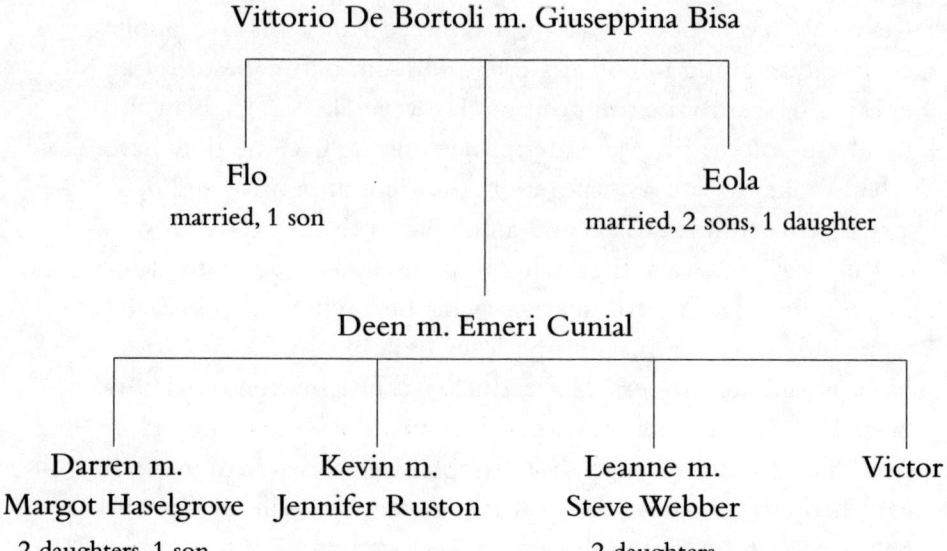

Vittorio De Bortoli m. Giuseppina Bisa

Flo
married, 1 son

Eola
married, 2 sons, 1 daughter

Deen m. Emeri Cunial

Darren m.
Margot Haselgrove

2 daughters, 1 son

Kevin m.
Jennifer Ruston

Leanne m.
Steve Webber

2 daughters

Victor

THE DE BORTOLIS

WINE critic Huon Hooke can still remember the first time he tasted Darren De Bortoli's dessert wine. The two men had been students together at Roseworthy, Australia's first viti- culture college, where they had forged a friendship based on a shared passion for wine, despite very different backgrounds. Huon, with a rowing blue from Geelong Grammar, had grown up in the Anglo-Protestant heartland of the Australian establish- ment. Darren was the grandson of an illiterate Italian migrant. Both had graduated in 1982 determined to make an impact on a burgeoning wine scene; however, while Huon moved to Sydney to work as a wine merchant, Darren returned to the family farm. A year later, Huon and his colleagues got a call out of the blue.

'He said, "Hey guys, I've got something to show you. Can I send you a bottle or something?" And we said, "What is it?" And he said, "It's a sweet wine." We were not that impressed, but Darren sent down half-a-dozen bottles of 1982 botrytis semillon, just taken as samples out of the tank. No label, nothing, and I think they sat in a corner for a few days. We really weren't that interested in opening the bottles. And when we did, just out of curiosity, and poured a glass of this stuff, which was like nectar, golden in colour and very sweet and rich and honeyed, our jaws hit the floor. It blew our heads off.'[1]

That wine, made from a grape infected with what winemakers call the 'noble rot', put the De Bortoli family on the map. Up until then, sweet wines in Australia had been of the cheap, poor-quality variety, like the hock produced in Griffith where the De Bortolis had their winery. But here, for the first time, was a dessert wine of world standard—something to compare with the best that Europe had to offer. In fact, the De Bortoli dessert wine would outclass its more expensive rivals in international competitions and sales. It was yet another triumphant chapter in a family saga that had seen the De Bortolis go from strength to strength over three generations.

These days, the De Bortolis are among Australia's top ten wine producers and exporters, with an estimated worth of more than $100 million. A casual visitor to their headquarters in Griffith could be forgiven for thinking themselves on the set of *Dallas* rather than a family winery. Huge stainless steel tanks loom above a vast production site that dominates its rural surroundings. In a tiny corner, enclosed by well-tended gardens of flowers and herbs, sits the family home. This modest house is still the setting for the family's business meetings, which generally take place over lunch. Here too is where friends gather to play *bocce* and eat, for the De Bortolis are part of a vibrant rural community that has been shaped by successive waves of Italian immigration. And it is this shared history that, up to now, has been the wellspring of the family's good fortunes.

Indeed, the family's rags-to-riches story, notwithstanding the scale of its trajectory, is a relatively common one among Australia's migrant communities, not least among those arriving in the latter half of the twentieth century from continental Europe or Asia in search of the good life. What makes the De Bortolis' story different from most of the dynasties featured in this book is that their success was not achieved in a single generation by a founding patriarch alone. Rather, the family has built its achievements over three lifespans, with each generation stamping its individual mark on this ascendancy.

This may reflect the fact that, in many respects, this family had further to climb than many, originating as it did from such humble peasant beginnings with few expectations. But it may also suggest that progress up the ranks has slowed as the upper rungs of Australian society have become increasingly crowded with established players. Certainly, the family until now has looked strongly to its own local community for its peer group. And its connections to a shared Italian heritage remain an essential part of the family's character and cohesiveness today.

It is only now, in the third generation, that the family is in the process of being absorbed into an increasingly diverse national elite. Although still headquartered in Griffith, their success has made them tall poppies in the district, and pushed the family onto a national stage. These changes, in turn, will undoubtedly have a profound impact on the family's identity as it negotiates its progress through the ranks.

Today, the De Bortolis celebrate their peasant ancestry. But three generations ago when the family patriarch, Vittorio, embarked on one of the first migrant ships to leave Italy for the new worlds of Australia and the Americas, he was set on escaping provincial hardships. Vittorio grew up in a small village in the Veneto region of northern Italy, the youngest of six children in an impoverished family of cattle farmers. Over the generations, the family's land had been divided to a point where Vittorio knew there was nothing left for him to inherit. To make matters worse, the village and its surrounding countryside, which lay on the mountainous border between Italy and the former Austro-Hungarian empire, had been devastated in World War I. There was no work to be had and even though the family had its own farm, putting enough food on the table was difficult. Faced with such bleak prospects, Vittorio pinned his hopes on a voyage into the complete unknown. It was purely coincidental that the boat on which he sailed was destined for Melbourne. The year was

1924 and he was just eighteen years old. He would never see Italy again.

On arriving in Australia, Vittorio, along with many of his compatriots, immediately set off for Griffith in south-west New South Wales, where the Murrumbidgee Irrigation Scheme had turned an arid interior into an area of high-density farming. They were peasants in search of land to work, and the city held no appeal. Nor, one imagines, would Griffith have done. With only a few low hills on the horizon and a network of irrigation channels to define the landscape, the countryside is flat and featureless. Indeed, it would be hard to envisage a greater contrast to the mountains of northern Italy. Summer brought searing heat and dust storms, but land was plentiful and the advent of a reliable supply of water had made it a region of opportunity. Mixed farming, growing vegetables and fruit, ensured there was work for all.

Just one small, grainy photograph remains in the family's possession of those early days. It shows Vittorio's first Australian home underneath a three-metre high water tank that the young man had helped build. 'They used to bring the big rocks down from Scenic Hill, smash them, and all these people would sit down with sporting hammers and make these little piles of rock, which were then used in the concrete of the tanks,' observes his son Deen today. 'These tanks are an unusual design, but he lived there for six or seven months, had a nice big vegie garden, and used to be able to swap vegies for other things he needed.'[2]

After two years of labouring on local farms, Vittorio had saved enough money to buy one of the small properties that were going cheap. Griffith had been a focal point for the government's soldier-settlement scheme, in which out-of-work veterans from World War I were given land to farm. It was a well-intentioned failure, as old-timer Keith McWilliam recalls: 'Unfortunately those people weren't farmers and they nearly all went broke. There wouldn't be more than 2 or 3 per cent of the original farms still held by the soldier-settlers or their descendants. A lot of the people that were given blocks weren't healthy people. They had been gassed and all sorts of things in the war, and they just couldn't cope. But then the Italians came in around the mid- to late 1920s. They came in the hundreds and they could buy farms very, very cheaply because you had to take over some of the debt as well.'[3]

Keith's own family of Scottish immigrants had bought land in the district before the war and had been the first to grow grapes. At the time of Vittorio's arrival, the McWilliams were Griffith's wealthiest and most influential family by far. Theirs was the only winery and their business was the lynchpin of the local economy. In addition to their own harvests, they bought grapes from local farmers, including Vittorio who, by 1928, four years after his arrival, owned three farms.

'That was when people were walking off farms because they couldn't get anything for their produce,' recounts his son Deen today. 'My father, coming from Italy, thought that was a waste.' Vittorio took over the farms and prospered, growing a variety of fruit and vegetables, including grapes. While elsewhere Australia was in the grip of the Depression, for Vittorio things had never looked brighter. Life was frugal, but there was always plenty of food on the table. Best of all, his childhood sweetheart Giuseppina had joined him. She had spent the last three years working in France as a nursery maid to pay her passage. 'They virtually got married by proxy, they were sort of married by mail, you could say. But then they had a wedding when she came out.'

This belated ceremony was not without a sense of occasion. Despite financial constraints Giuseppina, as was proper, had brought a trousseau with her, including a satin-and-lace wedding dress that she had embroidered herself. It is among the family's most treasured keepsakes—a tiny dress, almost child-sized, classically simple, and now yellowed with age. Impeccably attired in their formal best, the young couple gaze out of their wedding photograph with a sense of solemnity and portent.

In them, as with all her other photographs, Giuseppina looks like a much larger woman for she exudes a wiry strength and holds herself with dignity and pride. Her strong features are dominated by a pair of dark almond eyes that stare at the camera. Intensity and willpower emanate. In contrast, her husband is as soft-featured as she is angular. Today, Vittorio's portrait holds pride of place above the De Bortoli cellar door as the founder of the family's fortunes. But this is no stern-faced patriarch. Instead, eyes twinkling, he laughs up at a kitten perched precariously on his straw hat—the picture of the contented peasant farmer. It is an image the family is keen to cultivate, particularly in today's corporate world, but most observers agree that Vittorio knew the value of a dollar and anxiously tended the family's fortunes.

Nevertheless, while friends remember Vittorio as a shrewd operator, most agree that Giuseppina was the one with steel in her bones and the determination to make good. 'Father always claimed she was the boss. He used to call her "bossa". Whenever he wanted to know something he'd say, "Hey, Bossa! What do you think of this?" And it was always bossa, rather than her calling him boss, because she was the mouthpiece. He was the hard worker, but she was the one with the brains, and so the combination worked brilliantly for many years.' Adds Deen's eldest sister Flo, 'I think my mum has been underrated a lot, because if she were in a different situation she would have been a great woman. She had power that people didn't realise.'[4]

For Vittorio and Giuseppina, life was the farm and they devoted their energies to it. In this they were no different to most other Italian migrants who had been able to purchase land in Griffith. Keith McWilliam still credits these new citizens with 'getting the town moving' and transforming the Griffith area from a sluggish backwater into a food bowl for the nation. 'They worked extremely hard. Their women and kids were out there in the blazing heat. They worked ungodly hours, I can tell you. Eighteen hours a day would be nothing for these people. They worked with their wives all day, with their kids after school, and in the packing sheds at night—packing all the stuff they were producing.'

By the time the tide of depression turned, the land and hard work were paying off. Vittorio and Giuseppina ran their farms along traditional Italian lines, growing a mixture of produce to sell. But they had also made their first wine the year they married. Today, their descendants salute this decision as serendipitous. It had been a bumper harvest, they say, and so as not to see grapes wasted, the couple made wine for their home table. Others recall it as an opportunity grasped. Keith McWilliam can remember his uncle, as early as 1928, admiring a parcel of grapes on the De Bortolis' farm, only to be told this batch was not for sale—they were keeping the grapes for themselves.

Rough and ready though it was, the De Bortolis' wine found an appreciative audience among the Italian community. In those days many Australians drank beer with their meals, if they drank anything. Wine fell into one of two categories: either it was 'plonk', drunk by derros, or it was an aperitif. Unlike the rest of the population, however, Italians did not like sherry, port or other fortified wines. Very little table wine was being produced by commercial wineries such as McWilliam's who catered to the Anglo-Australian mainstream. The De Bortoli farm was one of the few places where migrant Italians could get the kind of wine they had grown up drinking. Keith McWilliam remembers the attraction: 'There were a lot of people who used to live within four or five miles of the place. And on a Saturday and Sunday particularly, they'd walk over to De Bortolis' with any kind of container at all—they'd have ordinary petrol tins, anything—and they'd buy their four or eight gallons. It was only about a shilling or two a gallon in those days. They'd take them off home. We could hear them singing, often at two or three in the morning.'

Among the De Bortolis' keenest customers were the migrant Italian workers who followed the harvest, coming to Griffith to pick fruit and vegetables before returning to Queensland where they worked cutting sugar cane. This itinerant community began buying 270-litre barrels of wine to take with them on their return journey north. Soon they were the mainstays of the De Bortolis' winery, as son Deen recalls: 'The Italians from the cane fields wanted dry wine, so my father made this Clarendon hock, which he was able to sell to the cane cutters. When they'd come down, they'd buy barrels and barrels of this, and they'd send it up by rail to Queensland, because in those days probably 95 per cent of all wine in Australia was fortified. It just got bigger and bigger and bigger from there.'

Family history has it that it was Giuseppina who pioneered the family's earliest commercial vintages—directing her husband's efforts by reading out instructions from the wine-making books she had ordered from France. Like most Italian farmers, Vittorio could make wine for the home table, but he had no idea how to preserve or refine it for his customers. Nor could he read or write. Giuseppina, fluent in Italian and French, was the educated one. She also became the more conversant of the two in English as she bartered private tuition from the local schoolteacher in exchange for French lessons. 'My mother learnt to speak English. She learnt to do all the accounts and she was able to run the business. I remember as a kid at night sleeping under the desk because she was doing the winery work, writing letters,' says Deen, the middle of three children. Only his eldest sister Flo, born in 1931, can remember the days before Giuseppina began working a double-shift on the farm and in the office. She remembers these as relatively carefree times, before paper-work and the demands of a growing business consumed all of her mother's time.

By the time Deen was born in 1936 and his sister Eola five years later, the family enterprise was well established and had become the centre of a small but thriving community as Vittorio and Giuseppina sponsored friends and relatives wanting to emigrate from Italy. New arrivals in Griffith would often be taken as a matter of course to the De Bortoli farm as their first point of call. Many would help out on the farm and vineyards in exchange for food and lodgings. 'My father had a lot of people come out from Italy and they had all these little huts at the back of the house, and they used to stay there. And, of course, in those days there was no money, they used to just work for their dinner and on the weekends they'd have their parties and play their *bocce*,' recalls Deen De Bortoli of an idealised past. 'I can remember as a kid still, there was a lot of fun, a lot of singing at least every night or second night, and it was sort of a period you remember, which you don't see any more. We try to resurrect it a bit now, but it's not like it was. Everybody was in the same boat. Nobody had any money, so everyone was equal, and I think there weren't the jealousies that you probably got later on. Everyone seemed to be happy.'

This labour built the farm, but there was also a sense of extended family, heightened by the fact that almost all who worked there came from the same village or nearby, and spoke the same regional dialect. When harvest and vintage brought in workers from interstate, and from other parts of Italy, they too became part of the family's life. Recalls Flo, 'Especially in the vintage, the men who came to work were also fed at home on long tables on the verandah, and they would come for their three meals a day, up to fifteen people.' While Giuseppina divided her time between the farm and the office, Vittorio divided his between the farm and the kitchen. 'I think Dad always realised the help that my mother gave to him, and quite often he'd try and help out. My dad was a great cook, so he quite often took over the cook's role if she needed to do other things.'[5]

Home was now a small brick cottage, rather than the original lean-to in which the couple had first lived. Although a mark of the family's new prosperity, the building of this new house coincided with an uncertain time in its fortunes: war had broken out in Europe, and Australia and Italy were in opposing camps. Migrant Italians were classified as enemy aliens, and many were interned for the duration of the war, or had their property confiscated. Vittorio and Giuseppina had already become naturalised Australians and as farmers were deemed to be making a valuable contribution to the war effort, so they avoided detention— unlike many of their workers and neighbours. But there were a few close calls. Flo still remembers her fear at being questioned by police because she had been boasting at school of the radio her father had bought for their new home, the family's first. From this point on, great care was taken to avoid suspicion, and the family dutifully reported in at the police station every week.

Despite these anxieties, World War II and particularly its aftermath saw a steady rise in the family's fortunes. By staying out of the internment camps and on their land, Vittorio and Guiseppina were well placed to meet the growing demand for farm produce and wine. Still, there were other battles. Strict licensing laws ensured that the large established brewers had a virtual monopoly on liquor sales, particularly if retailed in smaller quantities, most of which was sold through affiliated hotels. The family kept its head down and continued to produce wine in bulk for its migrant consumers. Nevertheless, as is quietly admitted, much was done unofficially. The local Italians in Griffith, and no doubt elsewhere, ran their own bootleg pubs or *osterias*. Liquor was also sold from the back door, although never to the plain-clothed undercover inspector who came to the front, wanting to buy brandy 'for his ailing wife'. A favourite Griffith folktale is of Vittorio finally being paid a visit by an official from the taxation department, and meeting their demand for years of back taxes by unearthing a small fortune in savings from a rusty tin can.

By the end of the war, Vittorio had the family's future clearly in his sights. He was determined that his three children would receive the opportunities he had been denied. Giuseppina was equally motivated. 'She was quite determined that whatever we wanted to do as girls, we would be allowed to do it. She gave us the feeling that to be educated and going to school was not our right, but a great privilege,' agree her daughters today. While both girls went to work in the family business, they would never labour on the land. The De Bortolis were peasants no longer.

'One good thing about Dad, he didn't want me to work on the farm, like a lot of farmers' daughters did. So I started off in the office,' recalls Flo, who still muses at what the future might have held had she been a boy. Both she and her younger sister always knew that when it came to the family succession, their brother Deen came first. 'Dad was determined to have a boy, and he was lucky the second child was a boy, because the family name was a big thing to him. From the day Deen was born, it was never left in doubt that he would take over.'

Today, it is hard to imagine Deen anywhere else. As his wife fondly points out, 'He was born actually here at the winery. His mother didn't make it into hospital. She was one of those very fortunate women who didn't have a lot of problems with child-birth. So we always feel that Deen, if he ever dies, is going to come back and haunt the place.' And, unlike his sisters, Vittorio's son from the start worked the land. 'When I was six years old, I was driving the truck down the farm, you know, if we needed to pick up the grapes, things like that,' he recalls. Despite lucrative offers to sell the farm and retire, Vittorio was adamant that in time-honoured Italian tradition the property would go to his son. However, although Deen grew up knowing where his future lay, his prospects as the heir apparent did not go unquestioned.

Indeed, if local hearsay is to be believed, Vittorio and Giuseppina's boy came of age as one of the leaders of the town's brat pack. Rock-and-roll had just hit town and Deen was an avid follower. He also loved fast cars and drove a gleaming shark-finned convertible, which he drag-raced out past the local dam. Griffith, like many country towns, is built for young men to cruise through, with an impossibly wide double-barrelled main street. It's still a place where boredom and alcohol fuel high-octane teen spirits. Few old-timers, however, have forgotten the day that young Deen De Bortoli drove over the police con-stable's toes. It's hard to dismiss this small-town gossip when photographs of the time show a cocky young man, who in features, attitude and slick-backed hair resembles no one more closely than James Dean.

It's also hard to reconcile this fashionable young man with Deen De Bortoli today. Although still a sharp dresser when occasion demands, Deen's youthful polish has largely worn off.

In his day-to-day stubbies and flannel shirt, his appearance is very much that of the ruddy-faced, salt-of-the-earth farmer. A ute has taken the place of the convertible. But all who know him will tell you that in personality little has changed. Confident, headstrong and opinionated, he can, according to his family, be stubborn to the point of perversity. And while he enjoys a challenge, Deen loves nothing more than to win— whether it is an argument, a Friday night *bocce* game among friends, or a business outcome.

Even as a young teenager Deen was determined to map his own path, irrespective of his parents' wishes. Despite Vittorio and Giuseppina's deeply felt belief in the value of education, their son dropped out of high school as soon as he could. He remains unrepentant to this day. 'I left school when I was in third year, on the day I turned sixteen, which was 17 August 1952. My father didn't want me to, but I felt I knew more than the teachers did, and I just wasn't interested. I was interested in the winery, and I think I made the right move.'

And yet Deen's focus was not on the fine art of winemaking. As he says himself: 'The wine didn't interest me in those days. It was more the mechanical side of it. I was just intrigued by the fact that you crushed the grapes, put them in a tank and they'd ferment and all this red stuff would be bubbling over. Selling wine didn't enter my head at all. I just liked the way it was made.' The following decade would see a gradual phasing out of the family's fruit growing endeavours to winemaking alone.

While Deen indulged a fascination with the mechanics of winemaking, his father was anxiously aware of the need to reach drinkers. With no opportunity to sell wine through the usual channels, he had to create his own distribution centre and home-delivery service. A small corner shop in the Sydney suburb of Kingsford, next door to the local undertaker, put him in easy reach of the growing migrant communities in the city's inner-west. It also became a means of providing for his daughters through the family business, without compromising his son's inheritance. 'Deen would take over the winery end, and the Sydney end was left to Flo and me—that was something we always knew,' says Eola today.

It was the short end of the straw. Particularly as the enterprise was designed to advantage the family winery rather than operate as a viable concern in its own right. Although Vittorio would eventually upgrade to a larger site in Annandale, his daughters agree that 'as far as Dad was concerned it didn't matter if Sydney made any money as long as the winery was benefiting from it'. Both girls were sent to manage the business with their respective husbands. Today they are joint landlords of a building that no longer has an affiliation to the winery, managing it as a rental property, and agree that the time they spent working there could have been better spent elsewhere.

'It was a great sacrifice, and there was a time that I said to my husband Silvio, you know, this is a little bit too much. But he said, "Oh, I can't let your dad down, he needs this help." So we battled on, but I wouldn't do it today. I would have just walked out!' says Flo, who still remembers the backbreaking work involved in unloading and redistributing the 270-litre barrels. 'I hope Deen appreciates the sacrifices we made on his behalf because we could have been putting that energy into our own business. But I suppose it's what you do for your family. It's very fortunate really that we did stick by Dad, because look at the business today.' Despite their contribution to the winery's success, neither sister has any involvement in the business today, nor a share in its profits. They have never returned to live in Griffith, although they keep in close touch with their brother and his family, returning for holidays and family occasions.

Vittorio's embryonic distribution system put the winery on a more secure footing, but years of work and worry had taken their toll. In 1957 he was hospitalised with ulcers. His son was determined to make things easier. The answer, Deen believed, lay in increasing mechanisation. He was sure that with the aid of his beloved machines, the farm could produce more wine, more cheaply and more efficiently. 'I always felt that you needed to get to a certain level to make it viable and to modernise it,' says

Deen, who still applauds himself for acting accordingly. 'I virtually put it all in myself. I built the actual crusher pit—or designed it myself and helped the concreters—and then set up all the elevators and conveyors with a local blacksmith.' In that year alone, the size of the winery doubled, with a corresponding jump in wine production from 700 to 1900 tonnes.

This flurry of activity coincided with a personal milestone in Deen's life. In 1958 he married his local sweetheart, Emeri Cunial. His new bride was also from an Italian family, and her parents had come from a village across the valley from Vittorio's and Giuseppina's. Like Vittorio, Emeri's father had been among the first to settle in Griffith. But unlike this peasant farmer, he was a natural linguist who spoke English without an accent, and he soon assumed a leadership role in the community as an interpreter and facilitator with Australian officialdom. Although Deen had met his match—for Emeri's elegant blonde looks and softly spoken, precise English camouflaged an equal determination and fiery temper—business always came first. 'At the time the family was extending the winery and building extra tanks, so Deen required new machinery. That meant our honeymoon was taken in Adelaide because that's where the equipment came from,' recalls Emeri with a wry smile. 'I spent my honeymoon going through machinery shops! I was still a good little bride at the time, and doing the right thing, because I knew Deen had a job to do.'[6]

Like most of her generation, Emeri would not work in the vineyards or winery, but instead made home and the family her focus. In keeping with older traditions, the new bride also joined her husband in the parental home. The two generations lived together for six years, until Vittorio decided to build himself a flat above the winery. 'I don't know about Deen's mother being very happy about leaving the house. I don't think she was. I mean, I wouldn't have been,' confesses Emeri today. 'I think Vittorio wanted to get away from all these screaming children. The family was growing, and I had three [of four] children, all under five.'

While Deen dates his stewardship of the family business from his father's illness, others believe it coincided with the arrival of this third generation. (Until that time, a passion for model trains and aeroplanes is rumoured to have competed with the winery for his attention.) Either way, in the decade that followed the birth of Deen and Emeri's children, the family winery was transformed. Not only were production levels almost doubled every year, but for the first time there was a trained winemaker on board. Louis Del Piano had arrived in Australia from Italy in the early 1950s, part of a new generation of Italians who sought a better future far from the rubble of war-torn Europe. Unlike his predecessors in Griffith, he was not from the villages but a university graduate who had celebrated the end of the war with overnight road trips to Paris and the Folies-Bergère.[7] Keeping quiet about his professional qualifications, Louis applied for a visa as a labourer and, with thousands of others, was encouraged to emigrate as part of a new manual workforce. An acquaintance directed him to Griffith where he immediately found work at the McWilliams' winery. Three and a half years later, in 1959, Vittorio De Bortoli wooed him over with the promise of an additional £5 a week and an insistence that all Italians should stick together.

Arriving in Griffith in the mid-1950s, recalls Louis, was like finding oneself on the far side of the moon, and the De Bortoli winery, despite its growing capacity, was primitive at best. 'There was no laboratory, no refrigeration. They had one decent pump and a couple of small filters, pumping wine from one bigger tank into two or three smaller tanks. In those days, they didn't even have numbers on the vats. It was amazing. I told old Mr De Bortoli, "I've got to know from which tank into which tank the wine is going." Eventually I got the stencil made myself, got some orange paint, and painted the numbers on.' More difficult was finding the funds for a basic laboratory. 'I kept insisting that I needed some laboratory equipment—you know, some flasks, a couple of Bunsen burners, things like that. I kept asking a couple of times a week. In the end, he said, "All right, all right." He took some money out of his back pocket and he gave me a ten-pound note and said, "Go buy yourself a laboratory".'

Despite these initial frustrations, Louis Del Piano remained with the De Bortolis for almost nine years. As the wine became more refined, so too did its packaging, Louis designing a family crest for the labels, which proclaimed the motto *Semper ad Majora*—'Always striving for better'. But progress was painstaking. Vittorio did not see the need to become more sophisticated and, with vivid memories of childhood poverty, he loathed spending money unnecessarily. Moreover, while not as outspoken as his son, Vittorio could be equally hard-headed. Recollects Louis, who is nothing if not loquacious: 'He would listen to me without saying anything, nod his head a bit, and then when I finished, he'd say, "You're making a long story out of nothing. Tell me in six or seven words what advantage is coming to me. If you can prove to me that I get an advantage, and I can make more money and improve the position of the winery, we'll do it." I found that he was very cunning. He knew what he was doing, and he always knew what he wanted.' Nevertheless, Louis often required Giuseppina's assistance in bringing her husband on side and credits her with being the more far-sighted of the two when it came to embracing change.[8]

Louis would also find an occasional ally in Vittorio's heir, despite a clash of egos, as Deen's ambitions now far surpassed his father's. Although he shared Vittorio's taste in wine, Deen was impatient for growth. It was in part, he says, an expression of youthful exuberance. 'As a young person you want to do things a lot quicker. At the time my father sort of pulled me into line a bit. I'd slow down for a year, but then away we'd go again, building more tanks.' Deen's incessant need to keep building—a trait still jokingly remarked on by the rest of his family—invariably meant that he also had to turn his attention to finding customers. 'I used to go out and sell wine myself in those days,' he recalls. 'I remember selling wine off the back of the truck because things were pretty hard in the early Sixties.

We went through a bad era in the industry, when things were pretty slow. But being young you just wondered why people were closing down and felt, well, that means there's more room for us.'

Confident to the last, Deen continued expanding and diversifying, putting in a bottling line and a distillery to make fortified wines like the McWilliams family. Inevitably this put him on a collision course with his father. 'We'd have a lot of rows because, typical father and son, I wanted to move on quicker than he did. So we used to have some good ding-dong battles. But they were pretty friendly,' reminisces Deen today. Adds his wife: 'Sometimes I would be in the house and I would hear Deen and Vittorio fighting out in the middle of the yard, and they would be really arguing hammer and tongs. You'd think they were going to murder each other.'

Increasingly Deen would wait for his parents to make their annual excursion to Sydney to visit their daughters and to keep an eye on the distribution business, before he embarked on his next building project. These prolonged absences became the focus of frenzied activity. 'Vittorio would go away, and Deen would have everybody lined up to do extensions. And Vittorio would come home and he'd find all these things that were done. First he would walk around the winery to see what had happened while he was away, and then there'd be an almighty explosion, and then he'd go off and he'd shake his head and he'd have to accept it. He exploded a lot, but I could relate to that because I probably am a little bit like that myself. But once he exploded, he was all right,' remembers Emeri cheerfully.

Unlike her mother-in-law who found their fights distressing, Emeri would regularly join in.[9] She and Deen had their fair share of battles too, which often culminated in smashed crockery. 'We would never really fight over business. I think that what we'd fight over were trivial things, and it was probably the pressure brought on by business and other outside things.' Even today, their disagreements are legendary among their friends. 'They have the most volatile arguments—they're Olympic standard.

They're gold medallists and you can work as hard as you can, but you can't quite get to their level. Typical Italian style—it just explodes! Then bang, it's gone, the plate's smashed, it's over.'[10]

While others could easily be left traumatised by such vehement outbursts, these arguments are simply regarded as part of the culture of the family. No matter how violent their dis-agreements, Deen and Vittorio never stopped taking their meals together. 'They'd come in, have lunch or dinner, or whatever, and discuss something else completely,' comments Emeri. Mealtimes, then as now, brought the family together, and the day's business was reviewed and discussed round the table. Not that this ensured agreement or cooperation. 'Vittorio and Deen never agreed on anything,' she confesses. 'Deen would suggest something, and Vittorio would say, "No, no, no, no", and he'd go off on a tangent. Deen's good at that now too some-times, but he is a little more lenient in giving our boys more responsibility.'

For Vittorio, who trusted only what he could see and grasp, his son's willingness to gamble on the future bordered on the reckless. Deen's constant search for improvements, his eager-ness to try new things, his delight in buying more and more equipment, and his determination to keep growing could bankrupt the business they had so painstakingly built from nothing. 'I think he was frightened of going into debt and expanding too much and sort of losing everything. I suppose, too, as he got older the technology got beyond him,' reflects Emeri today.

Deen, on the other hand, was equally sure that his investments in infrastructure would pay off. He was counting on a growing market and an escalating demand for table wines. And he began to reap dividends in the late 1960s when changes to the Trade Practices Act opened up the lucrative liquor trade to full com-petition. Bottle shops sprang up around the country, and hotels and pubs were no longer restricted in whom they could buy from. Most importantly, however, these reforms coincided with a second, quieter groundswell of change. Australia's flood of

Southern European migrants in the 1950s and 1960s, or 'wogs' as they were disparagingly known, had introduced Australian tastebuds to the delights of wine, olives and garlic. Henceforth, the country would look increasingly to Europe, not England, for its culinary inspiration. In 1972 table wines outsold fortified wines for the first time in Australia. Traditional winemakers, such as the McWilliams, were caught on the back foot. 'We were known, and known well, as a fortified wine company. Our ports, sherries and muscats were top-class, and we held a big portion of the Australian sales at that point. When people started to drink these dry [table] wines, both white and red, we were left with an enormous amount of grapes because we didn't have the market for the unfortified wines. People like the De Bortolis had a market built up there. It was very, very difficult,' recalls Keith McWilliam with some chagrin.

For Deen it was a golden opportunity. The De Bortolis had always produced inexpensive wines for people to drink with meals on an everyday basis. It was perfectly suited to this new mass market, and Deen's production lines were already in place. As wine consumption grew exponentially, so did the winery, crushing from 20 000 to 30 000 and 40 000 tonnes of grapes a year from their own and surrounding vineyards. The winery went from barrels to flagons, and then Deen led the way into cask wine by being one of the first to bag-and-box.

Vittorio, however, remained cautious to the last. His most memorable intervention came when Deen hired the company's first sales reps to address this emerging market. As far as Vittorio was concerned, these blokes in their fancy ties and suits were bludgers; he simply could not abide paying salaries to employees who did not do any useful physical work. When his son went on his first overseas trip that year, to the Munich Olympics, Vittorio called in the reps and set them to work putting in fence posts and wiring the vines. They resigned en masse. Deen, on his return, had to set up a whole new sales team. Nevertheless, Vittorio was mellowing with age, and despite his occasional outbursts, his son was well and truly in charge.

In the course of a two-decade transition, Deen had established himself as a second, perhaps even more forceful patriarch than his father. As a result, in contrast to many dynasties, this next generation would prove itself to be as adventurous and entrepreneurial as the first. Vittorio had achieved his ambitions in creating a prosperous farming venture to pass on to his son, but Deen's vision far exceeded his father's.

'Vittorio was the old school,' observes John Taylor, the De Bortolis' printer and a family friend. 'Deen had to go over his father in a lot of ways to develop. He couldn't have achieved what he did with his father's outlook.' Deen's passion for building and his mechanical aptitude reflect a faculty for numbers that makes him a natural businessman, says John, who has served as official roaster at almost every De Bortoli family occasion, and who considers Deen his mentor. 'He knows all his invoices to three decimal points. He's got the most incredible memory for detail and those types of things; he knows how much everything costs. He actually taught me the basis of costing. Another thing he taught me was not to have a wages mentality. You've got to take risks, to take the plunge. Have your vision, and achieve it bit by bit, but don't get the wages mentality.'

Despite Deen's run-ins with his father, his business acumen harks back to an old-fashioned way of doing things. As Keith McWilliam observes: 'My parents taught me the value of a quid, and I'm sure old man De Bortoli did the same with Deen.' Indeed, Deen's appetite for a bargain equals his enthusiasm for mechanisation. Most of the De Bortolis' equipment has been picked up at a fraction of the market price. Often it is second-hand and has been adapted to the job at hand. The winery's cooling apparatus, for example, was salvaged from BHP and simply made to work on wine vats rather than mines. It is both a point of honour and a source of enormous pride to Deen that he can produce wine as cheaply as anyone else in Australia. There is nothing boutique about his approach.

In fact most visitors to the winery walk past Deen, not realising they've just brushed shoulders with the owner and not the handyman. It's an impression he's happy to cultivate, and that he will often use to direct unwanted guests elsewhere, sending them on an elusive search for a more appropriately attired proprietor. Recalls John Taylor of their first introduction: 'When I met him, I knew him only as the chap who picked up the labels. He'd come in with a truck and throw them on. I always thought what a wonderful worker they'd got in this fellow. He'd be under the machine, he'd be round with a broom sweeping, every job there was, he'd be doing it. Anyway, he came in one day and picked up these labels and said they needed to order a few extra hundred thousand, which was an enormous order at that time. And I said, "I'll have to get official confirmation, I'll have to get Deen De Bortoli to authorise this." He said, "I am Deen De Bortoli."

'There he was in his usual greasy shirt and shorts from doing all the work around the winery. I still laugh about it. But Deen's never changed. He's down-to-earth. He knows every driver, every worker, and he makes it his business to get around with everybody, and I think that's the secret of his success and probably his knowledge.'

Deen's wife is less appreciative, attributing her husband's work ethic to an inability to delegate based on his unswerving conviction that no one else could do a better job. Particularly in the early years of his stewardship, Deen was the winery's troubleshooter: a one-man band who fixed the machines, ran the bottling line and oversaw the vintage. This had its downside, as Emeri is quick to point out. 'We didn't have a life because the winery just controlled everything. You just couldn't plan to go anywhere in case something happened. And invariably it always happened at school-holiday time, when you had planned to go somewhere. So we bought a caravan and it was packed and Deen would come in and say, "I think we can go tomorrow".'

Hopes too of a house of their own faded. 'We'd so many plans of houses but there was always a new extension to the winery. There was always a piece of machinery to be built or bought. I can remember when we got the first centrifuge, I used to go and look at it and I'd say, "That is my house." In those days it was nearly $200 000 for the centrifuge, and I'd say, "That is my house, that's my house".' Instead, new rooms were added to the original cottage and the old verandah enclosed, as a third generation grew up in the shadow of the winery. Their lives too would be shaped by the dynamics of the family business. 'All I can remember as a kid is my father coming home yelling obscenities and abuse about my grandfather because he had made some decision and his dad was completely against it,' says Darren, the eldest, who was born on 1 January 1960.[11]

'It was a very difficult time for the family,' recollects his sister, Leanne, 'because the business was going through a transition and Dad was taking it to that next level. There was a time, before we started to get people in with specialist skills, that he was effectively carrying the burden of the whole place on his shoulders. And there were times, as kids, when he was asleep on the couch after spending all night at the winery when you'd tiptoe through, being very mindful that you didn't want to wake him, because you knew you'd cop the wrath of him if you did. Looking back at it now, I think he just wanted to make sure the place was set up for us to slide into.'[12]

All four of Deen's children, like their father before them, worked in the winery. They might have been more hindrance than help, but pocket money was earned grape picking or sticking labels on bottles. There was still a sense of family, for most if not all of the workers had been employed on the property for most of their lives. At the same time, this third generation would have a significantly different upbringing and outlook. Fair like their mother, they grew up as part of an upwardly mobile, Anglicised mainstream, beginning with their names: Darren, Kevin, Leanne and (with a passing nod at the family patriarch) Victor. None learnt to speak Italian. Their education too would be different.

At the age of twelve, Darren was sent to board at St Joseph's College in Sydney, marking the start of a new tradition among the males in the family. 'Joeys' is among the country's most prestigious Catholic boarding schools, with a distinguished alumni of old boys, and a triumphant track record in schoolboy rugby union. After six years of Marist education and discipline, during which time he learnt to blend as unobtrusively as possible into the fabric of the school, Darren became the first member of his family to go to university when he went to Roseworthy College in South Australia to study winemaking. It was a course that had been charted for him at an early age, although not by Deen or Emeri. 'I always remember as a small child being told by my grandfather that I was going to be a winemaker. I never got those pressures from my parents, but I certainly understood from my grandparents that they had mapped out a future for me already.'

In 1979, having lived to witness his grandson's dutiful progress, Vittorio died. One wonders, however, what he would have made of Darren's contribution to the family enterprise, for his grandson would graduate from Roseworthy with a sophisticated palate, a passion for expensive wines and clear ideas of his own about the future of the business. Indeed, he would seize the opportunity to try something radically different just a year after his return in 1982, when a bumper harvest and a sluggish wine market once again left grapes on the vine.

'We made a lot of wine that year,' recalls his father. 'They were offering us grapes from everywhere. It was just a perfect year. It was virtually the same sort of year as the one when my father started in 1928. It was dry, and everything went right, and hundreds and hundreds of tonnes of grapes came in, and every tonne was better than the other.' Hectares were left unharvested, and there were rotten grapes aplenty. However, this was no ordinary rot, because, as his father suspected and Darren confirmed, Griffith by some sheer fluke of nature had the perfect climatic conditions for a fungal infection called botrytis. Indeed, the few bottles of wine that remained from Vittorio and Giuseppina's first vintage in 1928 had the telltale sweetness of having been botrytis affected. However, in Australia, unlike Europe, the infection was regarded as a scourge not a blessing because nobody drank sweet dessert wine, let alone prized it. This all changed when Darren received his father's blessing to attempt a French-style sauterne.

It was a tremendous gamble. By breaking new ground, Darren would fly in the face of entrenched prejudices, assuming his experiment in making the dessert wine succeeded. Looking back, even he finds it extraordinary that his father was prepared to take the risk. 'You must remember the wine industry was in a fairly poor state, so it wasn't really the time to be encouraging or doing something new. I was very fortunate I had the full support of my father. I can't imagine a big multinational conglomerate making a decision like that because it represents a serious amount of money to buy the fruit. You still have to pay the going rate, and the wine might turn out to be absolute rubbish. Not only that, there was strong consumer resistance to sweet wines because they were equated to being cheap wines, although Noble Rot actually makes some of the world's greatest and most expensive wines.'

That first vintage, in 1982, became one of them. 'That 1982 sauterne has won more medals and trophies internationally than any wine in world history,' boasts John Taylor gleefully. In fact, it proved so successful that it quickly encountered the fierce opposition of French winemakers who used the industry's strict labelling laws to try and see off the challenger. The De Bortolis were eventually forced to abandon the name 'sauterne' in favour of the sobriquet 'Noble One'. Despite such obstacles critical acclaim ensured sales, and this groundbreaking dessert wine henceforth became the family's calling card as it moved into new markets in Australia and overseas.

It did not succeed, however, in circumventing a prolonged battle of wills between the next generation of father and son. 'Those first four or five years tended to be extremely vocal,' confesses Darren of his early working relationship with Deen. 'You know, sort of tantrum-throwing, yelling matches. I'd make a decision and my father would disagree with it and I'd be severely reprimanded, and I'd insist it was the right decision. I think what happens after a period of time is that you get more of those right than wrong, and therefore you get a level of respect or tolerance maybe.'

'It's nice to know some things don't change,' smiles his aunt Eola, who witnessed those early exchanges on her visits to the winery. For Emeri, who had also seen it all before, those out-bursts were only to be expected. 'I think when the young ones come up out of schooling, or whatever, they do think they know it all, and they have all these different ideas. And, of course, you have the old bulls that have got their ideas and are not willing to concede to the younger ones. It's inevitable that Darren wanted to prove he could do things, and Deen didn't think he could.' At the time, however, there was little room for complacency as relationships were stretched to breaking.

'I remember one major argument with my father, to the extent that that was it. I was heading off. I didn't have to put up with it so I was packing the car and in the process of leaving,' recalls Darren. It was only Emeri's intervention that saved the day. 'My mother stole my keys. By the time she handed the keys back everyone had calmed down and we were able to approach things in a rational light. But I always think what would have happened had she not pinched the car keys.' (In fact Emeri had been so worried about her son's intentions that she had hidden the keys of every vehicle on the property.)

One of their most trenchant debates was over where the family could expand to next. Although Griffith now produced one of the world's great dessert wines, there was not the same potential to generate premium table wines. Darren had his heart set on buying land in the Yarra Valley, which he had visited while still a student. He believed the area could become one of the great winemaking regions in the country. Not only was its cool climate suited to producing some of Europe's greatest varieties, including chardonnay, cabernet sauvignon and pinot noir, it was perfectly positioned at just over an hour's drive from Melbourne. Sydney had the Hunter Valley and Adelaide the

Barossa, but this promising Melbourne hinterland was still devoted primarily to dairy farming.

While Deen was always looking for new ways to expand, the Yarra was an ambitious undertaking. There was little in the way of infrastructure, and cool-climate viticulture was still relatively new to Australia. His son 'ranted and raved and kicked doors' before finally throwing down the gauntlet. 'Darren said at the time, "Well, if we don't get a cool-climate property, I'm leaving",' recalls his mother. It could not have come at a worse time personally, for Emeri and Deen were now caring for Giuseppina who had Alzheimer's disease. The indomitable woman who had been the matriarch of a dynasty would struggle with the disease for more than a decade, eventually dying when she was ninety-one. While little else remained of the individual she had once been, Giuseppina's strength of will persisted to the very end.[13]

Despite these pressures, Deen and Emeri began making the five-hour drive south to explore the possibilities. Shortly thereafter, in 1987, they bought their first property in the Yarra and began the capital-intensive process of establishing vineyards, and a winery with its own restaurant to encourage tourists from Melbourne.[14] 'Deen conceded Darren was right,' says Emeri, but only 'after the usual arguments of course.' This time it was her husband who'd been found lagging behind youth. 'I think in the back of Deen's mind, he probably knew it was the right decision all along. It was inevitable. But to do it was hard at the time—very hard.'

In fact, the investment could have been better timed from a financial as well as personal point of view, because it came just before the 1989 recession. Cash flow was tight and the family, like many others, came perilously close to being overextended. Nor was the family's presence entirely welcome. Despite Noble One, the family had a down-market reputation and, as Darren's sister Leanne reflects: 'There were quite a few people who felt that we would come in and bastardise the region. I suppose, in some respects, we had a lot to prove.' Prove it they did, and the gamble paid off. The family's first vintages suggested enormous potential and, as others quickly followed the family's lead, the Yarra became—as Darren had predicted—one of the most sought-after tourist destinations and wine-producing regions in the country. Stephen Shelmerdine of Melbourne's Myer dynasty, who also has vineyards in the Yarra and is a family friend, insists that the De Bortolis should be given much of the credit for this.

Once again the Yarra venture demonstrated the family's ability to anticipate a new trend in consumer habits and tastes. While bulk wine continues to make up 70 per cent of the Australian market—and over 60 per cent of the company's turnover—an upsurge in consumer spending over the next decade and into the new century found expression in a tourism and gastronomy boom. The Yarra Valley and the wines it produced thus added a vital new string to the dynasty's bow.

'It's very important for De Bortoli to be in the premium wine market,' points out Huon Hooke, who has kept close tabs on the family's progress since his days at Roseworthy with Darren. 'It's a very important, growing section of the market, and a very profitable section. Certainly a much more profitable segment than the cheap wine market.' He believes the family's decision to expand into the Yarra reflects its synthesis of the personal with the commercial. 'I think the main reason Darren's parents did it was twofold. Firstly, to give the younger generation an extra interest—something to focus on that was more interesting to produce than what they'd been doing before. And premium wine is much more interesting to make than bulk wine. At the same time, it did wonders for the image of De Bortoli. If a company produces a flagship wine then that glory rubs off on all their other products, and I think that's definitely happened with De Bortoli. In fact, I couldn't think of a better example of that than De Bortoli.'

The family's feted and expensive Yarra Valley table wines have made the name De Bortoli synonymous with the best vintages Australia has to offer—most strikingly in 1997 when the winery was given the country's most prestigious wine award, the Jimmy Watson Trophy, for Best Young Red. Despite the plaudits, Deen has remained an ardent champion of cask wine, loudly defending its quality against the more expensive tastes of his son. 'It's a bit of a family joke that, in terms of wine styles, what my father likes and what I think are good are poles apart,' admits Darren. Observes his sister, 'Darren certainly has a far better palate than Deen has, but then Deen's quite happy, like many Italians, just drinking the wine he's made here.'

Father and son's divergent drinking tastes have brought them to different understandings of the family business, at least according to the son. 'Deen's position was to be one of the largest wine companies in Australia, whereas my position was to be one of the better winemakers in Australia, and not try to be big for the sake of being big.' According to his mother, however, the contrast is not quite so stark. 'Darren's and Deen's ideas have fused together. Sometimes both of them will argue and I will say, "Don't you realise you're arguing about the same thing?" They're both so keen to get their point across that they don't realise it's the same point.'

Certainly the two men seem to have forged a comfortable working relationship since Darren took over as CEO of the family company in 1994. In their shared office, across the road from the family home, Deen's schoolboy-sized desk, covered in a mountain of paper and receipt butts, sits alongside Darren's more typical computer-focused work space. While Darren has taken responsibility for most of the day-to-day operations of the company, Deen has continued to oversee major new projects and acquisitions. Even he acknowledges that his son's greater expertise in winemaking has freed him to concentrate on the things he likes best. While Darren is likely to be found having a cigarette on the office balcony as he struggles with the pressures of running a multimillion-dollar business, Deen is more often than not out and about—'building something', says his son.

Their different work spheres reflect the two men's enormous differences in style. Unlike his father's workmanlike shopfloor approach, Darren espouses the ethos of the contemporary corporate executive and stresses the importance of delegation and reliable, skilled staff. But father and son's segregation, says Darren, also ensures that both men have their distinct areas of responsibility and each does not encroach on the other's domain. The same holds true for each of Darren's three siblings, all of whom followed their older brother into the family business. While Darren is based at the company's Griffith head-quarters, his sister Leanne has managed the Yarra Valley winery with her husband, Steve Webber, since 1988. Steve, whom she married in 1987, is also the family's chief winemaker. Closer to home, middle brother Kevin runs the family's vineyards in Griffith. Unlike his eldest brother, Kevin is very much the farmer, with little time for office politics; unlike his father, he is also 'the quietest one of the family'. In contrast Victor, the youngest, is perhaps the most fiscally qualified of the family with a degree in accountancy. He has joined Darren in the office where he works in exports. Deen, who swore off advising his children what to do, takes a matter-of-fact view. 'It was good they all landed back in the place and we've made sure there was enough expansion so that if ever they got in each other's way, you could send them anywhere. But they've always gone very good, so there's never been a problem.'

His wife is less laconic. It's important to her that each of her offspring has found their niche in the business, and she has clearly had a firm but subtle hand in ensuring this outcome. When Victor wanted to try working in a particular sales area, it was his mother he spoke to about it. Although she is the only family member not to have an official position in the company, all agree that as everyone's sounding board, Emeri is crucial to how the family functions.[15] For her, this is simply a reflection of a mother's traditional role. 'I think that most mothers tend to be the centre of the family because we love each of our children equally and, if you love your husband, you can relate to him as well. You can see where the faults lie, and who's to blame, and you manage to try and calm the waters.'

But Emeri is more than a mediator. It is she who has shaped the family's traditions and, by extension, its future direction and progress. She, perhaps more than any other family member, has also determined the way in which business is conducted, with decisions still being made round the kitchen table. Father, sons and their respective spouses still have lunch together through the week and talk shop. As always opinions can become heated, but are tempered by an abundance of good food and wine. Other family traits have also become manifest. 'Darren can be a little bit like Deen,' observes Emeri. 'When somebody mentions an idea he'll just say, "Oh no, no, no." But then he'll go off and think about it and see its possibilities. We all recognise that. Knowing each other's personalities helps to make decisions, and it helps us accept each other and know how to handle each situation.'

While daughter Leanne and husband Steve are generally a phone call away in the Yarra, they are included in all major discussions and make regular visits to the family home. More often than not, Darren and Steve have found themselves in opposing camps, including recently on the need for the business to take a more structured marketing approach. In the end, however, a strong consensus operates. And all agree that the family's administration, ad hoc and organic as it may be, has worked well up to now in ensuring a flat management structure with a short chain of command and good communication channels. 'You can have a lot of misrepresentation if you're a bigger bureaucracy, whereas if we see that something needs to be taken care of, it's done immediately,' points out Emeri.

She hopes this communication and decision-making process will continue once she and Deen are no longer there to referee. For her, the lunch table will always be where the family gathers to touch base and discuss business, irrespective of the cook or the quality of the meals. 'I think they'd come over regardless of whether it was a sandwich or whatever. It's the convenience of having lunch and an acceptance of a family tradition. It always has been. I mean, when Deen and I got married that was the way things were done. Whoever comes into this house will have to end up cooking because it just seems the tradition of this house.'

Who that will be, however, is open to question. None of her three sons still lives at home. Victor has an apartment in town, and the two eldest live across the road from the winery with their wives, who both work in the family business. Neither has married a local girl: Darren's wife, Margot, is from a South Australian winemaking family, and Kevin's partner, Jennifer, is from Canada. Each brings her own contemporary sensibility to their role in the family. Moreover, although as the eldest, 'it seems to be the logical conclusion that Darren will take over from his father', he will not be the sole inheritor of the family business. Instead, it will be equally divided among all four siblings, as his sister Leanne makes clear. 'With my three brothers and myself, I think that in my parents' eyes we all contribute equally to the business and at the end of the day we'll all be treated equally. And certainly that is quite different to the way it was in the past.' In this instance Deen, with his wife's support, is adamant about breaking with tradition. 'I'm a bit different to most Italians. They always give preference to the boys and the girls always miss out. But I think that's wrong.'

Such progress will bring its own challenges, at least in the eyes of his eldest son. 'This is really the golden period for me,' acknowledges Darren of his parents' ownership of the company. 'Being the eldest, I really have got a fairly free rein. When my brothers and sisters come on board, and my father and mother are no longer around, I am going to look back on this period with great fondness because of the degree of autonomy I've got.' But while this period of Darren's stewardship may be charmed in some respects, it has been turbulent in others, not least perhaps because of the family's growing power and influence.

Today Griffith is one of the most prosperous towns in regional Australia. Many of its migrant families have made good, and the De Bortolis are only one of its many rags-to-riches stories, which include the Miranda wine family and the

Bartha family, who recently became Australia's largest chicken producers when they bought out Steggles. The district's disproportionately high number of agricultural entrepreneurs means Griffith has always enjoyed full employment, and a steady stream of new migrants—largely from Fiji and India—are replicating the Italian experience. Meanwhile many of its earlier immigrants are seen as part of a growing local establishment. Despite their modest lifestyle, the De Bortolis, along with the McWilliams, are considered the cream of this very wealthy crop.

While the family has always enjoyed a high local profile, its new status has placed considerable strain on old community ties, particularly in the face of harsh economic realities. In 2001, a booming market for table wine finally reached saturation point. Darren, with his father's approval, was determined to keep volume and prices down. While the family saw itself as hostage to market forces, this perception was not always shared. 'It's very difficult when we set grape prices because we have to make a business decision and you know it can affect your friends. You don't want that to happen, but it also means that if we don't make that decision we won't be around in years to come,' reflects Emeri. 'I don't think the wider community understands the struggle we go through in making the decisions we make. They think we are just trying to get prices down so that we can make big profits. But you know in your heart that you're not really the bad person, it's just the market.'

As vintage approached tempers flared, including Darren De Bortoli's when he found himself faced with growers hostile to the winery's pricing decisions at a company-sponsored dinner. 'Unfortunately I didn't anticipate the resentment the growers felt over the price reductions, which was probably a major mistake and very naive on my behalf. While I was trying to explain what I felt the future held, I got heckled by a few of our younger growers. At which point all the emotion and pent-up tension suddenly found an outlet, and I proceeded to lose it completely.' His response was to tell growers that those unhappy with the company's terms could take their grapes elsewhere.

It was bitter medicine and his outburst—which according to one grower included 'every expletive in the book'—set the gossip mills churning. With an annual crush of close to 50 000 tonnes, the De Bortolis were responsible for buying up approximately 20 per cent of the local harvest. Now speculation abounded that the family was in difficulty and abandoning its growers; some even went so far as to say that Darren had been assigned bodyguards in the face of escalating hostilities. These rumours were wildly overblown, but they mirrored the shifting sands of community expectations and antagonisms.

'Sometimes there's an expectation that if there's a problem, it's okay, De Bortoli will take it. And I find that the most frustrating, gut-wrenching sort of emotional pressure because the reality is we're not going to take grapes if we can't sell them,' insists Darren. 'My job is to ensure that the company remains in a strong, healthy, viable position, and it is very difficult when you have an emotional relationship with your grower base, because that complicates the decision-making process. It shouldn't, but the reality is of course it will.' Most grape growers consider Darren a tougher businessman than his father. As John Dal Broi, whose family has sold grapes to the De Bortolis for two generations, observes: 'Deen's the sort of guy who's very friendly out in the field. He loves being out on the farm and talking to growers. So we have a difference here. They're both good businesspeople, but under current pressures and given the size of the business now, you can't be Mr Nice Guy all the time.'[16]

While he may no longer be a regular at the local Catholic Club—in the interests of avoiding business arguments—Deen has grown up among the Griffith community alongside many of his growers. John Dal Broi is a regular guest at his home and a fellow *bocce* player. He is one of a close circle of friends who, says Emeri, 'know us as people, as friends, and not as someone who owns a business'. As her sister-in-law Eola points out: 'I think that Deen and Emeri have a very strong family in the Griffith community. I think they are very well thought of.

Sometimes that can be quite difficult for sons and daughters to keep up with.'

Certainly one suspects that their eldest son leads a more isolated existence. As one local farmer observed, 'He's the third generation, Darren is, and he probably hasn't had it as tough as what his father did.' For a town built on migrant labour, earning one's position in the community remains a key point. 'I don't think you'd be accepted in this society if you were old money, because unless you worked to achieve it I don't think they want to know you,' reflects John Taylor. But more than having to constantly prove himself, as did his father before him, Darren by virtue of interests and associations no longer seems one of the lads.[17] His peer group, one imagines, is in the cities among those who share his tastes in expensive wine and his corporate outlook. Taller and heavier-set than his father, he also looks more suited to the boardroom than the farm. As sister Leanne points out, 'I think Darren has a different style to Deen's that no doubt comes from going through university and studying, but then Darren has something quite different to contribute to the company.'

Up to now that contribution has entailed giving the family business a higher, more up-market profile at home and abroad. But as the company continues to grow, so too does the pressure to put it on a more corporate footing. The winery now employs more than two hundred staff, many with highly specialist skills. At the same time, the family is getting bigger as a fourth generation of De Bortolis grows up with aspirations of its own. When prompted by her grandfather, Leanne's daughter Kate pertly responds that she'd like to be vice-president one day. Meanwhile Darren's eldest son Ben is 'adamant he's going to be the boss', says his father. This has its advantages in encouraging Ben to do his homework, but 'whether that happens' remains to be seen.

'If he can do it on merit: fantastic,' says Darren. But he also believes that 'at some point, we're going to have to draw the line in terms of nepotism because you can't keep employing family members irrespective of their talents. It's a difficult issue to resolve. But there may come a time that there may not be a generation or group of De Bortolis coming through who are capable of taking the company to the next step. It may even be that I'm incapable of taking the company to the next step and that's just the harsh reality of life.'

For Darren, recent efforts to diversify the company's interests outside winemaking have not been successful. The family was one of the big losers when the insurance giant HIH collapsed, having bought twenty-three million shares only a year before the company went into receivership. (Town gossip was quick to respond, dubbing Darren 'Steve Austin, the Six Million Dollar Man', because of the estimated loss. This sturdy irreverence and cynicism no doubt has gone a long way to keeping the family's feet firmly on the ground.) Irrespective of his own abilities as CEO, however, Darren believes it is inevitable that as the family and company grow larger, success based on the characteristics of the various family members involved will no longer hold sway. With this in mind, he and his siblings have kept a close watch on McWilliams' wines where shares in the family business are held by four separate companies, each representing the descendants of the founding patriarch's four sons. While some family members still work in the business and a representative from each branch of the family sits on the board of directors, it is run virtually as a public company with an independent CEO. This has made things somewhat restrictive and impersonal, says Keith McWilliam who still harks back to the good old days, but it has ensured the long-term stability and success of the family company. Now stretching over five generations, McWilliams' Wines remains a market leader, valued at more than $140 million.

For Deen, the De Bortoli winery has always been an expression of the people behind it. 'It's the family that makes the business. I think it's important that family can carry out what they're capable of carrying out rather than the other way around.' According to his son, however, the interests of the company must eventually take precedence over those of individual family members. Much as he likes history, he says, there is no room for sentimentality in business. While selling out to a public corporation is anathema to Deen, as it was to his father, his son believes even this may be inevitable as the sums of money on offer become too tempting to refuse. (In 2001 Rosemount Wines, one of the staunchest family companies in the business, accepted a billion-dollar offer by Southcorp to merge into the public corporation, which now owns a handful of old family names.)

It seems inevitable, when looking at the history of dynasties past, that the flavour and character of the De Bortoli dynasty will eventually become absorbed into a mainstream business elite. Certainly Darren, if not his father, appears resigned to this possibility. 'I wouldn't want to see De Bortoli become a public company, but I'm also a realist and I know that it's going to occur—it's just a question of when.' In financial terms, such a deal could well be the De Bortolis' crowning achievement, but many believe the family will not make such a final break with the past. (Keith McWilliam remains convinced that it will stay a family-owned company, but that it will have to change its outlook, perhaps mimicking the path his family has taken.) Certainly there seems little doubt that with each generation the family will continue to revise its dynastic traditions as it makes steady progress away from its rural Italian roots. The only thing they can not afford to change are the arguments.

ENDNOTES

THE MACARTHURS

1 John Macarthur-Stanham, interviews, Camden Park, September 1999 and November 2000. All quotes from John Macarthur-Stanham are taken from these interviews.

2 Beverley Kingston, *Elizabeth Macarthur*, Historic Houses Trust of New South Wales, Sydney, 1984, p. 3.

3 Lennard Bickel, *Australia's First Lady: The Story of Elizabeth Macarthur*, Allen & Unwin, 1991, p. 16.

4 Elizabeth Macarthur, 'Journal of the Voyage to New South Wales', Macarthur Papers, vol. 12, Mitchell Library. Elizabeth in later writings would never offer any comment on the harshness of convict life in the penal colony.

5 J.B. Hirst, *Convict Society and its Enemies*, Allen & Unwin, Sydney, 1983, p. 151.

6 Alan Atkinson, interviews, September 1999 and November 2001.

7 Beverley Kingston, op. cit., p. 5.

8 M.H. Ellis, *John Macarthur*, Angus & Robertson, Sydney, 1955, pp. 207–208.

9 John Macarthur, Memorial to Lords of the Committee of the Privy Council, London, January 1804 as cited in S.M. Macarthur-Onslow, ed., *The Macarthurs of Camden*, Rigby, Sydney, 1973.

10 J.C. Garran & L. White, *Merinos, Myths and Macarthurs*, Australian National University Press, Canberra, 1985.

11 Despite the advantages of monopoly and his determination to invest in trading opportunities, Macarthur had not profited as much from his position as regimental paymaster as had similar officers in other colonial services, notably India. It is also perhaps

worth noting that Captain Anthony Kemp, Macarthur's successor as paymaster-general in the Corps, was considerably more aggressive in capitalising on his position. He maintained a shop in Sydney Town, from where he retailed goods (at considerable profit to himself), and paid his troops in kind. When any soldier collected his monthly pay, he would be invited to select goods from the shop to the value of his income. But if any soldier held out for money, 'Kemp turned on him furiously, called him a "damn saucy mutinous rogue", and threatened to have him flogged for his impertinence. Against this bullying, the soldier had no redress; he was forced to take his pay and dispose of the goods as best he could.' M.C. & T.B. Kemp, 'Captain Anthony Fenn Kemp', *Journal of the Royal Australian Historical Society*, vol. 15, March 1965, p. 11, as cited in Ross Fitzgerald & Mark Hearn, *Bligh, Macarthur and the Rum Rebellion*, Kangaroo Press, Sydney, 1988, p. 42.

12 C.M.H. Clark, *A History of Australia*, vol. 1, Melbourne University Press, Melbourne, 1962, p. 138.

13 Ross Fitzgerald & Mark Hearn, op cit., p. 72.

14 As well as questioning Macarthur's land grants, Governor Bligh alienated many of his would-be allies among the colony's new settlers and emancipated convicts by consistently refusing them land grants. Meanwhile, he himself had embraced entitlements of over 400 hectares which he enthusiastically developed at government expense.

15 As cited in Lennard Bickel, op. cit., p. 63.

16 Ross Fitzgerald & Mark Hearn, op. cit., p. 115.

17 Colonel Johnstone, the officer who led the coup at Macarthur's behest, was courtmartialled and cashiered. Easygoing and easily influenced, he eventually returned to his property, Annandale Farm, on the outskirts of Sydney Town.

18 Beverley Kingston, op. cit., p. 9.

19 Quentin Macarthur-Stanham, interview, November 2000, Camden Park. All quotes from Quentin Macarthur-Stanham are taken from this interview.

20 Beverley Kingston, op. cit., p. 7.

21 Jill Conway, 'Elizabeth Macarthur', *Australian Dictionary of Biography*, Melbourne University Press, CD-ROM, Melbourne, 1992–96.

22 Governor Macquarie's associations included his friendship with the convict architect Francis Greenway who, under commission to the crown, would bestow on Sydney several of its finest public buildings.

23 S.M. Macarthur-Onslow, op. cit., p. 34.

24 Perhaps John Macarthur's most audacious venture was his 1824 establishment of the Australian Agricultural Company, ostensibly designed to oversee colonial wool production. Despite the enthusiastic subscription of British shareholders, the enterprise was viewed with great scepticism in the colony where it was seen as little more than a vehicle for bolstering the family's fortunes— and, indeed, it soon foundered.

25 Ross Fitzgerald & Mark Hearn, op. cit., p. 123.

26 'William Charles Wentworth', *Australian Dictionary of Biography*, op. cit.

27 *Sydney Gazette*, 15 April 1834.

28 M.H. Ellis, op. cit., pp. xiv–xvi.

29 Beverley Kingston, op. cit., p. 8.

30 Ibid., p. 9.

31 Ibid., p. 7.

32 Lennard Bickel, op. cit., p. 176.

33 A.T. Atkinson, 'John Macarthur Before Australia Knew Him', *Journal of Australian Studies*, no. 4, June 1979, p. 37.

34 Alan Atkinson, interviews, September 1999 and November 2001.

35 Lennard Bickel, op. cit., p. 177.

36 A.T. Atkinson, 'The Political Life of James Macarthur,' PhD thesis, Australian National University, 1976, p. 1.

37 'John Macarthur', *Australian Dictionary of Biography*, op. cit.

38 S.M. Macarthur-Onslow, op. cit.

39 'John Macarthur', *Australian Dictionary of Biography*, op. cit.

40 John Macarthur-Stanham, interview.

41 As Quentin Macarthur-Stanham observes of Camden Park: 'The heyday of the place undoubtedly started at John Macarthur's

death, when James and William managed the place and this house was being finished and furnished, and the property developed and expanded.'

42 A.T. Atkinson, 'The Political Life of James Macarthur', op. cit., p. 1.

43 John Wrigley, Camden Historical Society, interview, November 2000.

44 Beverley Kingston, op. cit., pp. 7, 11.

45 'James Macarthur', *Australian Dictionary of Biography*, op. cit.

46 Elizabeth resisted most invitations to visit her son and daughter-in-law at Camden Park, preferring to remain at Elizabeth Farm which she now shared with her youngest daughter Emmeline and Emmeline's husband Henry Parkes.

47 *Some Early Records of the Macarthurs of Camden*, edited by Sibella Macarthur-Onslow, was first published by Rigby Ltd in 1914.

48 'Sibella Macarthur-Onslow', *Australian Dictionary of Biography*, op. cit.

49 Sibella's social achievements included the founding of the Ladies' Empire Club in London and (with her brother, George) the People's Reform League of New South Wales to raise the standard of morality in public life.

50 'Sibella Macarthur-Onslow', *Australian Dictionary of Biography*, op. cit.

51 Other land around Camden had by now been sold off, including to ex-employees, giving rise eventually to the town of Camden.

52 J.B. Hirst, op. cit., p. 150.

53 'James Macarthur-Onslow', *Australian Dictionary of Biography*, op. cit.

54 Helen's younger sister, Elizabeth, had been living at Camden Park after their father's death and had hoped that Helen would not take up her inheritance, but rather pass it on to her. Ironically, Elizabeth had been left a family house in Surrey, England, which she could have offered Helen in compensation, but she sold this without consulting her sister or offering her first refusal. Had Helen been offered the house in England, she might have chosen not to return to Australia, and the family history would have been quite different.

55 Andalusia Richardson, *Andy's Annals*, Christopher Blackstone, 1997, p. 71.

56 Marion Millwood, interview, Sydney, November 2000 and January 2001. All quotes from Marion Millwood are taken from these interviews.

57 Mark Macarthur-Stanham, interview, Cowra, January 2001. All quotes from Mark Macarthur-Stanham are taken from this interview.

58 Anne Jeffreys, interview, Cowra, January 2001. All quotes from Anne Jeffreys are taken from this interview.

59 Mark still sees many of the former estate workers, their sons and families in Camden and—as he muses with some irony on his own landless position—many of them have their own farms these days.

60 Edwina Macarthur-Stanham, interview, Camden Park, September 1999 and November 2000.

THE DURACKS

1 Ernestine Hill, *The Territory*, Angus & Robertson, Sydney, 1951.

2 Interview with Mary Durack, *National Times*, 2–8 September 1983, p. 32.

3 Interview with Anne Barker (nee Durack), Perth, 31 March 2001. All quotes from Anne Barker are taken from this interview.

4 Mary Durack, *Kings in Grass Castles*, Constable, London, 1985, pp. 80–81.

5 Ibid., pp. 296–97.

6 Ibid., p. 242.

7 Mary Durack, *Sons in the Saddle*, Constable, London, 1983, p. 1.

8 Ibid., p. 50.

9 Mary Durack, *Kings in Grass Castles*, p. 347.

10 Ibid., p. 409.

11 Interview with Professor Geoffrey Bolton, Pro-Vice-Chancellor, Murdoch University, Perth, 1 April 2001.

12 Mary Durack, *Sons in the Saddle*, pp. 152–55.

13 Patsy Millett & Naomi Millet (eds), *Pilgrimage: A Journey Through the Life and Writings of Mary Durack*, Bantam, Sydney, 2000, p. 37.

14 Ibid., p. 13.

15 Interview with Enid Durack, Perth, 31 March 2001. All quotes from Enid are taken from this interview.

16 Chips Mackinolty, *Sydney Morning Herald*, 28 August 1991, p. 15.

17 Interview with John Durack, 7 April 2001.

18 Victoria Laurie, 'Unfinished Business: The Legacy of the Durack Dynasty', *HQ* magazine, March/April 1998, p. 56.

19 Elizabeth Durack created a public furore in 1997 when she announced to a journalist she had used the pseudonym 'Eddie Burrup' for some of her recent work. She also created detailed 'biographical' notes about Eddie to accompany his art on show. Elizabeth didn't regard the use of a pseudonym or the 'biographical' details as deception. She argued she was indeed painting as 'Eddie', an Aboriginal elder, and that her life in the North provided her with an understanding of Aboriginal life. Elizabeth had always used Aboriginal motifs and this was merely taking the practice a step further. Elizabeth was firm in her belief that just as it was acceptable for Aboriginal painters to paint in a European style, it was equally acceptable for her to use an Aboriginal style and pseudonym.

20 Interview with Ben Ward and Jeff Chunuma, Cockatoo Springs, 4 April 2001.

THE DOWNERS

1 Tony Staley, a long-time king-maker in the Liberal Party, was 'an expert at political destabilisation', Mike Steketee, 'The day of the dream team', *Australian Magazine*, July 23–24, 1994.

2 Alexander Downer, ABC-TV News, 23 May 1994.

3 John Hepworth, interview, Adelaide, October 1999 and December 2000. All quotes from John Hepworth taken from these interviews.

4 Stella Downer, interviews, Sydney, September 1999 and Sydney and Adelaide, December 2000. All quotes from Stella Downer are taken from this interview.

5 Alexander Downer as cited in Peter Ward, 'Born of the Liberals', *Australian*, 11 June 1994.

6 Dennis Grant, interview, Canberra, November 2000. All quotes from Dennis Grant are taken from this interview.

7 John Hepworth, interview.

8 *Australian Dictionary of Biography*, Melbourne University Press, CD-ROM, 1992–96.

9 Robert Lacour-Gayet, *A Concise History of Australia*, Penguin Books, Melbourne, 1976, p. 148.

10 Fayette Gosse, *The Gosses: An Anglo-Australian Family*, Brian Clouston, Canberra, 1981.

11 Robert Lacour-Gayet, op. cit., p. 170.

12 Bishop John Hepworth, interview.

13 Ibid.

14 Fayette Gosse, op. cit., p. 97.

15 Marjorie Barnard, *A History of Australia*, Angus & Robertson, Sydney, 1962, p. 200.

16 Robert Lacour-Gayet, op. cit., p. 172.

17 Bishop John Hepworth, interview.

18 as cited in *Famous Australians*.

19 John Bannon, interview, Adelaide, December 2000. All quotes from John Bannon are taken from this interview.

20 *Australian Dictionary of Biography*.

21 Ibid.

22 Ibid.

23 Alexander Downer, interviews, Adelaide, October 1999 and Canberra, November 2000. All quotes from Alexander Downer are taken from this interview.

24 *Australian Dictionary of Biography*.

25 Ibid.

26 John Bannon, interview.

27 'My father was a great believer in the sort of Menzian vision of building Canberra as the national capital—not the sort of attitude you often find towards Canberra, which is that it's an unfortunate necessity—and he wanted to make a contribution. He was very excited about the suburb that had been named after his father. He liked that sort of thing.' Alexander Downer, interview.

28 Stella Downer, interview.

29 Alexander Downer, interview.

30 Alexander Downer, *Six Prime Ministers*, Hill of Content Publishing Company, Melbourne, 1982, p. xi.

31 Fayette Gosse, op. cit., p. 190.

32 Sir Alexander's glowing view of Empire as a bastion of democratic freedoms—at least compared with the rest of the world—was shared by many others of his background, not least by his half-cousin Sidney Downer, Sir John's grandson by his first marriage. Sidney would pen a heartfelt tribute to the Empire and its values, with the signature line 'Let us be grateful for what we stand', while also imprisoned in Changi. Unlike Sir Alexander, however, Sidney had joined the RAF as an officer.

33 Lady Mary Downer, Interviews, Adelaide, October 1999 and December 2000. All quotes from Lady Downer are taken from these interviews.

34 Bishop John Hepworth, interview.

35 Confirms family historian and relative Fayette Gosse: 'They gave without prejudice and without fuss. For years efforts were made to complete St Peter's Anglican Cathedral which lacked its towers. One morning the officers of the diocese were electrified by the receipt of a cheque for £10 000, signed by the Presbyterian Robert Barr Smith . . . To university, schools, charities, hospitals and all manner of private need he gave huge sums, often anonymously. But he resisted any political or civic duties and the only public body with which he would associate was the Botanical Gardens. In early days he loved to hunt and play polo and the hunt met at Torrens Park. The Barr Smiths were hospitable but in a private, almost secret way. They liked fun rather than formality. One guest remembered on arrival at the house everyone was given a pair of stilts and how hilarious it was as everyone teetered round the lawns and surrounding paddocks with them.' op. cit., p. 157.

36 Lady Mary Downer, interview.

37 Clyde Cameron, interview, Adelaide, December 2000.

38 Alexander Downer, *Six Prime Ministers*, p. 1.

39 Clyde Cameron, *The Cameron Diaries*, Sydney, 1990, p. 334.

40 Ibid.

41 Stella Downer, interview.

42 Alexander Downer, *Six Prime Ministers*, op. cit., p. 66.

43 Ibid., p. 7.

44 Ibid., p. viii.

45 Ibid., p. 45. True to his progressive South Australian roots, Sir Alexander also admitted to finding Menzies's attitudes to 'social questions . . . rather narrow. During a Cabinet discussion I amazed him by stating that DH Lawrence's *Lady Chatterley's Lover* should be allowed to circulate freely: he was all for its suppression . . . He would certainly never have countenanced nude bathing beaches or the prevailing dismantling of most of the censorship.' p. 31.

46 Alexander Downer, interview.

47 As cited in Mary Kalantzis and Bill Cope, 'Downer's backward sense of our past', *Australian*, 16 June 1994.

48 Alexander Downer, *Six Prime Ministers*, op. cit., p. 55.

49 ibid., p. 55.

50 Stella Downer, interview.

51 Alexander Downer, interview.

52 Alexander Downer as cited in Christine Wallace, 'Downer makes a difference', *Australian Financial Review*, 9 December 1993.

53 Alexander Downer, interview.

54 As cited in Michael Davies, 'A Class of His Own', *Age*, 3 December 1994.

55 Alexander Downer, op. cit., p. 56.

56 Ibid., p. 56.

57 Michael Davies, op. cit.

58 The company manufactures medicinal bandages and paper products.

59 As cited in Peter Ward, 'Home and dry with the Downer family', *Australian*, 28 May 1994.

60 Ibid.

61 Clyde Cameron, op. cit., p. 334.

62 Christine Wallace, op. cit.

63 Mike Seccombe, *Sydney Morning Herald*, 26 May 1994.

64 *Bulletin*, 16 August 1994.

65 Other puns included the suggestion that the Liberals' footwear policy could be called 'the thongs that matter' and so forth.

66 Alexander Downer, ABC–TV, '7.30 Report', 26 January 1995.

67 Richard Farmer as cited in Mike Seccombe, 'Keating fails in first thrust at Downer', *Sydney Morning Herald*, 2 June 1994.

68 Dennis Grant, interview.

69 Michelle Grattan, interview, November 1999.

THE MYERS

1 Interview at First Step, Melbourne, 20 March 2001.

2 Interview with William Shelmerdine, First Step, Melbourne, 20 March 2001.

3 Interview with Patrick Myer, First Step, Melbourne, 20 March 2001.

4 Ambrose Pratt, *Sidney Myer: A Biography*, Seven Seas, Melbourne, 1993, p. 52.

5 Interview with Stephen Shelmerdine, Myer family office, Melbourne, 15 March 2001. All quotes and comments by Stephen Shelmerdine are taken from this interview.

6 Margaret Paul, ' "For He's a Jolly Good Fellow!"': Sidney Myer's Statements of Philanthropy for Melbourne, 1926–1934,' Master of Arts thesis for the Department of History, University of Melbourne, 1999, p. 29–30.

7 Stella Barber with Margaret Paul, 'Sidney Myer: A Life, a Legacy', unpublished manuscript, 1998, p. 77.

8 Interview with Stephen Shelmerdine.

9 Stella Barber with Margaret Paul, ibid., p. 83.

10 *Bendigo Advertiser*, 1 September 1934, p. 5.

11 Interview with Lady Marigold Southey, Toorak, Melbourne, 13 March 2001. All quotes and comments by Lady Southey are taken from this interview.

12 Ambrose Pratt, ibid., p. 72.

13 Robert G Menzies, 'Forward' in Ambrose Pratt, *Sydney Myer: A Biography*.

14 Ambrose Pratt, op. cit., p. 105.

15 Ambrose Pratt, op. cit., pp. 119, 120.

16 See Percey E Joske, *The Laws of Marriage and Divorce in Australia and New Zealand*, Butterworth, Sydney, 1952.

17 Kenneth Baillieu Myer interviewed by Heather Rusden for the

National Library of Australia, 23 November 1990–13 February 1992. All quotes and comments by the late Ken Myer are taken from these interviews.

18 *Punch*, 19 February 1920, p. 310.

19 Letter from Lee Neil to Sidney Myer, 22 March 1920, as documented in Margaret Paul, op. cit., p. 44.

20 Interview with Anne Cordner for ABC Radio National, October 1999.

21 See, for example, Corrie Perkin, 'Myer's Melbourne' *Age*, 21 May 1999.

22 Neilma Gantner interviewed by Jane Cadzow, *Good Weekend*, 19 May 2001, p. 37.

23 *Argus*, 26 December 1930, p. 4.

24 Interview with Pamela Warrender for ABC Radio National, Melbourne, October 1999. All quotes and comments by Pamela Warrender taken from this interview.

25 Pamela Warrender, *Prince of Merchants: The Story of Norman Myer*, Gold Star Publications, Melbourne, p. 100.

26 Interview with Pamela Warrender.

27 Interview with Neilma Gantner, op. cit., p. 40.

28 Interview with Vallejo Gantner, St Kilda, 17 March 2001.

THE MURDOCHS

1 Interview with Anna Murdoch Mann, the *Australian Women's Weekly*, August 2001, pp. 13–22. All quotes and comments by Anna Murdoch Mann are taken from this interview, unless otherwise stated.

2 Interview with Rupert Murdoch, Los Angeles, 22 August 2001.

3 *Business Review Weekly*, 10 March 1997, p. 46.

4 Inteview with Dame Elisabeth Murdoch, Cruden Farm, Langwarrin, 5 May 2001. All comments and quotes by Dame Elisabeth Murdoch are taken from this interview unless otherwise stated.

5 John Monks, *Elisabeth Murdoch: Two Lives*, Pan Macmillan, Sydney, 1994, pp. 21–27.

6 Ibid., p. 24.

7 William Shawcross, *Rupert Murdoch: Ringmaster of the Information Circus*, Pan Books, London 1993, p. 33.

8 Ibid., p. 35.

9 Ibid., pp. 41–42.

10 Former editor-in-chief of the Adelaide *News* John Hetherington, in Neil Chenoweth, *Virtual Murdoch: Reality Wars on the Information Highway*, Secker & Warburg, London, p. 26.

11 Ibid., p. 25.

12 Interview with Janet Calvert-Jones, Melbourne, 5 May 2001. All quotes and comments from Janet Calvert-Jones taken from this interview.

13 John Monks, op. cit., p. 144.

14 Keith Murdoch was knighted in 1933 for services to journalism.

15 For more information on this deal see Neil Chenoweth, op. cit., pp. 26–7.

16 See Andrew Neil, *Full Disclosure*, Pan Books, London, 1997, pp. 197–240 and Neil Chenoweth, op. cit., p. 21.

17 Rupert Murdoch interviewed by William Shawcross, *Vanity Fair*, October 1999, p. 272.

18 Rupert Murdoch, Los Angeles, 22 August 2001.

19 William Shawcross, op. cit., p. 62.

20 Chris Patten's memoirs, *East and West*, was later published by Macmillan.

21 William Shawcross, *Vanity Fair*, p. 321.

22 Ibid., p. 272.

23 Philip Townsend, *Punch*, July 2001, p. 20.

24 Interview with Lachlan Murdoch, Sydney, 26 March 2001. All quotes and comments from this point are taken from this interview, unless otherwise stated.

25 Interview with Elisabeth Murdoch, London, 11 September 2001. All quotes with Elisabeth Murdoch are taken from this interview unless otherwise stated.

26 Interview with James Murdoch in *Vanity Fair*, July 1997, p. 64.

27 Geraldine Brooks, *HQ*, October 1999, p. 140.

28 Interview with Rupert Murdoch, Los Angeles, 22 August 2001.

29 Andrew Neil, op. cit., p. 198.

30 Interview with Matthew Freud, *Guardian*, 3 July 2001, p. 11.

31 The *Guardian*, 3 July 2001, p. 12.

32 Leslie Chang, John Lippman and Robert Frank, the *Asian Wall Street Journal* and the *Washington Street Journal* and reprinted in the *Australian Financial Review*, 3 November 2000, pp. 80–81.

THE DE BORTOLIS

1 Huon Hooke, interview, Sydney, January 2001. All quotes from Huon Hooke are taken from this interview.

2 Deen De Bortoli, interview, Bilbul, October 1999 and February 2001. All quotes from Deen De Bortoli are taken from this interview.

3 Keith McWilliam, interview, Griffith, October 1999 and February 2001. All quotes from Keith McWilliam are taken from these interviews.

4 Flo and Eola De Bortoli, interview, Sydney, January 2001. All quotes from the sisters are taken from this interview. The two sisters tell a story from their mother's childhood, when Giuseppina was only five or six and stricken with fever. The local doctor advised the family to prepare themselves for the worst for their child was not long of this world. As soon as he left, Giuseppina is said to have hopped out of bed and informed her parents, 'Well, he's gone and I'm still here.'

5 Flo and Eola De Bortoli, interview.

6 Emeri De Bortoli, interview, Bilbul, October 1999 and February 2001. All quotes from Emeri De Bortoli are taken from this interview.

7 Even today, Louis is something of an outsider among Griffith's Italian community—not least because as a Piedmontese he does not speak the dialect of the villages. Today, he and his son run a million-dollar business supplying winemaking equipment and machinery. Louis Del Piano, interview, Griffith, October 1999 and February 2001. All quotes from Louis Del Piano are taken from this interview.

8 'When I had some problem and I couldn't get Mr De Bortoli to do what I wanted, I used to go and chat with Giuseppina, and

she would say, "Don't worry, Louis. I'll talk to the boss. If not tomorrow, then in the next week it will be done. Don't say anything more, just leave it to me." And maybe after a few days, or a week, it was done. That was it.' Louis Del Piano, interview.

9 Emeri remembers Giuseppina being quite envious of her appetite for argument. 'Quite often she'd say, "I wish I could have been more like you and let them all have it, rather than go off and brood about it".'

10 John Taylor, interview, Griffith, February 2001. All quotes from John Taylor are taken from this interview.

11 Darren De Bortoli, interview, Griffith, October 1999 and February 2001. All quotes from Darren De Bortoli are taken from this interview.

12 Leanne De Bortoli, Interview, Griffith, February 2001. All quotes from Leanne De Bortoli are taken from this interview.

13 Giuseppina's daughters, who were summoned to Griffith as their mother's death approached, recall being telephoned several times by hospice staff with the news that she was drawing her last breath. On rushing down, they would find that Giuseppina had made another miraculous recovery. 'It was funny and terrible at once', says Eola, who urged her mother to 'let go', for this determination to hang on at all costs was typical of her mother.

14 Today the De Bortolis' restaurant in the Yarra serves some forty thousand customers a year. However, as the Yarra has become more and more sought-after, the family has turned its attention to the nearby King Valley. They are now planting extensive vineyards in this little-known region of dairy farms, and extraordinary beauty, in the foothills of the Snowy Mountains.

15 'My mother is the Rock of Gibraltar round which the family is built up,' says Darren succinctly.

16 John Dal Broi, interview, Bilbul, February 2001.

17 Brothers Kevin and Victor seem to have a more comfortable social network locally, perhaps because, unlike Darren, they are not seen as the family's business head.

ACKNOWLEDGMENTS

We would like to thank first and foremost all the members of the Murdoch, Macarthur, Downer, Durack, Myer and De Bortoli families who gave so generously of their time and assistance, and in doing so made this book possible.

We would also like to thank the following people for their expertise: John Wrigley, Beverley Kingston, Alan Atkinson, John Hepworth, Dirk Von Dissell, Stella Barber, Stafford Sanders, John Dal Broi, Louis and Joyce del Piano, Huon Hooke and Michael Collins-Persse.

At the ABC, we would like to thank our television colleagues, particularly Janet Bell, Tim Clark and Stephen Ramsey; and at ABC Books, Jenny Mills. Special thanks to Marjorie Wearne at the ABC Federal Reference Library for her tireless efforts, research skills and patience.

Last but not least, we would like to thank our editors, Jacqueline Kent, Julie Stanton and Susan Morris-Yates for ensuring we were in such good hands.

BIBLIOGRAPHY

UNPUBLISHED PAPERS AND THESIS

Stella Barber & Paul, Margaret, Sidney Myer: A Life, A Legacy, unpublished manuscript, 1998.

Paul, Margaret, For he's a Jolly Good Fellow!: Sidney Myer's Statements of Philanthropy for Melbourne 1926–1934, MA thesis, University of Melbourne, 1999.

BOOKS

Atkinson, Alan, *Camden*, Oxford University Press, Sydney, 1988.

Australian Dictionary of Biography, Melbourne University Press, CD Rom, Folio for Windows, 1992–1996.

Barnard, Marjorie, *A History of Australia*, Angus & Robertson, Sydney, 1963.

Bickel, Lennard, *Australia's First Lady: The Story of Elizabeth Macarthur*, Allen & Unwin, Sydney, 1991.

Blake, Nelson Manfred, *The Road to Reno: A History of Divorce in the United States*, Macmillan, New York, 1962.

Blakeney, Michael, *Australia and the Jewish Refugees, 1933–1948*, Croom Helm, Melbourne, 1985.

Cannon, Michael, *The Land Boomers*, Thomas Nelson Ltd, Melbourne, 1966.

Chenoweth, Neil, *Virtual Murdoch: Reality Wars on the Information Highway*, Secker & Warburg, London, 2001.

Clark, C M H, *A History of Australia*, vol 1, Melbourne University Press, Melbourne, 1962.

Cusack, Frank, *Bendigo: A History*, Heinemann, Melbourne, 1973.

Davison, Graeme, *The Rise and Fall of Marvellous Melbourne*, Melbourne University Press, Melbourne, 1978.

Downer, Alexander, *Six Prime Ministers*, Hill of Content, Melbourne, 1982.

Durack, Mary, *Keep Him My Country*, Bantam, Sydney, 1999. (First published 1955)

Durack, Mary, *Kings in Grass Castles*, Constable, London, 1985. (First published 1959)

Durack, Mary, *Sons in the Saddle*, Constable, London, 1983.

Dutton, Geoffrey, *The Squatters*, Currey O'Neil Ross Pty Ltd, Melbourne, 1985.

Ellis M H, *John Macarthur*, Angus & Robertson, Sydney, 1955.

Fitzgerald, Ross & Hearn, Mark, *Bligh, Macarthur and the Rum Rebellion*, Kangaroo Press, Sydney, 1988.

Garran, J C, & White, L, *Merinos, Myths and Macarthurs*, ANU Press, Canberra, 1985.

Gitelman, Zvi, *A Century of Ambivalence: The Jews of Russia and the Soviet Union, 1881 to the Present*, Penguin, London, 1988.

Gosse, Fayette, *The Gosses: An Anglo-Australian Family*, Brian Clouston, Canberra, 1981.

Hill, Ernestine, *The Great Australian Loneliness*, Imprint, Sydney, 1995. (First published 1937)

Hirst, J B, *Convict Society and its Enemies*, Allen & Unwin, Sydney, 1983.

Joske, Percy, *The Laws of Marriage and Divorce in Australia and New Zealand*, Butterworth, Sydney, 1952.

Kingston, Beverley, *Elizabeth Macarthur*, Historic Houses Trust of New South Wales, Sydney, 1984.

Lacour-Gayet, Robert, *A Concise History of Australia*, Penguin Books, Melbourne, 1976.

Lancaster, Bill, *The Department Store: A Social History*, Leicester University Press, London, 1995.

Macarthur-Onslow, S M, ed, *The Macarthurs of Camden*, Rigby Ltd, Sydney, 1973.

Marshall, Alan, *The Gay Provider: The Myer Story*, FW Cheshire, Melbourne, 1961.

Millett, Patsy & Millet, Naomi (eds), *Pilgrimage: A Journey though the Life and Writings of Mary Durack*, Bantam, Sydney, 2000.

Monks, John 1994, *Elisabeth Murdoch: Two Lives*, Pan Macmillan, Sydney.

Neil, Andrew, *Full Disclosure*, Pan Books, London, 1997.

Pratt, Ambrose, *Sidney Myer: A Biography*, Seven Seas, Melbourne, 1993.

Riley, Glenda, *Divorce: An American Tradition*, Oxford University Press, New York, 1991.

Rubinstein, Hilary, *The Jews in Victoria*, Allen & Unwin, Sydney, 1986.

Shawcross, Wiliam, *Rupert Murdoch: Ringmaster of the Information Circus*, Pan Books, London, 1993.

Warrender, Pamela, *Prince of Merchants: The Story of Norman Myer*, Gold Star Publications, Melbourne, 1972.